UNCLE TOM

UNCLE TOM

From Martyr to Traitor

ADENA SPINGARN

Stanford University Press
Stanford, California

Stanford University Press
Stanford, California

Printed in the United States of America on acid-free, archival-quality paper

Library of Congress Cataloging-in-Publication Data

Names: Spingarn, Adena, 1981– author.
Title: Uncle Tom : from martyr to traitor / Adena Spingarn.
Description: Stanford, California : Stanford University Press, 2018. | Includes bibliographical references and index.
Identifiers: LCCN 2017045103 | ISBN 9780804799157 (cloth : alk. paper) | ISBN 9781503606098 (epub)
Subjects: LCSH: Uncle Tom (Fictitious character) | Stowe, Harriet Beecher, 1811–1896. Uncle Tom's cabin. | Stowe, Harriet Beecher, 1811–1896—Adaptations—History and criticism. | African Americans in literature—History. | Stereotypes (Social psychology) in literature—History. | American literature—Social aspects—History. | United States—Race relations—History. | Racism—United States—History.
Classification: LCC PS2954.U6 S67 2018 | DDC 813/.3—dc23
LC record available at https://lccn.loc.gov/2017045103

Typeset by Bruce Lundquist in 01.25/15 Adobe Caslon Pro

To Dvora Cyrlak and Neil Spingarn, who gave me the words.

CONTENTS

FOREWORD

AS IS TRUE OF MANY PEOPLE OF MY GENERATION, my first encounter with Uncle Tom and his cabin occurred through popular culture. In the late 1950s, I saw the 1932 Our Gang/Little Rascals film *Spanky*, which featured the Rascals producing a barn-theater version of the novel. To tell the truth, I wasn't so focused on Uncle Tom as much as I was on Eliza and her desperate but nimble balancing act as she fled for her freedom across ice floes in the Ohio River, simulated quite effectively by empty crates. About the same time, I remember seeing another child-centered version of *Uncle Tom's Cabin*: a 1933 Walt Disney cartoon short with Mickey playing Tom and Minnie playing Little Eva. Eventually, I actually read Harriet Beecher Stowe's *Uncle Tom's Cabin* as part of my eighth-grade course in "Prose and Poetry," proving West Virginia's high valuation of the novel as well as an optimistic attitude about their students' willingness to read a century-old, sentimental novel ostensibly about race and the Civil War.

During the "Black Power" revolutionary years of the late 1960s, I shared the popular black militant view of an "Uncle Tom" as a shuffling, subservient race traitor. Further, James Baldwin's essay "Everybody's Protest Novel," a scathing 1949 critique of the novel's sentimentality and Harriet Beecher Stowe's inability to imagine a black fictional character as complex as she was, only served to reinforce Uncle Tom's place in the racial imaginary. Yet even for those who had read neither the novel nor Baldwin's essay, Uncle Tom became the despised symbol of racial attitudes that we sought to reject. Later, as a literary critic, I kept up with shifting views of the novel that evolved through the decades, and then, at Robert Weil's urging at W. W. Norton, I decided to reevaluate my own relationship both with the novel and with the much-maligned Uncle Tom himself. In 2007, I published with Hollis Robbins at Johns Hopkins *The Annotated Uncle Tom's Cabin*, in which we trace the continued scholarly fascination with this endlessly intriguing novel and offered my own reading of Uncle Tom and his function within this work.

Obviously, I am one of a large number of scholars of American literature and culture who continue to redefine our views of Stowe's profoundly influential novel. However, it does not take familiarity with the scholarship and the ups and downs of the literary canon for someone to be very aware of the cultural meaning of "Uncle Tom." As Adena Spingarn points out in this brilliant new study, the negative connotations of "Uncle Tom" continue unabated in the public discourse and have expanded beyond its application to African Americans to connote "race traitors" for other ethnic groups through terms such as "Uncle Tomahawk" and "Uncle Chan." Grounding her work in exhaustive archival research, Spingarn is the first scholar to explore in detail how Uncle Tom was transformed from a model of Christian humility, purity, and self-sacrificing goodness into the archetype of a selfish race traitor. By employing an emerging resource of digitalized source materials, especially historical newspapers and periodicals, Spingarn has developed a database of important references both to Uncle Tom and to *Uncle Tom's Cabin* that she deploys with impressive nuance throughout this riveting book.

One of the groundbreaking results of Spingarn's meticulous research is the relocation of the vilification of Uncle Tom to black political rhetoric as early as the 1910s, at the height of what the historian Rayford W. Logan famously called "the nadir" of American race relations. A rhetoric of black political resistance needed to attach itself to a familiar and well-defined figure if it was to carve out a space as a trope in the political language of the time. As Spingarn beautifully details in her book, it was "Jim Crow's retightening [in the 1890s] of many of the social, economic, and political shackles of the antebellum era" that led to an African American revolt against the racist concept of the patient, submissive slave, not only content with her or his lot but loyal to the order in which she and he were hereditarily enslaved. Spingarn identifies how a group of black men and women, staking their claims to the rights of citizenship and sovereign identity severely under assault, needed more than just persuasive language to articulate who they were and how they wanted to be seen. They were "New Negroes," and the epitome of all they were not—the "Old Negro"—was none other than long-suffering Uncle Tom, who quickly became the symbol of the *opposite* of this new black identity. For its identification of this critical shift alone, *Uncle Tom: From Martyr to Traitor* will be a major contribution not only to the study of *Uncle Tom's Cabin* but also—and perhaps just as significantly—to the study of emerging black identity politics in the early twentieth century.

In the spirit of full disclosure, I have been following Spingarn's career for a long time. It was during her meticulous research into the theatrical representations of *Uncle Tom's Cabin* that she discovered James Weldon Johnson's outline for an "operatic cantata" based on the novel in the James Weldon Johnson Papers at Yale University's Beinecke Library. I was not alone in thinking that we had access to all theatrical interpretations of the novel already, so this was an extraordinary discovery, with the potential to bring this novel to life again, and for a new generation. There is a leitmotif here: Adena Spingarn finds what other scholars have missed, and she then explicates these materials with impressive sensitivity and insight. In this book, her in-depth analysis of Johnson's outline, as well as other theatrical works based on Stowe's novel, displays not only her depth of scholarship but also her masterfully readable critical prose style.

Each American generation must freshly confront the legacy of America's original sin and the attendant problems of our society's legacy of racism; this is certainly true of our time and place. What W. E. B. Du Bois, riffing on a term coined by Frederick Douglass in 1881, famously called "the color line" is still very much with us. As we reach for symbols to help us grapple with these issues and deconstruct anti-black racism, Uncle Tom has become, as Spingarn argues, far beyond the pages of Stowe's novel, "a kind of Rorschach inkblot for American race relations: what this figure has meant tells us less about him than it does about those who have responded to him." Spingarn, in her impressive first book, provides both the general reader and her scholarly peers with a brilliant researched, superbly written seminal analysis of the history of everyone's racial protest metaphor, the most popular black character in the history of American literature, the self-sacrificing Christ-like character whom people simply called Uncle Tom.

Henry Louis Gates, Jr.

UNCLE TOM

INTRODUCTION

> Literature may be viewed in two aspects—as an expression of life, past and pres-
> ent, and as a force directly affecting the conduct of life, present and future. . . .
> History is instructive, and may warn or admonish; but to this quality literature
> adds the faculty of persuasion, by which men's hearts are reached, the springs of
> action touched, and the currents of life directed.
>
> Charles Chesnutt, "Literature in Its Relation to Life" (1899)[1]

IN THE FALL OF 1967, a young man wearing a black leather jacket and a black beret parked his motorcycle outside of a party at Iowa's Grinnell College and went inside to talk with Ralph Ellison about *Invisible Man* (1952). The conversation became heated, and before long the young man shouted, "You're an Uncle Tom, man! You're a sell-out. You're a disgrace to your race." For the moment, Ellison maintained his cool, but once the young man rode away, he broke down, sobbing, "I'm not a Tom, I'm not a Tom."[2] How could a century-old literary character provoke such a response? Even now, more than 165 years after the publication of Harriet Beecher Stowe's anti-slavery novel, *Uncle Tom's Cabin* (1852), those words still pack a punch. Far from an esoteric literary allusion, Uncle Tom is, as Henry Louis Gates Jr. aptly describes, "the ultimate instrument of black-on-black derogation."[3] Stowe's character, written as a Christ-like martyr who refuses to divulge the whereabouts of two fugitive slaves, has taken on a uniquely dynamic cultural life beyond the pages of *Uncle Tom's Cabin*, becoming a widely recognized epithet for a black person deemed so subservient to whites that he betrays his race.

Today, this conception of Uncle Tom as a submissive race traitor has largely eclipsed Stowe's character, becoming a powerful political and cultural symbol to many who have never read, or even heard of, the novel. The situation is neatly summed up in a scene between two black characters in a 2007 episode of the critically acclaimed television show *30 Rock*. Tracy, a famous

actor who grew up in the projects, and Toofer, a preppy, Harvard-educated
television writer, butt heads over racial representation.[4] (In an edgy joke,
Toofer's nickname comes out of his "two-for-one" value as both a Harvard
graduate and an African American.) When Tracy and Toofer are told to work
out their differences by writing a scene together, their opposing views on appropriate behavior and language make it seem as if they don't even speak
the same language. ("Yeah, that's right," says Toofer, "I'm speaking English.")
Each man sees the other as bad for the race: Toofer tells Tracy that his comic
skit in drag is the modern equivalent of minstrelsy, while Tracy criticizes
Toofer for acting white. "Who raised you?" he asks. "Look at you, standing
there with your pants that fit, using a wallet, drinking Starbucks. . . . Come
on, where's your heritage, my brother, my homeboy, my n——"—the N-word
is drowned out by the convenient drone of a vacuum cleaner. The implication is that Toofer, by embracing mainstream white fashion and habits, has
lost connection to his race.

When the two are forced to address their conflict in sensitivity training,
Tracy again criticizes Toofer for his lack of racial solidarity, calling to the
group, "Dude wears khakis. Uncle Tom, party of one! Uncle Tom, party of
one!" Tracy's comment underscores the tangling of racial authenticity and
solidarity embodied in the Uncle Tom figure. Wearing khaki pants rather
than street fashion is not simply a sartorial choice but a symbol of complicity
with white—and therefore anti-black—values. Khakis make him stand apart
from his race as a "party of one" working for his personal advancement rather
than the collective interest. But Toofer is exasperated by Tracy's reference to
Uncle Tom. "You can't call someone that if you've never read the book," he
sneers, asserting his own authority by way of education. Still, Toofer's objection doesn't make much of an impact on the group: in a sly punchline to the
scene, an onlooker calls out, "What book?"

What book, indeed. *Uncle Tom's Cabin* was the best-selling book of the
nineteenth century after the Bible, selling 300,000 copies in the United
States in its first year alone and a million copies between the United States
and Britain. Translated into more than a dozen languages, it was a sensation
all over the world. Yet even the huge popularity of Stowe's novel was eclipsed
by the vast and enduring network of responses the novel and its protagonist inspired. Continuing into the present day, these responses have taken

shape in virtually every medium imaginable, from children's playing cards to lavish theater productions, from radical black political movements to minstrel song-and-dance numbers, from Limoges figurines to rap music.[5] And they have taken substantial freedoms with Stowe's original text, sometimes expanding upon it, sometimes contradicting it, and sometimes altogether ignoring its existence. Somewhere along the way, the brawny, martyred hero of Stowe's novel came to be known as a submissive, old race traitor.

Early critics of the novel described Uncle Tom as a character whose "rich[] spiritual beauty" and "loft[y] moral grandeur" was unmatched in literature.[6] As Stowe introduces the character, Tom, "the hero of our story," is a deeply Christian man who is confident in himself even as he is humble before God, "his whole air self-respecting and dignified, yet united with a confiding and humble simplicity."[7] His humility does not stop him from asserting himself verbally, especially when it comes to his Christian faith. To mid-nineteenth-century African Americans, Uncle Tom connoted a pious Christian whose Christ-like submission merited respect, even if not, for some, emulation as a protest strategy. Frederick Douglass rejected this character as a personal model but also expressed appreciation for him in his second and third autobiographies, *My Bondage and My Freedom* (1855) and *The Life and Times of Frederick Douglass* (1892). In both, he described the beloved "spiritual father" of his youth, Father Lawson, as "in christian [*sic*] graces, the very counterpart of 'Uncle' Tom. The resemblance is so perfect, that he might have been the original of Mrs. Stowe's christian [*sic*] hero."[8] Although Uncle Tom was a fictional creation, for Douglass he was quite real, and he had made a lasting impact: Lawson's message of liberty through faith in God influenced Douglass' thoughts so deeply that, he admitted, "they have never entirely diverged."[9] To Douglass, as to many other black activists of his time, the community was enriched both by those who survived by religious faith and by those who survived by resistance. One could disagree with Uncle Tom's patient, self-sacrificing Christianity, and at times one could even mock it—and Douglass did both—but one could not deny its fundamental role in the survival of the race.[10]

Uncle Tom's modern connotation turns his original identity on its head: where Stowe's Christ-like hero sacrifices himself in the process of protecting two escaped slaves, the contemporary Uncle Tom sacrifices his race for his own interests. The figure has also undergone an enormous physical transformation, from the broad-shouldered "behemoth," as the novel's Marie St. Clare describes Tom when she first sees him, to a doddering, white-haired geriatric with a cane. Critics have long pondered this dramatic change, wondering "how a book whose avowed and successful purpose was to champion an oppressed people came to stand as a major symbol of that oppression."[11] The most convenient, if largely unexplored, explanation has been that the transformation was the result of the myriad theatrical adaptations of *Uncle Tom's Cabin* staged virtually without pause from 1852 through the 1930s and appearing intermittently ever since.[12] These adaptations, critics have almost universally assumed, turned Stowe's Christ-like hero into a submissive old fool.[13]

The contemporary force of the Uncle Tom slur has veiled the complicated story of this figure and thus of an important through-line of American racial politics. The dominant narrative of the *Uncle Tom's Cabin* dramas holds that they quickly lost their progressive political power, becoming a debased, retrograde spectacle of happy plantation scenes and minstrel comedy. One scholar has even gone so far as to argue that the plays "did more to hamper than to help the cause of the blacks in the United States."[14] This explanation posits an Uncle Tom figure created, like Aunt Jemima, entirely "in the fantasy world of whiteness, the only place where they were possible."[15] And it requires a marked shift in the way we think about *Uncle Tom's Cabin* in relation to American culture and politics. If we understand the novel and the plays of the 1850s as agents of social change, as works with the power to transform a nation's attitude toward a longtime institution and to demand recognition of the humanity, if not the equality, of a race that some had classed with animals, then it doesn't quite make sense to think of the continuing tradition as simply receiving and then reifying American racial prejudices. And as I show in this book, the historical record reveals a far more progressive assessment of the *Uncle Tom's Cabin* dramas than scholars have assumed.

Ever since the publication of Stowe's novel, Uncle Tom has been a central figure in American conversations about race and racial representation. This book tells the story of how these changing conversations transformed Stowe's character into a widely known derogatory slur. By tracking this transformation, I shed light on a history of American debates about the reality and legacy of slavery, the viability of various strategies for racial progress, and the appropriate attributes of black characters in literature, theater, and film. I argue that the figure's derogatory meaning did not emerge on the stage, where in fact black audiences received the *Uncle Tom's Cabin* dramas as works with radical political potential some years into the twentieth century. Rather, Uncle Tom became a slur within the black political rhetoric of the 1910s because the figure encapsulated a traumatic slavery past that reverberated through twentieth-century American race relations. Developing in the context of unjust and inhumane structures of oppression, this transformation was shaped by demographic, educational, cultural, and political shifts that made a younger generation of New Negroes increasingly assertive in its resistance to Jim Crow as well as more disparaging of the "old Negroes" who came before them. Uncle Tom, I suggest, is as much a product of black discourse as of the white imagination, a figure drawn upon and shaped by fundamental debates within the black community over who should represent the race and how it should be represented.

Blurring the lines between fiction and fact, Americans received Stowe's character as both a representat*ion* by a creative writer and a representat*ive* of the people enslaved in the South. This dual status ultimately produced two different cultural manifestations of Uncle Tom. One was the character as featured in literature, theater, and film, often though not always tied to Stowe's novel. The second was an approximation of a living, breathing person, a political, moral, and behavioral type to be embraced or critiqued. In both politics and cultural production, the derogatory denotation of this figure developed in the context of systematic racial injustices, through a particular kind of intraracial critique of an older generation by a younger one. Uncle Tom became a slur at the moment when the past was no longer seen as the building block of future progress nor as something to be ignored, but instead as a powerful contemporary adversary.

Race and Racism in American Culture

Although Uncle Tom has long been a slur, this book is the first to investigate Uncle Tom not just as a character within the cultural history of *Uncle Tom's Cabin*, or even within the many works "descended" from Stowe's novel, but also as a figure with an active life outside of expressive culture.[16] By integrating cultural and political analysis of this figure in the American imagination, *Uncle Tom: From Martyr to Traitor* fills a longtime gap in the scholarship on the political and social impact of what John William DeForest famously called the nation's nearest prospect for a "Great American Novel."[17] Covering a vast span of media and movements, the story of Uncle Tom enables a holistic analysis of what it means to "represent" a race in creative and sociopolitical terms. Critical race theory has shown us that race is socially constructed in complex and historically contingent ways. As the story of Uncle Tom makes clear, so, too, is racism. We often think of a stereotypical character as a static figure; indeed, repetition of sameness is fundamental to what makes a character a stereotype in the first place. Yet the changing responses of readers and critics to *Uncle Tom's Cabin* and the shifting rhetoric of Uncle Tom highlight the historical contingency of the concept of stereotype itself. Not only did attitudes toward this character and type change, so did the grounds for approval or objection.

Part of the attraction and the challenge of making a definitive assessment of Uncle Tom and *Uncle Tom's Cabin* in the American imagination is the broad extent of the character's cultural penetration. This is especially the case when it comes to the dramatic adaptations, which have been staged tens of thousands of times in an astounding variety of theatrical forms (including minstrelsy, melodrama, farce, opera, burlesque, vaudeville, and variety) by hundreds of theatrical companies, using an untold variety of scripts and sometimes nothing more than memory. As one critic observed in 1896, "If there is any one play in existence that has been abused, mutilated, and presented in every conceivable shape, it is 'Uncle Tom's Cabin.'"[18] If you follow the life of *Uncle Tom's Cabin* on the American stage, you get something pretty close to a history of the American popular theater.

My account of Uncle Tom's transformation relies on significant archival research in library and museum collections, where I have located previously undiscussed adaptations of *Uncle Tom's Cabin* by African Americans, as well as in digitized historical newspapers and periodicals.[19] The recent digitization of many historical American newspapers from cities large and small enables a more thorough historical tracking of the *Uncle Tom's Cabin* plays through contemporaneous accounts and advertisements. Providing access to an enormous trove of previously unexplored documents that substantially expand the already large amount of source material (playbills, posters, scripts, etc.) in library and museum archives, these digitized collections are especially useful for performance studies scholars who have in recent years paid increasing attention to the multiplicity of any given work in what is ultimately an ephemeral art form. Historical newspapers illuminate not just where and when the plays were performed or how they were marketed, but also, and perhaps more suggestively, how critics and audiences received them. Research in black periodicals is particularly relevant to this story because the black press was a key arena for the debate and creation of a common black culture. Spending hundreds of hours combing through references to Uncle Tom and *Uncle Tom's Cabin* in digital collections, I've created a database of thousands of significant mentions and used them as empirical evidence of sometimes surprising cultural attitudes. Of course, the archive is always partial. Many newspapers and books have not been digitized, and many if not most shows were never memorialized in print. Even so, the collection of thousands of digital records enables a fuller picture of what Uncle Tom and *Uncle Tom's Cabin* have meant to Americans than previous scholarship has provided.

Stage adaptations of Stowe's novel are overdue for a fresh investigation using these new resources. Until recently, scholarly discussion of the Uncle Tom stage shows relied heavily on the 1947 account of Harry Birdoff, an amateur historian and collector of Uncle Tom show paraphernalia. Birdoff's account is a useful starting point for research, but it is, as the author subtitles one section of the book, "An Informal and Affectionate History of America's Folk Play," and it has significant limitations as scholarship.[20] John Frick's *"Uncle Tom's Cabin" on the Stage and Screen* (2012) has partially addressed the need for a replacement for Birdoff's book by situating *Uncle Tom's Cabin* in theater history, but his account neither connects this tradition to the Uncle Tom character's enduring incorporation into American politics nor makes use of new digital research methods that would more fully address its performance and reception history.[21] David Reynolds' *Mightier Than the Sword: "Uncle Tom's Cabin" and the Battle for America* (2011), on the other hand, offers a more progressive reading of the *Uncle Tom's Cabin* plays and films. While my account shares with his an attention to the liberatory politics of this stage tradition, I am interested here in the ways that these plays both challenged and participated in the cultural forces that enabled and perpetuated Jim Crow. Moreover,

I show how the cultural history of *Uncle Tom's Cabin* contributed to the African American political conversations that turned Uncle Tom into a slur.

My archival methodology charts the transformation of Uncle Tom primarily through the words and actions of the readers, writers, artists, and everyday people who found meaning, whether positive or negative, in this figure. Some of these responses are extremely discomfiting from a twenty-first-century perspective. For example, the many *Uncle Tom's Cabin* playbills that advertise a lavish "great plantation scene" and, in the case of an 1877 performance in Boston, trumpet the involvement of "100 Genuine Southern Colored People who were slaves before the War. . . . Illustrating in a most realistic manner Life in the South Twenty Years Ago," strike a contemporary scholar as obscenely racist.[22] By framing black performance within a supposedly "realistic" plantation celebration, these scenes clearly reflect and participate in the racist structures that delimited black life in the United States. At the same time, however, newspapers such as the Indianapolis *Freeman* regularly published reports on the successes of members of various *Uncle Tom's Cabin* companies, showing an obvious pride in their accomplishments. For example, the paper reported of Stetson's Big Double Uncle Tom's Cabin Company that "Mr. Gus Collins is receiving lots of compliments and numerous press notices for his wonderfully natural portrayal of the famous part of Uncle Tom."[23] To be sure, the plays reinforced elements of a racist social order and damaging notions of racial difference. Yet here, as in the blackface minstrel shows of the nineteenth century, there were "contradictory racial impulses at work."[24] However offensive such performances are in our eyes, they meant something to those who had few opportunities to see the creative talents of black artists recognized and compensated.[25] As is clear from the stories of these performers and their audiences, human beings find ways to experience pride and dignity within horrifically unjust systems. When we dismiss these performances as nothing more than harmful capitulation to racist white standards, we deny black performers and audiences these feelings, rob them of their agency, and do a kind of violence to their memory.

By locating Uncle Tom's transformation on the stage, scholars have posited essentially two iterations of the character: Stowe's humble Christian and the boot-licking minstrel fool who hobbled onto American stages. This binary narrative does not adequately reflect the complexity of race in America. It

does not explain why a number of white Southerners at the turn of the twentieth century responded to *Uncle Tom's Cabin* plays as if they would violently
unravel the social order, nor why black commentators interpreted those same
productions as relevant to protests against lynching. Reliance on the category
of racism has a tendency to cut off analysis precisely at the point at which it is
most needed. We've seen this recently in the many deaths of unarmed black
men and women at the hands of law enforcement. The binary of racism and,
for lack of a better term, not-racism, in which racism is a clearly identifiable
bad thing (a Confederate flag, for example, or use of the N-word) engaged
in only by bad people, has helped create a society in which many, albeit not
enough, Americans explicitly deny the existence of an innate racial hierarchy.
Yet removing the Confederate flag from state buildings in Charleston is not,
of course, the same thing as removing racism. The racist/nonracist category
has discouraged Americans from acknowledging the unseen structures of racism that persist. In order to address these complicated structures, in this book
identifying racism is not a conclusion but rather a starting point for investigating how race worked at a particular moment. I use Uncle Tom as a kind
of Rorschach inkblot for American race relations: what this figure has meant
tells us less about him than it does about those who have responded to him.

The Birth of Uncle Tom

If Uncle Tom had, like Sister Carrie or Huck Finn, remained safely inside
the literary work that created him, his name probably would not have become a slur, and certainly not as widely known and referenced as it is today.
But Harriet Beecher Stowe's Tom was only the first of many, and his name
permeated American culture with a breadth and frequency unmatched in
American literary history. Stowe's blockbuster novel had several popular
characters, among them Eva, Topsy, and Eliza, whose ice-crossing became
one of the most famous scenes in the adaptations. But it was Uncle Tom that
came to stand in for everything the novel represented. Part of this may have
been syntactic happenstance, a result of the English language's unfriendliness
to doubling up possessives. ("*Uncle Tom's Cabin*'s popularity" sounds more
awkward than "Uncle Tom's popularity.") When writing about the novel,
critics often shortened its title to *Uncle Tom* in the service of more fluid prose.

But Uncle Tom was much more than a convenient abbreviation for a book title. He was also the most contentious character in a spectacularly well-known and controversial book, one that, as Jane P. Tompkins notes, deployed "the culture's greatest religious myth, the story of the crucifixion," and "its most cherished social beliefs—the sanctity of motherhood and the family" to encapsulate the greatest political and cultural conflict in American history.[26] Slave narratives published before 1852 gave white readers a chance to consider the humanity of black people, but these sold in limited numbers, and generally to readers who already held abolitionist sympathies. Frederick Douglass' 1845 *Narrative of the Life of Frederick Douglass*, for example, sold 30,000 copies during the 1840s while aided by a vigorous lecture tour, a total that is just 3 percent of the first-year sales of *Uncle Tom's Cabin* in the United States and Britain. In an era in which slaves counted as three fifths of a person and the superiority of the white race over the black race was widely considered a fact, Uncle Tom was the first humanized, even glorified representation of a black person that many whites had encountered. (The light-skinned George Harris, who explicitly attributes many of his characteristics to his Anglo-Saxon ancestry, perhaps did not present the same challenges to white audiences.) In his strength and submissiveness, in his commitment to God above both himself and his master, Stowe's Tom was the novel's exemplar of Christian virtue. If the reader had any doubts about the character's Christliness, Stowe made it explicit by titling the chapter in which he dies "The Martyr."

With the spread of *Uncle Tom's Cabin*, people from every walk of life and from all over the world wept in sympathy for the cruel plight of American slaves, from the working-class Frenchman who bought his bread at an Uncle Tom bakeshop to British royalty like the Earl of Shaftesbury, who announced himself a fan. George Sand's breathless review of the novel proclaimed, "This book is in all hands and in all journals. It has, and will have, editions in every form; people devour it, they cover it with tears. It is no longer permissible to those who can read not to have read it."[27] *Uncle Tom's Cabin* became the first great American success in the international cultural marketplace. The novel's centrality to the coming of the Civil War and the abolition of slavery was suggested by none other than Abraham Lincoln, who was rumored to have said, upon meeting Stowe, "So this is the little lady who wrote the book that started this great war."[28] Although the Lincoln story is probably apocryphal, the sentiment was a common one. Many Americans—black and white, across regions and the political spectrum—believed that Stowe's novel was a fundamental impetus for the Civil War.

The novel's political impact also reached far beyond the issue of slavery, to the very humanity of black Americans. Although others had argued for the equality of the races, most notably Frederick Douglass, who presented himself as a prime example of black achievement, Uncle Tom was the first black hero in American literature to capture the minds and hearts of a large audience. George Eliot, for one, wrote that Stowe had "*invented* the Negro novel," meaning not that Stowe was the first novelist to include black characters, but rather that she was the first one to reach a wide readership while taking blacks seriously as human beings.[29] In what Philip Fisher identifies as a characteristic strategy of the sentimental novel, Stowe's novel extends "normal states of primary feeling to people from whom they have been previously withheld."[30] Fueled by the revolutionary power of this novel, Uncle Tom became the center of the first major national conversation about the humanity of African Americans as well as a catalyzing figure in debates about abolitionist strategy.

From the moment *Uncle Tom's Cabin* entered American culture, it inspired wave upon wave of political and material responses. Southern whites protested that Stowe's book got both the institution of slavery and the character of slaves entirely wrong. They insisted that such horrors never (or rarely) happened, and that no black man could be as virtuous as Uncle Tom. Meanwhile, writers, artists, and entrepreneurs adapted Stowe's work in virtually every medium, from literature and theater to card games and plates. Whether adaptors of *Uncle Tom's Cabin* prioritized politics or profit, they could not help but grapple with the novel's two most shocking notions: that the institution of slavery was unjust and unchristian and that black slaves were human beings. Stowe's novel and its adaptations became a key arena in which Americans debated the fraught, twin issues of slavery and race, issues that would prove no less complicated or controversial once the question of slavery was legally settled.

One might have expected *Uncle Tom's Cabin* to fade in popularity with the abolition of slavery and the end of the Civil War. It had once been about a pressing political issue, one for which hundreds of thousands of Americans were ultimately willing to die. But even when the nation was officially reunited and slavery was abolished, *Uncle Tom's Cabin* didn't disappear—far from it. The novel continued to be reprinted nearly every year through the 1920s and regularly even after that, with some libraries reporting that Stowe's novel was one of the most popular items among patrons.[31] Stage adaptations of Stowe's story, which first appeared shortly after the novel's initial serialization in the *National Era*, flooded the nation into the 1930s. So did film adaptations, as the technology developed. Stephen Railton counts nine cinematic versions of *Uncle Tom's Cabin* between 1903 and 1927, from a one-reel Edison-Porter version that preceded even *The Great Train Robbery* to a big-budget thirteen-reel Universal film.[32]

If the abolition of slavery was the primary goal of Stowe's novel and that goal had been achieved, why did *Uncle Tom's Cabin* remain so prominent in American culture for so long after the Civil War? Certainly, Americans appreciated Stowe's work as a good story, full of romance and violence, comedy and tragedy, happy families and those torn apart. It is doubtful that the novel or its many adaptations would have caught on or remained popular if they had not been a pleasure to read and watch. Indeed, *Uncle Tom's Cabin* is not only genuinely moving—a feature that Leslie Fiedler was loathe to admit—but also a surprisingly funny book, filled with dry humor. Even so, *Uncle Tom's Cabin* was never simply a work of fiction or drama, and Uncle Tom was never simply a character; *Uncle Tom's Cabin* and its hero were verdicts, truthful or not, about the real nature of American chattel slavery, the South, and African Americans. Even once the passage of the Thirteenth Amendment settled the issue of slavery's legality, the institution's legacy remained open for discussion, as did the fate of the four million newly freed blacks. Stowe's novel and the many adaptations it inspired served as a central, ever-contested site for the nation's continuing racial and sectional debates, offering a space and vocabulary in which the nation could wrestle with the many cultural disruptions that had not been resolved with Appomattox. The persistent visibility of *Uncle Tom's Cabin* and its many popular adaptations made Uncle Tom the one black person that virtually every nineteenth-century American "knew."

If for whites Uncle Tom was a broad representative of blackness in America, black Americans more specifically saw this figure as the symbol of a traumatic collective history that many experienced as degrading, humiliating, and shameful. Unlike guilt, which develops from an individual's belief that she has violated her own accepted standards of behavior, shame is an externally oriented affect, coming from a feeling of personal inadequacy according to accepted standards. Guilt allows the subject to maintain a distinction between the self and the violating behavior. Shame, however, collapses the two, such that the violation *is* the self, and it manifests as "fear of exposing one's defective self to others."[33] Shame about slavery provoked some black Americans to approach the spirituals, and later the blues, as "part of a vernacular culture that needed to be left behind, an embarrassing remnant."[34] Even W. E. B. Du Bois, a firm believer in the importance of preserving the memory and cultural productions of slavery, described the period of the race's enslavement as "The Valley of Humiliation" in his historical pageant, *The Star of Ethiopia* (1911). The figure of Uncle Tom allowed irrational but nevertheless deeply held feelings of shame about the slavery past and continued oppression to be translated into blame. This psychological function distinguishes Uncle Tom from other influential literary characters and help explains why other oppressed groups have adapted this figure for their own intraracial critiques: "Uncle Tomahawk" for Native Americans, "Uncle Chan" for Asian Americans, "Aunt Tom" for feminists.

A Literary Phenomenon

In order to explain how a nineteenth-century literary character took on such an active life of his own, it's important to set out the technological advances, market changes, and national and international politics that pushed Stowe's novel and its hero into nearly every facet of American culture. At the end of 1852, less than a year after the publication of *Uncle Tom's Cabin*, the New York *Literary World* described the novel's instant and enormous popularity as "a phenomenon in the literary world, one of those phenomena which set at naught all previous experience and baffle all established and recognized principles."[35] In the first year of its publication, *Uncle Tom's Cabin* sold a record-making 300,000 copies in the United States alone, the equivalent of close to seven million copies in today's market. (The number becomes even more impressive when one considers that each copy is estimated to have had eight to ten readers.)[36] First-year international sales were also staggering, reaching close to one million in the United States and Britain, with more copies sold all over the world as translations came out.

From the beginning, the astonishing success of *Uncle Tom's Cabin* mystified critics, who often posed a version of the question asked by *Christian Parlor Magazine* a few months after the novel's publication: "What is in it to make it so wonderful?"[37] Explanations of the novel's success have varied tremendously, but all have tended to be vague and not quite adequate, circling around the novel's mysterious influence without arriving at any real conclusion about the origins of its immediate and lasting power. The *New York Evangelist* offered a typically inexact account, locating the novel's indubitable popularity in either its subject, its spirit, or its readers:

> Criticism may smile or frown, may dislike "the plot" and call the whole "absolute and audacious trash"; yet nothing can beat Uncle Tom in the art of finding readers. There is something in the book, in its theme, in the spirit with which it is executed, or in human nature, or in all these put together, that has given it an unprecedented popularity.[38]

Whether or not one liked the book or thought it was accurate about American slavery, there was no doubt that it excelled in "the art of finding readers." With almost preternatural timing, Uncle Tom entered a world that was singularly poised for the massive circulation of his image and a society that had just become ready for him. The *Uncle Tom's Cabin* phenomenon that made this character a household name came out of a perfect storm of factors both within and outside of the novel. With the recent passing of the Fugitive Slave Law, part of the Compromise of 1850, slavery had become a heightened concern in American politics. The law required all Americans, even those living in states where slavery was illegal, to help return fugitives to their masters. United States marshals and deputy marshals who refused to do everything in their power to capture a fugitive slave would be fined one thousand dollars, and if a fugitive escaped under their watch, marshals were liable for the full dollar value. Any person who obstructed the arrest of a fugitive or attempted to help one in any way, even by providing food or shelter, could be punished with a one-thousand-dollar fine and imprisonment for six months.[39] Now Northerners who had been content to leave the slavery issue to the South were forced to become an active part of it.

Stowe was indignant about the Fugitive Slave Law, writing to her sister that it made her feel "almost choked sometimes with pent up wrath that does no good."[40] Shortly after the law's passage, when another sister wrote urging Stowe to use her writing talent to help the nation understand the wrongness of slavery, Stowe realized that fiction could be a way for her to channel her righteous anger into something productive. Upon reading her sister's letter in the parlor one evening, she stood up and declared to her children, "I will write something. I will if I live."[41] Fiction, she knew, had the power to influence people in a way that a political tract could not.

At the same time that Northerners were becoming more receptive to an anti-slavery message, new technologies promoted the unprecedentedly rapid spread and wide embrace of *Uncle Tom's Cabin*. Cost-saving technological advancements in printing made books available to an expanded readership. The steam-powered Adams Power Printing Press, patented in 1836, enabled much faster production of books and therefore drastically reduced their cost. With the invention of stereotyping in 1811 and electrotyping in 1841, new editions of books no longer required the resetting of type. Publishers could make permanent, relatively inexpensive metal plates and store them for subsequent editions. Other technologies that aided book production included two paper-making machines that came into widespread use in the 1830s: the belt-based Foudrinier (1799) and Thomas Gilpin's cylinder (1816). By allowing the production of continuous rolls of paper in large widths, these machines offered a significant savings of time over sheet-by-sheet printing.[42] Technological advancements outside of book production also promoted the wide circulation of *Uncle Tom's Cabin*. Beginning in the 1830s and continuing until the Civil War, a railway boom spread railroad tracks across the United States, connecting what had been regional publishing networks into a growing national print culture. As Ronald J. Zboray points out, because the railroad network was clustered in the Northeast, publishers and authors could and did ignore the preferences of Southern readers in favor of Northern markets.[43] Meanwhile, improved and cheaper domestic lighting and wider availability of eyeglasses expanded the hours for reading and made it easier for Americans to sit down with a book.

In its entrance to the growing American literary marketplace, *Uncle Tom's Cabin* also benefited from the unusually canny and extensive promotional strategies of the novel's first publisher, the small Boston firm John P. Jewett and Company. Boston's leading publisher, Phillips, Sampson, had already rejected Stowe's novel during its 1851–1852 serialization in the abolitionist journal *The National Era*, one partner holding that it "would not sell a thousand copies"—clearly a monumental misjudgment.[44] But Jewett's wife, who had started reading the serials in *The National Era*, urged her husband to publish it, insisting that it would sell well. Before even a third of the novel had been serialized, Jewett wrote to Stowe and secured a contract with her to print *Uncle Tom's Cabin*, not knowing how long the novel would ultimately become. As Claire Parfait has documented, Jewett was an unusually savvy marketer who capitalized on existing publicity practices to promote *Uncle Tom's Cabin* and developed effective new ones.[45] With a prophetic understanding of the power of advertising, he ensured extensive coverage of Stowe's novel before its publication by spending thousands of dollars sending advertisements and prepared notices about the novel to magazines and newspapers. Following the custom of the day, these publications would print Jewett's notices as editorial matter with little or no amendment, as compensation for purchasing advertising.[46] Though Jewett's firm was small and had limited resources, he advertised as much as firms more than five times the size of his own, and he did so with greater acuity. While other publishers tended to advertise a different title in each issue of a journal, Jewett repeated the same advertisement in several issues, building interest over time.

But Jewett's real innovation came once the novel was in print, in his sophisticated understanding that the choice to buy something was as much a social decision as a personal one. In paid advertisements and prepared notices, the publisher went beyond the usual advertising practice of informing consumers about the content and quality of *Uncle Tom's Cabin*. More crucially, he stressed the novel's immense success, going into detail not only about its record sales figures but also the complicated logistical demands of printing so many copies. By handling the novel's success as itself "an unprecedented event, a publishing phenomenon," as Parfait suggests, Jewett's advertising campaign built on its own success, using past sales to promote future ones.[47] Consumers who read about all the excitement over Stowe's novel could get swept up along with it. One of Jewett's reports, reprinted in *The Liberator* and *The Independent*, among other periodicals, announced that his publishing firm was having trouble meeting the high demand for *Uncle Tom's Cabin*, despite keeping three papers mills and three Adams power presses running twenty-four hours every day of the week except Sunday. Within three weeks of the novel's publication, 20,000 copies had sold.[48] By May, *The Independent* reported, 125 to 200 bookbinders were constantly at work binding 90,000 pounds of paper into 55 tons of bound volumes.[49] And by June, *Uncle Tom's Cabin* was in such high demand at New York's Mercantile Library that the institution purchased forty-five copies, which remained in constant rotation among the city's future merchants.[50] A few copies of the novel even found their way across the country to California, where miners paid 25 cents to take their turn at reading it.[51] Jewett, the first publisher to so heavily emphasize these kinds of facts and figures, anticipated what has become common knowledge in contemporary publishing, where magazines and mass-market trade books often trumpet numbers on their covers ("10 Ways to Cut Calories," *People* magazine's "50 Most Beautiful People," *The 7 Habits of Highly Effective People*) in order to increase sales. Though splashing numbers on the covers of magazines can produce a cluttered appearance, it is so effective in boosting newsstand sales that magazine publishers often embrace the tactic for copies sold from newsstands, while opting for a simpler version of the cover for the subscribers who have already purchased their copy in advance and therefore don't need to be convinced.[52]

When sales of *Uncle Tom's Cabin* began to level toward the end of 1852, Jewett responded by coming out with a cheaper "Edition for the Million," which helped sell more copies of the novel after the upper end of the market had become saturated.[53] And with sales of that edition calming by the end of 1853, the following year Jewett published Stowe's *Key to "Uncle Tom's Cabin."* Although the *Key* was positioned as a defense of the novel's account of slavery, it also helped keep Uncle Tom in the limelight. Moreover, Jewett understood the potential of finding new ways to expand the reach of the novel beyond Stowe's text. For further promotion, he hired the poet John Greenleaf Whittier to write a poem, "Little Eva: Uncle Tom's Guardian Angel," and then had the composer Manuel Emilio set Whittier's lyrics to music.

Even outside of Jewett's savvy publicity tactics, *Uncle Tom's Cabin* seemed to spur its own promotion, to an astounding extent. Jewett's effort at selling branded products—what has come to be called "merchandising" in contemporary parlance—ultimately constituted a small portion of what became a massive proliferation of *Uncle Tom's Cabin* spin-offs produced without his or Stowe's knowledge or consent. Indeed, within months of the publication of *Uncle Tom's Cabin*, J. S. Dwight's prominent music journal grumbled that every music publisher had to make his own "Little Eva" song, with composers paying more attention to song titles than to the quality of the music: "[A]ll the minor composers are as busy on this theme, as if it were the one point of contact for the time being with the popular sympathies."[54] If not the *only* point of contact with the popular sympathies, *Uncle Tom's Cabin* was certainly one of the more efficient means of accessing them. It was infinitely adaptable, providing a foundation of ready popularity on which any other creator or manufacturer could build.

Figure 1a. "Uncle Tom's Cabin: Vision of Uncle Tom," commemorative plate. Harriet Beecher Stowe Center, Hartford, CT.

Perhaps most important, the novel's fast-moving, multi-threaded plot, its archetypal characters, and its panoramic scope made it a uniquely rich source for adaptation and translation, suited to any genre and attractive to all audiences. Those interested in riding the wave of the novel's popularity found that it offered a treasure trove of source material: romance and violence, comedy and tragedy, happy families and those torn apart, angels and demons, convention and radicalism. And these elements could be selectively plucked and reimagined in a vast number of ways: moral theater for church groups, proslavery "anti-Tom" novels, playing cards for children, porcelain figurines and plates for display in parlors, fine paintings and sculptures for art collectors. (See figures 1a and 1b.) The easy adaptability of *Uncle Tom's Cabin* found a

Figure 1b. "Onkel Tom's Hutte playing card #8," ca. 1855. Harriet Beecher Stowe Center, Hartford, CT.

convenient complement in the mid-nineteenth century's rising middle class and consumer culture. As the popularity of Stowe's novel grew, artists and businesspeople capitalized on its success, using its basic premises and characters as the launching point for products across a variety of media and levels of cultural sophistication. Though these products were not approved by Stowe or her publisher and did not make them money directly, to some extent they fostered a mutually beneficial situation: Uncle Tom products sold well because of the novel's popularity, but they also helped sell copies by contributing to the worldwide Uncle Tom frenzy.

In an 1853 letter to Stowe, the English clergyman John Angell James called *Uncle Tom's Cabin* "the literary phenomenon which has fallen on us like the manna in the camp of the Israelites, adapted to every taste, and relished by every palate."[55] The clergyman offered an apt analogy in comparing the novel to the Israelites' manna, which is described so differently at various points in the Old Testament that, Biblical commentators concluded, its taste must have varied according to who ate it. Stowe's novel, adapted into a seemingly infinite number of forms and genres, was similarly molded into whatever Americans were most eager to purchase. It is striking to note that, even while writing to the novel's author, James described the creation of *Uncle Tom's Cabin* as a kind of divine miracle—a notion that Stowe would also promote in her claim that "I didn't write it, God did"—underscoring Stowe's limited control over the creations her novel inspired. His sense of the novel's unique versatility and adaptability anticipates the later observation of the novelist Henry James, who would describe Stowe's novel as "much less a book than a state of vision, of feeling and of consciousness," comparing it to "a wonderful 'leaping' fish" that had transcended the limits of the page and made itself at home wherever it landed, no matter the medium.[56] Adaptations of Stowe's novel varied significantly in their meaning and intent. At the same time that minstrel Uncle Toms cavorted on Bowery stages, Uncle Tom spin-offs purchased for display inside the home could be emphatically sentimental. In their numerous forms, these adaptations of Stowe's novel both reflected and created the culture surrounding it.

Stowe's story had a singularly active existence outside the pages of the text itself. Of course, the merchandising of popular works was not new; Dickens' fiction was quite popular in this arena, as were products related to the fashionable opera singer Jenny Lind. However, the freedom with which adaptations of Stowe's novel departed from the text was unique. Unlike the popular Little Nell merchandise from Dickens' *The Old Curiosity Shop*, for example, Uncle Tom products were inspired by ideological as well as financial considerations. By their very subject matter, these products were plugged into deep and enduring issues of race in America, and they could not help but engage with the pressing question of racial difference.

The cultural power of *Uncle Tom's Cabin* was immediately obvious to pro-slavery Americans, who worried that its instant popularity and sympathetic readership would help end slavery. To counter Stowe's attacks, they created their own ideological breed of fiction. "In order to meet the fallacies of this abolition tale, it would be well if the friends of the Union would array fiction against fiction," reasoned the *Pittsburgh Gazette*. "Meet the disunionists with their own chosen weapon, and they are foiled."[57] In an age before film or television, with a growing, increasingly literate middle class looking to spend its dollars on entertainment, fiction was, more than ever before, a means of reaching a large American audience. Within a few months of the publication of *Uncle Tom's Cabin*, a Southern writer hoping to set straight the record on slavery came out with *Life at the South: Uncle Tom's Cabin as It Is*. Several more anti-Tom texts followed; *The Independent* counted eight within six months, noting that Stowe's novel seemed to have produced a whole new school of literature from both sides of the slavery debate.[58] Indeed, before *Uncle Tom's Cabin*, as William R. Taylor notes, the Southern plantation novel (a genre that emerged in the 1830s) had concentrated on the lives of white planters, with slaves appearing only in bit parts. But Stowe's novel lastingly expanded the focus from planter only to master and slave.[59] The practice of giving significant attention to slave life and character continued for decades after the publication of Stowe's novel, most notably in the fiction of Joel Chandler Harris and Thomas Nelson Page. Twain's *Adventures of Huckleberry Finn* (1885), with its depiction of the interracial friendship between Huck Finn and Jim, might also be thought to descend from Stowe. With the popularity of *Uncle Tom's Cabin*, Stowe had set up a cultural battleground upon which the nature of both the institution of slavery and of African Americans would be hotly contested for many years to come.

"Uncle Sam Put to Open Shame by Uncle Tom"

Abroad, just as in the United States, *Uncle Tom's Cabin* rippled across various media. In London, on Christmas night of 1852, stage versions of *Uncle Tom's Cabin* played in no less than five theaters, with varying levels of faithfulness to Stowe's novel. An "equestrian version" at Astley's Amphitheatre ended not with Uncle Tom's tragic death but with a sword scene between Cassy and Legree. Across the Thames, a show at Sadler's Wells reached its peak with "a display of rival 'Uncle Toms,' each greater than the last."[60] At a Parisian cattle market's Carnival promenade, where traditionally the largest ox was named after the celebrity of the year, the leading ox of 1853 was called Uncle Tom, with the two smaller oxen accompanying him named Shelby and St. Clare.[61] Meanwhile, French choreographers composed a schottisch and a quadrille named after Uncle Tom, and licorice was now called "Uncle Tom candy"—as if Uncle Tom had come to define blackness.[62]

With the novel's translation into a multitude of languages—not just French and German but also Chinese, Welsh, Armenian, Finnish, and Hungarian, among others—Uncle Tom became perhaps the most widely traveled ambassador of American culture. Anti-slavery publications such as *Frederick Douglass' Paper*, *The National Era*, and *The Liberator* eagerly followed the novel's success abroad, but American slavery advocates were incensed by its enormous international popularity. A writer for *The Southern Literary Messenger* protested that Stowe, with "shameless disregard to truth," was slandering her own country to the world, "filling the minds of all who know nothing of slavery with hatred for that institution and those who uphold it."[63] By publicizing what many Southerners thought was a flagrantly unfair representation of slavery, Stowe was, they charged, giving foreigners an invitation to criticize the nation. Proslavery groups felt that Stowe's novel went too far in airing America's dirty laundry and complained that *Uncle Tom's Cabin* was popular only because it offered an American travesty that allowed the English to divert attention from the oppressive labor system in their own country. The *New York Herald* charged that Europeans who sympathized with Uncle Tom and condemned his oppressors failed to realize "that they themselves are the Legrees and the Haleys upon whom retribution must fall."[64] To supporters of slavery, Uncle Tom was nothing less than a traitor to his nation. "How they rejoice to see Mrs. Stowe's hand lifting up the veil, and exposing the nakedness of the republic—to see Uncle Sam put to open shame by Uncle Tom!" wailed one magazine.[65]

For those in favor of the institution of slavery, Uncle Tom was the most egregious fabrication in a book of slanderous lies, and his popularity in such a wide variety of media only made it worse. They described the Uncle Tom phenomenon as an uncontrollable disease that they were powerless to stop. Less than a year after *Uncle Tom's Cabin* was published, the Democratic magazine *Putnam's* reported that the entire world was becoming "Uncle Tomitized" by an "Uncle Tomific" that, "like the cholera, knows no distinction of climate or race."[66] In similar language, *The Literary World* complained that an "Uncle Tom epidemic" had swept the globe "with unabated violence," seizing men, women, and children from every walk of life: "The prevailing affection is universal, and all have the Uncle Tom."[67] Spreading as fast as cholera, *Uncle Tom's Cabin* brought together millions of people of different races and classes from all over the world in shared sympathy for slaves. In an age of international political revolution, the novel's deep penetration across cultures threatened to do serious violence to an already-precarious status quo. In the middle of the controversy over American slavery, Uncle Tom was both the personification of a growing movement that recognized the humanity of black people and the body over which that humanity would continue to be debated.

Character and Culture

This book investigates what happens when a literary character exits a novel and takes on an independent life. While I would argue that Uncle Tom has had a uniquely dynamic and controversial cultural life, his story nevertheless provides a case study of the kind of cultural work a literary character can do. Stowe's is not the only character who has enjoyed a life outside of the source text. Some characters have worked their way into common language: Miguel de Cervantes' Don Quixote, for example, constructed the quixotic type. Others, such as Shakespeare's Shylock, have become embodiments of ethnic and racial stereotypes. Still others have provided shorthand for personality types (Ebenezer Scrooge, Captain Ahab) or complex ideas (the monstrous creature in Mary Shelley's *Frankenstein*, now popularly believed to be the novel's title character rather than his inventor).[68]

Character, as John Frow and others have noted, is a crucial and yet strikingly undertheorized element of the novel, "both ontologically and methodologically ambivalent" because of its dual status as literary device, on the one hand, and cultural concept related to the individual or self, on the other.[69] As Alex Woloch usefully articulates, "literary character is itself divided," simultaneously pushing the novel to expand outward, toward an actual person who might exist in the world and who might think or do any number of things not represented in the novel (character's referential function), and inward, to the finite set of descriptions and social interactions contained within a narrative's structure (its structural function).[70] Of course, character is hardly the only element of fiction that is both referential and structural. The same might be said of fictional settings: consider, for example, Huck Finn and Jim's travel down the Ohio River; the river is both a geographical conduit between the slave South and ultimate freedom in the North and a liminal space in which the two characters can relate as human beings.

What ultimately distinguishes character from other novelistic devices is its three-pronged referentiality. Characters can represent human beings in three ways, all of which have social repercussions. One is through the amount of space they occupy in a given work of fiction. In the aggregate, if most black characters in fiction are minor, as was the case for many years in American literature, literature can imply the minimal importance of an entire race. The second mode of representation is at the individual level, in the personality traits and activities of a character. For example, a novel seriously portraying a black doctor might show a white reader that such types can and do exist, while one that pokes fun at such a character's delusions of grandeur might suggest that there is no such thing as black progress. This mode can also work historically, suggesting a certain assessment of the past. The third aspect of representation is social: when fictional narratives frequently repeat a set of power relations between characters, they can create a cultural script that perpetuates that power dynamic in real life.

That literary characters help us imagine complex social relationships is a crucial feature of fiction's cultural power that has received relatively little attention in the recent critical revival of character. This book builds on recent works including Deidre Lynch's *The Economy of Character*, Woloch's *The One and the Many*, and David Brewer's *The Afterlife of Character* by offering a wider scale of analysis: the relationship between character and culture.[71] Woloch's scale of analysis is the finite structure of the realist novel, which he suggests is destabilized by its "dual impulses to bring in a multitude of characters and to bring out the interiority of a single protagonist."[72] Through the concepts of character-space and character-system, Woloch richly theorizes the competition between characters for narrative space as a mirror of the struggle for economic resources. While this Marxian interpretation halts at the boundaries of the individual novel, such a competition for space must be reexamined when characters become part of a broader social struggle for resources, rights, and recognition. To that end, Lynch's scale of analysis extends to the imaginative space of the eighteenth-century British reader, who, she argues, used fictional characters as a "coping mechanism" in a rapidly changing, alienating society of complex class and gender divisions.[73] While Lynch's "pragmatics of character" identifies the individual psyche as character's most resonant cultural space, David Brewer posits a more communal function for character in what he calls "imaginative expansion," a practice in which communities of readers collaboratively envision extended lives for fictional characters. (Today we call this "fan fiction.") Brewer sees imaginative expansion as a function of domestic stability, in which fictional characters become "a common object to rally around."[74] Yet the case of *Uncle Tom's Cabin* offers a more complicated social alternative, in which a character becomes a common object over which to struggle. Indeed, Stowe's Uncle Tom functioned as an imaginative space in which a heterogeneous nation negotiated the most fraught, contentious, and deeply imbricated issue in its history: race.

Fiction is not simply "about" something; as Joshua Landy observes, "[f]ictions also give *form* to this aboutness; they instigate a *process* . . . and they have an *effect* that goes far beyond the mere delivery of information."[75] The "formative" function that Landy identifies works not only for the individual reader, who develops new capacities for seeing the world, but also for a society facing a seemingly intractable problem. Among the many features of the novel that inform the choices readers make in their daily lives, character holds an especially rich capacity for activating the imagination as a useful political and social space, thereby helping readers imagine and make sense of social transformation. Characters derive some of this potential power from their simultaneous fictionality and referentiality: they reference people, the basic unit of society, but they are not actual people, for whom reality imposes certain limits on the imagination. A character can take on an independent life with a flexibility that a real person cannot. By and large, the characters that do this are of the sort that E. M. Forster called "flat": sometimes called a "type," they are "constructed around a single idea or quality" and thus both "easily recognized . . . by the reader's emotional eye" and "easily remembered."[76] Sometimes, as Forster notes of Charles Dickens' characters in particular, a flat character is so skillfully written that she is also immensely vital. But that vitality alone cannot account for the cultural penetration of a character like Uncle Tom. Importantly, Stowe's character combined the easy classification of the type—the Christian martyr—with the previously unfathomable—a fully human black person featured in a widely read literary work—at a highly contentious cultural moment. At once familiar and radical, this flat character became ambiguous enough to invite multiple, opposing interpretations.

Organized chronologically, this book begins by situating the hero of *Uncle Tom's Cabin* in a nineteenth-century context of sentimentality and Christianity. In Chapter 1, I argue that Tom is both the novel's model for Christian political reform and its universal masculine ideal, and that, for African Americans, this character embodied the tension between Christian submission and political protest. Of course, Stowe's Uncle Tom was only the first of many. The next two chapters reveal Uncle Tom's dignified representation on the antebellum American stage, which I argue disrupted existing minstrel stereotypes to incite the North against slavery, as well as the enduring ideological controversies around the *Uncle Tom's Cabin* plays. Guided by records of the promotion and reception of these plays, in Chapter 3 I show that they remained politically relevant and inspiring to many black Americans and deeply threatening to some white Southerners well into the twentieth century. In Chapter 4, I return to the Uncle Tom literary character and its continuing presence in American literature. Here, I argue that pre–Harlem Renaissance black writers including Charles Chesnutt, Mary Church Terrell, and a young James Weldon Johnson saw Uncle Tom as a potential model of politically effective, emotionally powerful characterization that could be adapted to the injustices of modern black life.

To explain Uncle Tom's transformation, then, we must look beyond the expressive arts. In Chapter 5, I show how Uncle Tom became a slur in the mainstream black political discourse of the 1910s and situate the figure's transformation in the shifting rhetoric of the Old and New Negro at the turn of the century. Despite Uncle Tom's pejorative meaning, protests by African Americans against *Uncle Tom's Cabin* and its title character did not arise for another two decades. In Chapter 6, I suggest that while New Negro critics were confident that the days of Uncle Tom were over, during the 1930s research on the social and psychological impact of film made black Americans more alert to the complex ways that racial patterns in film and radio contributed to the continuing denial of rights to black people in America. An increasingly sophisticated critique of "Uncle Tom roles" in film developed, ultimately prompting widespread rejection of both *Uncle Tom's Cabin* and its eponymous character. Finally, in the Epilogue, I address Uncle Tom's cultural and political life after Stowe's novel lost its progressive reputation, showing how authors and activists drew on the figure to explore the enduring legacies of slavery in the black community.

Characters endure not just because they are pleasurable but also because they are useful, whether to the individual reader who wants to enjoy getting lost in a book, groups of readers gathered in book clubs, or a complex society attempting to navigate its deepest anxieties. Uncle Tom has always, in a sense, been a mixed-race figure. Whether as a white author's imagining of a black slave, or as a black person who submits to whites, this figure lives within the social space of the color line, an ever-present embodiment of perceived incompatibilities between the races. Despite significant advancements in civil rights and race relations, the fact that Uncle Tom is still so often referenced in popular culture suggests just how deeply drawn these racial divisions remain.

CHAPTER 1

A MANLY HERO

SINCE HIS BIRTH in Harriet Beecher Stowe's anti-slavery novel, Uncle Tom has appeared on thousands of stages and in a dozen or more movies; he has been painted, drawn, and sculpted; he has been re-imagined by pro-slavery Southerners and by black protest writers; he has crisscrossed the country and circuited the globe. After such a long and active life outside of Stowe's novel, it's no wonder that the original Uncle Tom tends to get lost in the crowd. Despite a wide critical acknowledgment that the hero of *Uncle Tom's Cabin* is not, in fact, an Uncle Tom, at least not in the way that we understand the term today, the large body of Stowe criticism has allowed contemporary ideas about race, gender, religion, politics, and even death to mask the consistently radical values of *Uncle Tom's Cabin* itself. It is worth noting that, during the decade and a half after the Civil War, when the lawyer and novelist Albion Tourgée had Stowe's novel read to a large number of "the most intelligent colored people in the former slave states ... almost every one of them noted the freedom of speech between master and servant."[1] One insisted that "Uncle Tom must have been raised up north!" To those formerly enslaved, Uncle Tom was not a figure of submission, but rather a man unrealistically assertive with his master.

Uncle Tom has had almost as many identities within the literary critical literature as he has had in American culture, but the resurgence of Stowe criticism since the 1970s has produced two prevalent agreements about Uncle Tom: first, that he is feminine—a "heroine instead of a hero," as Elizabeth

Ammons describes him—and second, that Uncle Tom's heroism is racially differentiated from white or even mulatto heroism.[2] If Uncle Tom is submissive
and self-sacrificing, the argument goes, then he is feminine, a central part of
the nineteenth-century domestic novel's feminine reorganization of culture.[3]
And if Stowe's full-blooded black protagonist is the novel's most submissive
Christian, then his Christ-like heroism must come from the color of his skin
and confirm what George Fredrickson describes as the novel's romantic racialism.[4] Both of these perspectives on Uncle Tom strongly differentiate him from
the novel's white men, positing a segregated system of values within the text.[5]
Critics have read this differentiation in many different ways: as Stowe's critique of the masculine world, as her misguided effort to argue against slavery
even while upholding racial difference, as a racist devaluation of black masculinity.[6] This chapter, however, reads Uncle Tom as Stowe's universal masculine
ideal and, ultimately, the novel's most radical assertion of both the possibility
of racial equality and the natural human right to freedom. Through the character of Uncle Tom, Stowe dramatizes a tension central to abolitionist debates of
the time: between natural rights and religious obligations. I begin by discussing the novel's representations of racial difference, arguing that alongside the
romantic racialist language noted by George Fredrickson, *Uncle Tom's Cabin*
often couches its racial generalizations in contingency, just as often attributing
racial characteristics to environment and experience as to biology. Moreover,
Uncle Tom's perfect moral character comes not from his race, I show, but from
his conversion to a Christianity that was widely praised by critics of the 1850s.
Next I address the character's position in discussions about the role of religion
in racial protest. Finally, I situate Tom among the novel's other characters,
both black and white, arguing that the novel embraces a shared notion of masculine Christian values for both races. This ideal, encapsulated in what Stowe
calls the "manly heart," combines deep emotional sensitivity with a willingness
to act selflessly. Although Tom refuses to make his own escape from slavery, he
recognizes the desire for freedom as both natural and right.

Race in Uncle Tom's Cabin

In 1971, George Fredrickson coined the term "romantic racialism" to describe
a racial attitude, virtually standard among mid-nineteenth-century anti-

slavery activists, that accepted racial differences but not a racial hierarchy.[7] According to romantic racialists, biology made black people permanently childlike and submissive. While some concluded from this merely that whites should not exploit blacks, others, most notably Alexander Kinmont and William Ellery Channing, went a step further, arguing that these qualities made black people natural Christians and therefore perhaps even inherently morally superior to whites.[8] After all, in the New Testament, Christ counsels his followers to model their faith after little children.[9]

In an argument embraced by many Stowe critics, Fredrickson presents *Uncle Tom's Cabin* as "the classic expression of romantic racialism," arguing that the novel offers the fullest and most influential representation of blacks as natural Christians.[10] Counterposing Uncle Tom's submissive Christianity to George Harris' aggressive spirit, Fredrickson further argues that Stowe's black characters are easily distinguished in their docility from the novel's mulattoes, who are "restive and rebellious" as a result of their Anglo-Saxon blood.[11] As "a naturally Christian black man," Uncle Tom can resist only passively, by refusing to commit an unchristian act.[12] This sense of a romantic racialist divide in *Uncle Tom's Cabin*, with the naturally Christian black characters in one category and the more aggressive mulattoes in another, has become a mainstay of critical discourse surrounding the novel.

There is no question that *Uncle Tom's Cabin* makes racial generalizations, both explicit and implicit.[13] Even so, Stowe departs from the romantic racialist attitude in a subtle but meaningful way: while the novel embraces the notion of racial difference and inherited racial traits, it often ascribes these to environment and experience.[14] In fact, Stowe's account of racial inheritance anticipates the biological framework of epigenetics, a growing field that suggests that people's inheritable DNA can be changed by their behavior and environment. By couching racial generalizations in the contingencies of behavior and environment, Stowe calls attention to the instability of racial categories, suggesting the potential for racial equality. Moreover, Stowe's novel cannily recognizes the performative aspects of race, especially the way that enslaved people can play into racial expectations and use them to their own advantage.

In *Uncle Tom's Cabin*, racial generalizations that might at first glance seem to support biological racial difference are frequently moderated by language of variation and change. Tom, for example, has "to the full, the gentle, domestic heart, which, woe for them! *has been* a peculiar characteristic of his unhappy race" (my emphasis).[15] The language here is tellingly contingent: not only can the extent of this "peculiar characteristic" differ (Tom has it "to the full," but the implication is that others may not), but the use of the present perfect tense ("has been") rather than the present (is) suggests the temporal instability of the characterization. In other words, this has been a racial characteristic, but it may not always be. The novel also asserts that experience can produce behavior at odds with general racial characteristics. Fear of being sold down South, for example, "nerves the African, naturally patient, timid and unenterprising, with heroic courage" (83) to attempt escape. Even the slave-trader Marks knows how physically assertive slaves can become when threatened with recapture: when Loker sneers that George Harris and his party would be "too plaguey scared" to shoot, Marks insists that "niggers *do* fight like the devil, sometimes" (170). Critics make much of the fact that George and several in his party are mulattoes, rather than full-blooded blacks, but this distinction never enters into Marks' reasoning.

Consider, furthermore, the language of causality and contingency in Stowe's sweeping statement about black sensuality: "The negro, it must be remembered, is an exotic of the most gorgeous and superb countries of the world, and he has, deep in his heart, a passion for all that is splendid, rich, and fanciful; a passion which, rudely indulged by untrained taste, draws on them the ridicule of the colder and more correct white race" (141). Here Stowe offers an experience-based explanation for the racial characteristics she perceives, crediting black sensuality to what she imagines as the richly beautiful nations of Africa. (This experience could in fact be very recent, since the United States did not ban the importation of slaves until 1808.) Compared to the Darwinian theory of evolution that would emerge only a few years after the publication of *Uncle Tom's Cabin*, Stowe's account of the development of racial characteristics is markedly more immediate and less functional. According to Stowe, the Negro loves beauty not for any useful purpose or because he is inferior, but because he, or his parents or grandparents or more distant ancestors, comes from a place full of it. This passion is, as Stowe describes, "deep in his heart." But in her acknowledgment that this passion, if "rudely indulged by untrained taste," can provoke "the ridicule of the colder and more correct white race"—an attitude for which she offers no endorsement—Stowe suggests that it can be changed with training.

Perhaps the novel's most insightfully developed manifestation of an environmental and experiential explanation for racial attributes is the character of Topsy, who has not only internalized the values and expectations of her cruel masters but also bears the weight of generations of servitude. In Stowe's comparison of Eva and Topsy, the girls are at once "representatives of the two extremes of society" and "representatives of their races" (213), a mirroring of the language that suggests an equivalence between race and social position. Stowe then offers a more detailed account of the generations of experience that have produced these racial differences, contrasting "[t]he Saxon, born of ages of cultivation, command, education, physical and moral eminence" with "the Afric, born of ages of oppression, submission, ignorance, toil, and vice!" (213). Eva, a privileged member of a fortunate race, and Topsy, an ill-treated member of an oppressed race, are characterized not so much by the color of their skin as by their positions in long social histories.

And yet Topsy, who I'd suggest is one of the novel's most psychologically nuanced characters, is not wholly a product of her ancestry; wise to Miss Ophelia's expectations of a little black girl in filthy clothes, she takes a gleeful pleasure in performing the role of a foolish ragamuffin. Stowe describes Topsy's facial expression as "an odd mixture of shrewdness and cunning, over which was oddly drawn, like a kind of veil, an expression of the most doleful gravity and solemnity" (207). This veil is not, however, the inborn kind that W. E. B. Du Bois would later describe in *The Souls of Black Folk* (1903). Rather, it is one that the girl consciously dons as she plays tricks on the unsuspecting Ophelia. Although Topsy is very bright, "learning everything that was taught her with surprising quickness" (216), she resists becoming the prim and proper young lady that Ophelia wants her to be. As soon as it seems that she's learned how to do something flawlessly, she makes a mess of it: she can make a perfect bed but sometimes decides to pull off all the covers instead. Topsy is an excellent reader but occasionally amuses herself by willfully misreading her catechism, blaming her misbehavior on a wickedness that is clearly contrived rather than inborn. As Stowe writes, "Topsy always made great capital of her own sins and enormities, evidently considering them as something peculiarly distinguishing" (217). If her enslaved position prevents her from using her brightness in the traditional manner, then she'll distinguish herself and exert her agency with wickedness.[16]

Meanwhile, St. Clare has his own explanation for Topsy's misbehavior. Describing how social forces shape racial identity, he argues that the experience of slavery can produce racial characteristics that initially seem to be biologically determined. "You see," he tells his cousin Ophelia, "from the mother's breast the colored child feels and sees that there are none but underhanded ways open to it" (185). Arguing against racial determinism, St. Clare explains that a slave is born into a society with racial divisions so deep and clear that, even before acquiring language, the child understands the limits placed on her by her blackness and behaves accordingly. According to St. Clare, the institution of slavery, not biology, produces racial difference. As such, Uncle Tom is "a moral miracle!" (185) and what is remarkable about him is not that he is a moral black man but that he has remained one despite the crushing circumstances of slavery.

Uncle Tom's Religion

There's a factual error in St. Clare's assessment of Uncle Tom's moral character, and it's one that many critics have repeated. Having known Uncle Tom for just a short time, St. Clare assumes that his new slave has always been like this, that he is one of the few who "Nature makes so impracticably simple, truthful, and faithful, that the worst possible influence can't destroy" his good character (185). But Tom was not, in fact, born this way. St. Clare's description contradicts a small but crucial detail in Stowe's characterization: Tom's Christian goodness is the result of a relatively recent religious conversion. As Tom's longtime master, Shelby, relates in the first pages of the novel, Uncle Tom "got religion at a camp-meeting, four years ago; and I believe he really *did* get it. I've trusted him, *since then*, with everything I have,—money, house, horses,—and let him come and go round the country; and I always found him true and square in everything" (2; second emphasis mine). "Since then"—as a result of his conversion rather than an inborn characteristic—Uncle Tom has become, as Shelby describes him, "an uncommon fellow . . . steady, honest, capable, manages my whole farm like a clock" (1–2). When the slave-trader Haley tries to qualify this praise, saying that Uncle Tom must be "honest, as niggers go," Shelby rejects this racial limitation. "No; I mean, really, Tom is a good, steady, sensible, pious fellow" (2), he insists, reiterating that Uncle Tom is an uncommon "fellow," not just a remarkable slave.

Moreover, Tom himself also believes that he has fundamentally changed as a result of his religious conversion. We see this later in the novel, when Cassy asks him to join her and Emmeline in their escape from Legree's plantation. For the second time, Tom refuses to run away, explaining that religious obligation must keep him on the plantation because there are souls that need to be saved. Yet he recalls a time when he would have been willing to escape, telling Cassy, "[T]ime was when I would; but the Lord's given me a work among these yer poor souls, and I'll stay with 'em and bear my cross with 'em till the end" (345). Although he once would have been willing to attempt escape, now that Uncle Tom has "got religion," as Shelby calls it, he believes that the spiritual needs of others must take priority over his own freedom. For Tom, religious obligation supersedes everything.

Of course, from a contemporary perspective, Uncle Tom's religious explanation for his refusal—twice!—to escape slavery is puzzling, to say the least. How can any reasonable interpretation of Christianity demand that a person remain enslaved? Why doesn't Tom's faith encourage him to lead an insurrection? Does he have to submit to cruel treatment just because he's black? Tom's self-sacrificing interpretation of Christianity probably doesn't appeal to a modern reader, and it rubbed a few radical abolitionists the wrong way, too, as I will discuss shortly. But for the most part, whether they were for or against slavery, readers of *Uncle Tom's Cabin* saw Uncle Tom as a universal Christian ideal, not one whose goodness was racially determined. The prominent abolitionist William Lloyd Garrison, for example, praised Uncle Tom's "Christian gentleness, forbearance, and love," going on to argue that if a slave was capable of such Christian virtue, slavery was wrong.[17] Another critic glorified Tom as the highest Christian ideal, making no qualification for his race: "[A] character of richer spiritual beauty, of loftier moral grandeur, than his cannot be painted. Wherever he moves a celestial halo seems to encircle his brow." At the moment of Uncle Tom's death, the critic observed, "we can almost see angel hands placing upon his bleeding temples the crown of martyrdom."[18] In this view, death was simply the moment when the martyr, already so close to God, joined his creator in heaven.

Even as pro-slavery critics questioned whether a black man could be so virtuous, they agreed that Stowe's Uncle Tom was an ideal Christian. Some argued that Tom was too perfect a Christian to be credible as a black man, that he was just another falsehood in Stowe's slanderous attack on the South. Complaining that Stowe's characterizations were unfair to whites and un-realistically favorable to blacks, a review in *The Southern Literary Messenger* asserted that this bias reached its pinnacle in the flawless virtue of Uncle Tom: "[A]n epitome of the cardinal virtues, a sort of ebony St. Paul . . . with all of the Apostle's meekness and fortitude. . . . [I]f there be any virtue, and if there be any praise, all these things were blended in Uncle Tom."[19] Like St. Paul the Apostle, a tireless preacher of the Gospel, Stowe's char-acter underwent extensive tribulations without shaking his faith. Coupling "meekness and fortitude," the character modeled unblemished moral perfec-tion and unwavering faithfulness to God. But according to this critic, this characterization of Uncle Tom showed an enormously mistaken understand-ing of black capabilities. The character's virtues were wild fabrications that confirmed Stowe's prejudice against whites and in favor of blacks. Seeking to eat his cake and have it too, the critic also argued that, even if a perfect black man like Uncle Tom could exist, only enslavement could have made him so: "It is, indeed, a triumphant vindication of the institution of slavery against Mrs. Stowe's assaults, that in a slaveholding community, a character so perfect as 'Uncle Tom' could be produced."[20] The argument that only a master's paternal care could make a slave a perfect Christian was not lost on the prominent abolitionist Thomas Wentworth Higginson, who pointed out that Stowe's idealized character made the case for "the absurd paradox, that slavery educates higher virtues than freedom." Indeed, he reasoned sarcasti-cally, "if it is the normal tendency of bondage to produce saints like Uncle Tom, let us offer ourselves at auction immediately."[21]

In the years following the publication of *Uncle Tom's Cabin*, those who crit-icized Uncle Tom generally did not take issue with Stowe's racial stereotyping. Nor did they believe that the novel's images of blackness were dangerous. Such objections would come much later, in the twentieth century. Rather, anti-slavery activists of the 1850s were concerned that Uncle Tom's interpretation of Christianity sidestepped the need for assertive and embodied protest. In a letter to *The Liberator*, the radical abolitionist Henry C. Wright complained that Uncle Tom's Christianity should not have encouraged him to submit, but rather should have compelled him to resist oppression. The real Christian spirit, Wright argued, was "an aspiration for freedom," and true Christian "justice, honesty, kindness, love and forgiveness in Tom towards his masters would have led him to have taken their money, their horses, their clothes, or anything they claimed as theirs, to aid him to free himself from the horrors, and them from the guilt of slavery."[22] Framing his comments in an opposing interpretation of Christianity rather than an attack on Uncle Tom's character, Wright asserted that the truly virtuous slave would enable his master's path to salvation by escaping; even if a master did not recognize the sinfulness of slavery, he would benefit in being freed from its guilt. Still, a respondent to Wright's critique of Uncle Tom's Christianity argued that the character was in fact the best example in fiction of Wright's own doctrine of nonresistance. Stowe's hero, Wright's respondent wrote, should be praised as a nonresistant even if "more enlightened views of religion would have made him a less submissive one."[23] The problem with Uncle Tom, then, was his religious interpretation. For this critic, who believed that "no person can be a Christian and consent to remain a slave," Tom was "not the highest type of Christian perfection, by any means, but only the best character that slavery can produce."

These discussions of Uncle Tom's religion reflected theological tensions within nineteenth-century Christianity. In an age of reformist energy, was Christ's advice to turn the other cheek really a viable option? William Lloyd Garrison certainly hoped so, and in fact he worried that white readers of *Uncle Tom's Cabin* would see the novel's hero as a model only for black people. In an unsigned review of Stowe's novel for *The Liberator*, Garrison extolled Tom's Christ-like nature, marveling that the character "triumphantly exemplifies the nature, tendency and results of CHRISTIAN NON-RESISTANCE."[24] Identifying Tom as a fictional embodiment of Christian nonresistance, Garrison suggested that the character's moral virtues would produce real-world "results" if only readers enacted them in their own lives. Yet he worried that whites would not understand that Uncle Tom was a model for them, too. Several critics have highlighted this review, in which Garrison asks whether there is "one law of submission and non-resistance for the black man, and another law of rebellion and conflict for the white man," as a critique of the novel itself, as a kind of predecessor to James Baldwin's later assessment of a racial dichotomy within the novel. But a reading of Garrison's comments in fuller context suggests that his concern was about a racial dichotomy in the minds of white Americans rather than in the novel itself.

> That all the slaves at the South ought, "if smitten on the one cheek, to turn the other also"—to repudiate all carnal weapons, shed no blood, "be obedient to their masters," wait for a peaceful deliverance, and abstain for all insurrectionary movements—is every where taken for granted, because the VICTIMS ARE BLACK. . . . But, for those whose skin is of a different complexion, the case is materially altered. When they are spit upon and buffeted, outraged and oppressed, talk not then of a non-resisting Saviour—it is fanaticism! Talk not of overcoming evil with good—it is madness! Talk not of peacefully submitting to chains and stripes—it is base servility! Talk not of servants being obedient to their masters—let the blood of tyrants flow! How is this to be explained or reconciled? Is there one law of submission and non-resistance for the black man, and another law of rebellion and conflict for the white man? When it is the whites who are trodden in the dust, does Christ justify them in taking up arms to vindicate their rights? And when it is the blacks who are thus treated, does Christ require them to be patient, harmless, long-suffering, and forgiving? And are there two Christs?[25]

As a nonresistant, Garrison objected to the idea of a submissive Christ for blacks and a violent one for whites. He believed that it was important for whites to understand the difference between "base servility" and Christly submission and hoped that they would embrace Uncle Tom's example of Christian nonresistance rather than seeing it as an ideal for blacks alone. To read this review as a diagnosis of a racial dichotomy in the novel is to embrace exactly the attitude against which Garrison cautions.

Ultimately, submission to God and willful selflessness are the crowning virtues of Stowe's Christianity. Uncle Tom's interpretation of Christianity epitomizes the religious ideal that *Uncle Tom's Cabin* champions for all people, regardless of race. In his humility and generosity, in his selfless commitment to his fellow men and women, Uncle Tom models himself on the self-sacrificing example of Christ in the Gospels. He has, as Stowe describes him, a deep connection to scripture, which "seemed so entirely to have wrought itself into his being, as to have become a part of himself, and to drop from his lips unconsciously" (26). Like Christ, Uncle Tom prioritizes his everlasting soul over his body, and he chooses to turn the other cheek and love his enemies as they beat him to death. A spiritual leader not only to his fellow slaves, but also to St. Clare, Tom is a Christian model for all.

"A Manly Heart"

As much as the novel's Christianity coincides with nineteenth-century ideals of feminine domesticity, Uncle Tom exemplifies the novel's moral ideal in a distinctly masculine form. Indeed, despite the contemporary critical tendency to describe Tom as a feminine figure, nineteenth-century visual culture did not envision a feminine Tom. The many popular drawings and figurines of Tom and Eva, which became the most popular and remade images from Stowe's story,[26] consistently emphasize the contrast between Tom's heft and Eva's daintiness. Hammatt Billings' illustration of "Little Eva Reading the Bible to Uncle Tom in the Arbor" (see figure 1.1) for Jewett's first edition of

Figure 1.1. "Little Eva Reading the Bible to Uncle Tom in the Arbor," illustration by Hammatt Billings for the first edition of *Uncle Tom's Cabin.* Courtesy Department of Special Collections, Stanford University Libraries.

the novel depicts a tall and broad Tom with arms at least twice as thick as Eva's, while in many mass-produced and fine art figurines of "Uncle Tom mania" (see figure 1.2), a tiny Eva stands or sits on Tom's lap as he holds his head high, looking off into the heavens. As Cynthia Griffin Wolff suggests, the empowerment of women and the domestic sphere in *Uncle Tom's Cabin* operates alongside a complementary but essentially different masculine power, one refashioned by Stowe's self-sacrificing Christianity. Rather than feminizing Tom, Stowe writes him as part of a radically revised conception of masculinity that eschews aggression in favor of Christ-like values.[27] Certainly,

Figure 1.2. Staffordshire figurine of Uncle Tom and Eva, ca. 1852. Harriet Beecher Stowe Center, Hartford, CT.

in the novel Uncle Tom is repeatedly associated with women, but the association comes with a meaningful difference when it comes to action. Consider the difference between Tom and St. Clare's mother, both of whom Stowe describes as embodiments of the Bible.[28] St. Clare's mother is an example of the kind of quiet Christian influence that *Uncle Tom's Cabin* champions for women. She never explicitly contradicts her husband, who lacks both religious sentiment and sympathy for his slaves, but nevertheless deeply impresses upon her son "an idea of the dignity and worth of the meanest human soul" (197). As St. Clare describes it, the Christian woman's role is to help shape the men around her into good Christians.

But men, as we see in the case of Augustine St. Clare, must do more than that. St. Clare admits that his greatest flaw is his failure to turn his innate sensitivity into real action. As a child, he was naturally sympathetic and kind, his character "more akin to the softness of woman than the ordinary hardness of his own sex" (132). Although he developed "the rough bark of manhood" (201) as he got older, this masculinity is, importantly, only on the surface, and it fails to penetrate deep enough for him to develop what Stowe describes both Uncle Tom and the young George Shelby as having: a "manly heart" (81, 362). St. Clare blames his weakness on his mother's premature death, musing that if only she had lived longer, she would have been able to complete the process of molding her son into an ideal man. For St. Clare, unlike his saintly mother, producing a divine child like Eva is not enough; his access to greater social and political power demands more of him. One Biblical passage that deeply resonates with and troubles him teaches, "they are condemned for *not* doing positive good, as if that included every possible harm" (272). The paraphrased passage is likely Matthew: 25.31–45, which he has just finishing reading aloud at Tom's request. Tom has marked this passage heavily in his Bible, and its message strikes St. Clare so forcefully that he reads it twice. Just as Matthew teaches that those who do not feed the hungry and clothe the naked are cursed to "everlasting fire," St. Clare's interpretation of Christianity judges his own casual kindness and right thinking inadequate. A believer must be willing to "throw[] the whole weight of his being against this monstrous system of injustice . . . if need be, sacrificing himself in the battle" (272), but St. Clare is more likely to lie on the sofa and talk than stand up and fight. His passive

unwillingness to act upon his moral convictions is what prevents him from
having a "manly heart."[29]

While Stowe's concept of feminine Christian influence expresses itself
in the care of the family and the domestic space, her ideal man, one with a
"manly heart," must use his deep feeling to act selflessly on a broader scale.
For example, when Tom finds out that he will be sold from the Shelby plantation, he reveals his own "brave, manly heart" by comforting his wife and
"smothering [his] own sorrow. . . . Tom spoke with a thick utterance, and
with a bitter choking in his throat,—but he spoke brave and strong" (81).
Conjoining sentiment and strength, Stowe's "manly heart" is one that feels
deeply but still does the right thing—in this case, sacrificing himself so that
others will not be sold. The manly heart is also a particularly effective agent
of Stowe's notion of political reform, in which "feeling right" translates into
social transformation. George Shelby models this mode of reform at the end
of the novel as he weeps at Tom's deathbed, his tears "[doing] honor to his
manly heart" (362). Shelby is not undone by his sorrow; upon Tom's death,
the young man vows to "do *what one man can* to drive out this curse of slavery
from my land!" (365). And indeed he does, freeing his slaves and offering
them wages and education in the novel's penultimate chapter. In the face of
Uncle Tom's death, George Shelby's "manly heart" moves him to act.

St. Clare's musing about the man he might have been had his mother
lived longer—"a saint, reformer, martyr" (198)—underscores the centrality of
Christian selflessness in the novel's conception of a powerful, ideal masculinity. In contrast to George Shelby, whose grief at Uncle Tom's death moves
him to action against slavery, St. Clare fails to use his deep emotion and
keen moral judgment as the impetus for action. Lacking a "manly heart," he
wastes his life on shallow pleasures and vices and ultimately dies before freeing his slaves as he had planned. More than anything, St. Clare is a model
of failed Christian potential. As he admits in his confession that he is "up
to heaven's gate in theory, down in earth's dust in practice," he is unable to
match his moral convictions with actions, and he focuses on earthly pleasures
rather than spiritual rewards. Although Eva is a perfect child, the rest of the
St. Clare household is alarmingly shallow and materialistic. In that sense,
perhaps his valet Adolph's error in putting on airs as another "*Mr.* St. Clare"
(187), in his "absolute confusion as to *meum tuum* with regard to himself and

his master" (177), comes not from imitating a white man but from imitating the wrong one: a gentleman who is more invested in cologne and cambric handkerchiefs than in Christian behavior.

Tom, on the other hand, knows to model himself after Christ and not St. Clare. Many critics have understood his Christian selflessness as less masculine than George Harris' aggressive militancy, arguing that Uncle Tom's Cabin presents different notions of masculinity for blacks and for whites, or even for blacks and mulattoes.[30] But although George explicitly attributes his more aggressive actions to his "hot and hasty Saxon" (376) blood, this does not mean either that George himself feels that these impulses are morally right or that the rest of the novel supports this racial differentiation of masculinity. Stowe's masculine ideal of the sympathetic and actively self-sacrificing "manly heart" extends across the novel: not only to Uncle Tom and to Shelby, but also to the novel's other characters, including George, who acts selflessly once he is free from the threat of slavery. Indeed, Tom and George have more in common than it might seem: while their levels of religious observance differ, both value what they see as a Christian imperative of self-lessness. George's early ambivalence about Christianity becomes much closer to Tom's Christian selflessness once Loker is shot and injured, the threat of capture dissipated. Eliza, a devout Christian, says that the group should "do something for that poor man" (174), making a suggestion that is selfless but vague. George, however, offers a more concrete plan to aid the injured slave-catcher. Following the example of the Good Samaritan, he proposes that the group "take him up and carry him on" to a place where he can recuperate. "It would be no more than Christian," he insists. And, with Tom-like compassion, he is deeply relieved to find out that the slave-trader will recover. "It would always be a heavy thought to me, if I'd caused his death," he says, "even in a just cause" (175).

Tom's Christian goodness also finds a complement in the two white men who do the most for the fugitives Georgia and Eliza: Senator Bird and Simeon, the Quaker. Both men embrace sympathy for others above asser-tions of dominance and aggression, and both channel their sympathy into selfless action. Senator Bird, who at first supports the Fugitive Slave Law, is self-sacrificing and sentimental: he "rather like[s] the idea of consider-ing himself a sacrifice to his country" (67) and is moved to tears by Eliza's sad story. Ultimately, his ready sympathy for the downtrodden trumps his commitment to upholding the laws of his nation; answering to a higher power than the federal government, the senator actively assists the fugitives. Likewise, the Quaker Simeon, another of Stowe's model men, is both deeply sympathetic and willing to sacrifice himself for others. Because he believes that slavery is wrong, Simeon risks fines and imprisonment to help slaves escape from bondage. Nevertheless, he tells his son that he would "do the same for the slaveholder as for the slave, if the Lord brought him to my door in affliction" (122). Simeon's readiness to care for a slaveholder just as he would for a slave is a manifestation of Christ's counsel to love one's enemies, and Tom, who prays for Legree's soul even as the slave-owner beats him to death, follows the same Christly imperative.

Uncle Tom's Politics

Uncle Tom's submission to God and his Christ-like love for his enemies should not be confused with a general submissiveness of character or a lack of self-respect. For Stowe, humility and dignity go hand in hand. As the novel introduces him, Tom, "the hero of our story," is a man confident in himself even as he is humble before God: "There was something about his whole air self-respecting and dignified, yet united with a confiding and humble simplicity" (18). While submission to white masters in the novel is just as often degrading as it is enriching (think of Cassy or Sambo and Quimbo on Legree's plantation, or even the shallowness of Adolph and Rosa at St. Clare's estate), submission to God, as we see in the case of Uncle Tom, is another matter entirely. Stowe distinguishes Uncle Tom's Christian submission from the "cringing subserviency" to other men that she criticizes as "one of the most baleful effects of slavery" (352). In describing these effects as "baleful," Stowe suggests that while submission to God enables virtue, subservience to men produces evil.

Moreover, Tom's belief that submission to his masters is part of his earthly duty does not stop him from strenuously urging St. Clare to behave in a more Christian manner. Tom's assertiveness may seem minor to a modern reader, but it was significant in Stowe's time, as is so tellingly suggested in the responses of Southern freedmen who noted the freedom of conversation between master and slave.[31] Indeed, Tom is hardly submissive when he faces Legree's unchristian requests. When Legree tells him to flog another slave, Tom boldly refuses, saying that while he's willing to work night and day, beating the woman is not right, "and, Mas'r, I *never* shall do it,—*never!*" (308). The force of his words surprises Legree, who, like some contemporary readers, has assumed that a respectful demeanor means a weak will: "Tom had a remarkably smooth, soft voice, and a habitually respectful manner, that had given Legree an idea that he would be cowardly, and easily subdued" (308–309). But, as Stowe shows, Legree's assumption is incorrect. Tom will give his body to Legree, but he will never give his soul; his submission to God does not translate into subservience to men. Legree can see this in Tom even as he beats him: "Tom stood perfectly submissive, and yet Legree could not hide from himself that his power over his bond thrall was somehow gone" (342). Even the devilish atheist can see the limits of earthly power over the love of Christ. Stowe suggests that there is real power in Tom's kind of submission, precisely because it can separate the ephemeral body from the everlasting soul.

Both for Uncle Tom and for Stowe, the personal payoff for Christian behavior comes in heaven, not on earth. In that sense, Tom's attitude is very much at odds with the radical abolitionist aspiration to create a heaven on earth.[32] As such, it has undeniable limitations as a political model. But this doesn't mean that suffering on earth is easy for Tom. It deeply pains him to leave his wife and children, and a night of prayer makes him only "sort o' reconciled" to his fate (48). Later, steeped in the horrors of Legree's plantation, Tom struggles to accept the earthly suffering required for heavenly blessings. In his one moment of serious religious doubt (a moment which, as Richard Yarborough points out, resembles the brief moment before the crucifixion when Christ questions his faith), Tom finds that a fellow slave's doubts about the existence of God affect his own faith; he struggles with the personal repercussions of a miserable life on the Legree plantation.[33] This projected misery must make an early death more appealing.

Tom also struggles with a powerful sense of the wrongness of slavery, of the "dire misrule, and palpable, unrebuked injustice" (303) inherent in the institution. He fully recognizes that slavery is disordered and unjust, and indeed his Christianity doesn't stop him from yearning for freedom or from feeling that he is entitled to it as a human being. With a radicalism that is often overshadowed by Uncle Tom's submission to God and focus on the next world over this one, *Uncle Tom's Cabin* consistently offers support for the existence of natural rights for blacks and whites alike, even as it dramatizes the clash between natural rights and religious obligations. Tom tells St. Clare that he has a deep desire to be free, no matter how kind his master might be: "Mas'r's been too good; but, Mas'r, I'd rather have poor clothes, poor house, poor everything, and have 'em *mine*, than have the best, and have 'em any man's else,—I had *so*, Mas'r; I think it's natur Mas'r" (265). Pushing against the pro-slavery argument that black people are materially better off under slavery than they would be outside of it, Tom argues that earthly possessions are no consolation for his absence of freedom. This "natur" desire to be autonomous is, Stowe shows, the same for blacks as for whites, part of the natural rights of man. When St. Clare dies before setting Tom free, Stowe mocks the notion that a black person would feel any better about enslavement than would a white man. "The poor old soul," she writes, "had such a singular, unaccountable prejudice in favor of liberty" (280). With the characteristic irony that is often overlooked by critics, Stowe suggests that Tom's desire for liberty is far from singular—it is, she implies, an intrinsic human desire.

And yet, according to Stowe's Christianity, this natural human desire for freedom must ultimately defer to religious obligation. Stowe dramatizes this conflict in Uncle Tom's two decisions to remain in slavery. When Eliza asks him to escape the Shelby plantation with her and Harry, he refuses, explaining his understanding that if he isn't sold, all the other slaves will have to be sold in his place. Like Christ, Uncle Tom sacrifices himself to save others. "It's better for me alone to go," he reflects, "than to break up the place and sell all" (34). But although Tom will not escape, he describes Eliza's response as both natural and right: "Let Eliza go—it's her right! I wouldn't be the one to say no—'t an't in *natur* for her to stay" (34). Tom's refusal to escape hardly means that he believes that slaves inherently belong under the rule of their masters; far from that, he argues that it is Eliza's "right" to escape and that "natur"—not just Eliza's nature but nature in general, or perhaps the nature of a mother concerned for her child—encourages her to do so. Uncle Tom, however, is determined not to give in to his human nature, which he explicitly contrasts with Christian imperative. Consider his response to Aunt Chloe and some other slaves when he hears them wishing ill upon the slave-trader: "It's natur, Chloe, and natur's strong," he says, "but the Lord's grace is stronger; besides, you oughter think what an awful state a poor crittur's soul's in that'll do them ar things. . . . I'm sure I'd rather be sold, ten thousand times over, than to have all that ar poor crittur's got to answer for" (48). Using the Bible to support his lack of anger at the slave-trader, Tom makes it clear that God's word, and not his own human desires, determines his position. Explicitly contrasting human nature with religious duty, he concludes that the suffering of enslavement in this world is preferable to suffering for all of eternity, as he is certain the slave-trader will. Getting to heaven is ultimately far more important to Tom than is trying to realize a heaven on earth.

For Tom, religious observance and racial solidarity are complementary practices, both rooted in selfless devotion to a community. During a second opportunity to escape slavery—this time from the horrors of the Legree plantation—Uncle Tom again chooses to fulfill his religious duty rather than to escape with Cassy and Emmeline. He explains that "the Lord's given me a work among these yer poor souls" (345) and he feels obligated to remain with his fellow slaves in order to administer to their spiritual needs. The necessity for spiritual guidance has recently become quite apparent: Legree's plantation is so miserable that not only does one slave insist to Tom that "de Lord an't here" (302), but her words also move Tom to question his own faith for the first time. While for a wavering moment the prospect of a lifetime of misery and injustice reorients Tom's soul toward earthly suffering, ultimately he finds comfort in a dream that reminds him that such affliction is just the prelude to heavenly riches. Tom's dream recalls a scene earlier in the novel, in which Eva reads the Bible to Uncle Tom in the garden by Lake Pontchartrain and first announces that she will soon go to heaven. Eva's favorite parts of the Bible, Stowe tells us, are the Revelations and the Prophecies, and in Tom's dream, the girl reads a passage from the Prophecies of Isaiah in which God promises his presence and protection even in man's darkest hours.[34] After Eva reads these comforting words to Uncle Tom, she turns into an angel, rising on "shining wings, from which flakes and spangles of gold fell off like stars" (303). The solace that Tom finds in this dream is twofold: while the passage from Isaiah reassures Tom that God is with him even amid the

utter horror of the Legree plantation, Eva's transformation into an angel—a
spectacular vision that would become the elaborate finale for stage versions
of the story—reminds him that there are spiritual rewards to come if only he
holds on to his faith.

Eva's desire to die for others is in fact what first suggests to Tom that a
Christ-like death might be a desirable option for him. While he is a devout
Christian from the beginning of the novel, it is only after Eva's death that
Tom becomes willing, even eager, to offer up his own life in the service of
others. While she is alive, Eva often joyfully expresses her desire to die, like
Christ, so that she can save others. She tells Tom, "I can understand why
Jesus *wanted* to die for us.... I've felt that I would be glad to die, if my dying
could stop all this misery. I *would die* for them, Tom, if I could. . . . I want
to go,—I love to go!" (240–241). Her enthusiastic vision of martyrdom both
mimics Christ's sacrifice on the cross and calls upon heaven as the site of
abolitionist triumph. As Eva describes it to the slaves gathered around her
deathbed, heaven is a racially integrated paradise, "a beautiful world, where
Jesus is . . . for you, as much as me" (251). Despite the racial divisions in this
life, all will be welcomed equally in heaven. And indeed, this vision of racial
equality in heaven resurfaces in St. Clare's death scene, in which Stowe's narrator asserts that "in the gates of eternity, the black hand and the white hold
each other with an equal clasp" (276). Eva's ecstatic passing, during which
Stowe writes that she "passed from death unto life!" (257), highlights the
novel's prioritizing of the next life over this one. As Jane Tompkins observes,
in *Uncle Tom's Cabin*, death is "not only the crowning achievement of life,
it *is* life," and it allows the enactment of a political and religious philosophy "in which the pure and powerless die to save the powerful and corrupt,
and thereby show themselves more powerful than those they save."[35] It is no
wonder, then, that ultimately Tom will regard death as an attractive exit from
the perils of enslavement. When he dreams of Eva becoming an angel, his
faith is renewed by the reminder that his suffering at the hands of Legree can
be meaningful—and maybe even soon over.

In Stowe's account of Uncle Tom's last moments, the glory of death over
life, and of heavenly triumph over earthly power, is clear. Tom has endured
much in this life, but he will receive great rewards in heaven. "Pity him not!"
Stowe instructs. "Such a life and death is not for pity! Not in the riches of

omnipotence is the chief glory of God; but in self-denying, suffering love. And blessed are the men whom he calls to fellowship with him, bearing their cross after him with patience" (365). Despite all of Tom's suffering, Stowe commands her readers not to pity him. Suffering and self-sacrifice are, under the novel's values, rich blessings that help men emulate Christ's martyrdom on the cross. In a radical redefinition of masculine power from dominance to love and self-sacrifice, Stowe asserts that God's glory is not in his omnipotence but in the power of Christ's "self-denying, suffering love." Ultimately, like Christ, Tom's greatest influence comes through his death, which effects not only the conversion of Sambo and Quimbo but also George Shelby's vow upon Tom's grave to free all of his slaves and "do *what one man can* to drive out this curse of slavery from my land!" (365). Accordingly, George begins these efforts by freeing all of his slaves and offering them wages and education to ease the transition to freedom.

But even Uncle Tom realizes that not everyone can be like him, and for those who cannot (Eliza, Cassy, and Emmeline), Tom himself advocates earthly resistance. When Cassy tells Tom that she wants to murder Legree, he begs her not to commit this sin, and instead suggests that she and Emmeline try to escape, as long as they can do it without violence. What's more, there's a strong suggestion that Tom's prayers, perhaps aided by a spark of divine interference, are what prompt Cassy to come up with the ingenious plan that allows the two women to escape: although Cassy has spent many hours trying to come up with a practicable flight plan, "at this moment"—at just the moment that Tom tells Cassy he'll pray for her to find a way to escape—"there flashed through her mind a plan, so simple and feasible in all its details, as to awaken an instant hope" (345). Through his involvement in Cassy and Emmeline's escape, Tom reveals his recognition that his own mode of Christianity is not possible for everyone and that there are other acceptable responses to slavery. Even in the novel, Uncle Tom is, like Christ, an ideal rather than an achievable goal.

As the years have passed, and as our ideas about race, gender, religion, and politics have changed, Uncle Tom's model of Christian self-sacrifice has become less and less widely appealing. Today, it can be difficult for us to imagine that being an Uncle Tom was ever a good thing. But Uncle Tom's bad reputation in contemporary American culture shouldn't prevent us from

recognizing the radicalism of Stowe's portrayal of a virtuous black man devoted to God and to his fellow human beings. The transformative power
of this loving, self-sacrificing character did not stop at the edges of Stowe's
novel. When dramatists adapted *Uncle Tom's Cabin*, Uncle Tom brought his
"manly heart" to the stage.

CHAPTER 2

UNCLE TOM ON THE AMERICAN STAGE

FROM THE MOMENT *Uncle Tom's Cabin* entered American culture, it inspired wave upon wave of response. Writers, artists, and manufacturers adapted Stowe's work in virtually every medium, from literature and theater to card games and plates. *Uncle Tom's Cabin* was, of course, the best-selling book of the nineteenth century after the Bible, selling 300,000 copies in the United States in its first year alone, and a million copies between the United States and Britain. But the readership of the novel paled in comparison to the number of Americans who went to the theater to see one—and often more—of the many popular dramatizations of Stowe's novel. Thomas Gossett has estimated that as many as fifty Americans attended stage versions of *Uncle Tom's Cabin* for every one who read the novel.[1]

Much like Stowe's novel, *Uncle Tom's Cabin* dramas garnered immediate and enduring success. Like most pious Christians of her time, Stowe believed that the theater was immoral. In 1852, she is said to have rejected the request of the temperance and anti-slavery performer Asa Hutchinson to adapt her novel for the stage, explaining that even a Christian play could become a gateway for young Christians to attend immoral theatrical productions.[2] In 1855, perhaps realizing that if you can't beat them, you might as well join them, Stowe composed her own stage version: *The Christian Slave*, a dramatic reading written expressly for Mary Webb, a free mulatto who had previously performed readings of scenes from Shakespeare and Sheridan and poems from Whittier and Longfellow.[3] (In her performance of Longfellow's *Hiawatha*, Webb, the wife of novelist Frank Webb, caused a stir by appearing in Native American costume.) Showing in Massachusetts, New York, and England, *The Christian Slave* didn't catch on the way that the other, more fully staged versions already had. Because Congress had not yet passed a law allowing authors to secure the copyright for adaptations of their work, Stowe had no legal recourse to prevent others from dramatizing her novel.[4] Free to take any liberties they wished with Stowe's work, producers put Uncle Tom on stage in every guise: serious moral dramas, pro-slavery revisions of Stowe's anti-slavery novel, comic variety skits with little resemblance to the original story. As Gossett rightly points out, Stowe's lack of control over the existence and contents of the many theatrical adaptations of *Uncle Tom's Cabin* is what makes them so interesting as social history.[5]

Although Stowe's novel is widely credited with helping turn the nation against slavery and hastening the Civil War, the theatrical productions based on it have precisely the opposite reputation. Many scholars acknowledge the initial anti-slavery influence of George L. Aiken's 1852 dramatization of *Uncle Tom's Cabin* but contend that the Uncle Tom plays quickly became more harmful than helpful to black Americans. The plays are also frequently blamed for turning Uncle Tom, the heroic Christian martyr of Stowe's novel, into the submissive race traitor his name connotes today.[6] In this account, once Uncle Tom stepped on stage, he quickly became a weak and submissive old man, a character in line with the minstrel convention of the "aged darkey." Contemporaneous accounts of the antebellum Uncle Tom shows, however, offer a very different narrative, one that emphasizes their radical departures from previous depictions of black characters. These accounts, which until now have not been investigated in comprehensive detail, note the sympathetic and respectable representations of black people in the Uncle Tom plays.

In the years leading up the Civil War, Uncle Tom's dignified representation on the American stage was a powerful force in turning the North against slavery. The one major change the adaptations made to his character was his age: pretty much from the beginning, the Uncle Tom of the stage was usually played as a white-haired old man with a cane. Producers may have aged the character because the sight of a vigorous black man—or a white actor in blackface—and a young white girl with their arms clasped around each other would have been too close to miscegenation for the comfort of nineteenth-century American audiences. Uncle Tom's age did not appear to have detracted from his dignity to these audiences, however, and might even have added to their respect and sympathy for the character.

Selling Uncle Tom's Cabin *on the American Stage*

Harriet Beecher Stowe wrote *Uncle Tom's Cabin* out of a passionate desire to end slavery, and although she hoped to make some money from it—her husband Calvin Stowe, according to their son Charles, "often expressed the hope that she would make money enough by the story to buy a new silk dress"—she never expected it to become such a sensation.[7] It is hard to imagine how she could have expected anything close to the "Uncle Tom mania" that quickly sprang up in the United States and around the world.[8] Until *Uncle Tom's Cabin*, no American book had found such international popularity and acclaim, and it is unlikely that anyone would have predicted that an anti-slavery novel written by the forty-year-old wife of a theologian would be the first.

Unlike the moral and political impulses behind Stowe's novel, however, the many dramatizations of *Uncle Tom's Cabin* were generally, as Sarah Meer rightly suggests, "commercial before they were political," created by people who saw the spectacular success of Stowe's novel and wanted to share in the profits.[9] For example, the most influential of the adaptations, by George L. Aiken, was commissioned by George C. Howard, manager of New York's Troy Museum, as a vehicle for his young daughter Cordelia, who played Eva—a circumstance that probably heightened Eva's central role in the resulting sentimental drama. Little Cordelia retired from the stage when she wasn't so little anymore, but Howard was able to turn *Uncle Tom's Cabin* into the backbone of lifelong careers for him and his wife: he took the role of St. Clare and proceeded to perform it sporadically for several decades, while Caroline Howard, the former Caroline Fox of the famous Boston stage family, became particularly well known for her Topsy.[10] Although Howard claimed to have anti-slavery sympathies, he was also open to amending his *Uncle Tom's Cabin* for a Southern audience. In 1855, a Baltimore theater manager, John E. Owens, asked Howard if his play could "be so adapted and softened in its style, without losing much of its interest, as to

be made not only acceptable, but telling to a Baltimore audience?" Could the
"very *objectionable* speeches and situations . . . be modified in their tone and
spirit, without materially weakening the plot and character of the play?"[11]
Evidently, the two were able to come to a compromise: Howard brought his
troupe to Baltimore the next month.[12]

Another prominent adaptation, commissioned by Boston Museum
theater manager Moses Kimball and written by the prolific but obscure
playwright H. J. Conway, was also a commercial venture. The England-born
Conway, who migrated to the United States in the 1830s, spent decades struggling as a "house playwright" who wrote commissioned works and peddled
his scripts for small fees.[13] Although Kimball was an opponent of slavery,
Conway's correspondence with him included no discussion of the play's politics. Instead it focused on the playwright's determined struggle to construct
a cohesive dramatic arc from a novel with multiple narrative threads. "I find
much difficulty in handling it dramatically, but there is no such word as *'fail'*
in my vocabulary," he wrote.[14] The Boston Museum's stage manager, William
Henry Sedley Smith (a struggling alcoholic who was author of the era's most
popular temperance play, *The Drunkard*), was a great admirer of politicians
Daniel Webster and Henry Clay, both of whom favored compromise on the
slavery issue rather than abolition. But he was far more concerned with the
house's profits than with the play's politics. "*This has been the greatest week ever
known in the Boston Museum*," Smith wrote in his diary a week into the show's
run. "Receipts a good deal over *three* thousand dollars! *So much for Uncle Tom.
The piece is certainly done gloriously.* I hardly need write here *my utter detesta-
tion* of its *political bearing*" (Smith's emphases).[15] The play's unprecedented
revenue ultimately outdid any concerns about its politics. By January, with
the play's seventy-third performance, Smith was delighted to report that the
show had been so popular that he had "turned scores away. *Wonderful piece!*"[16]
Uncle Tom's Cabin might even have shifted his political stance. Despite his
earlier admiration of compromise politicians, by 1854 Smith's diary recorded
deep disapproval of the Kansas-Nebraska Act, which opened the door for the
spread of slavery into the nation's new territories: "The infamous *Nebraska Bill*
pass'd the Senate 34 to 14! *Shameful.*"[17]

Of course, just because political agitation was not the primary goal of a
product did not mean it lacked political power. Commercial products that

capitalized on "Uncle Tom mania" gave hope to abolitionists and free blacks by calling attention to black humanity. Writing in *Frederick Douglass' Paper* under his "Ethiop" pseudonym, the black leader William J. Wilson described a welcome change in Brooklyn shop windows: where shopkeepers had previously "exhibited in their windows Zip Coon, or JIM CROW, with his naked toes kicking out the panes, for general amusement, profit and loyalty to the Southern God," the same shopkeepers were "now proud to illume these very windows through the windows of my Uncle Tom's Cabin; while good Old Aunt Chloe peeps out just to see what the matter is. May she continue to look out until every Uncle Tom is restored to his God-given rights—his full manhood—till every vestige of justice is done him."[18] For Wilson, Uncle Tom and Aunt Chloe so considerably improved upon earlier cultural representations of blacks that their appearance in local shop windows seemed to herald the restoration of the race's "God-given rights."

Wilson's view might help us understand why 1850s dramatic adaptations of *Uncle Tom's Cabin* drew black audiences so large that some theaters expanded their segregated sections to meet the growing demand.[19] Certainly, the politics of the *Uncle Tom's Cabin* plays and other commercial productions could be ambiguous, often resulting as much from the individual viewer's point of view as from the work itself. There were many Uncle Toms and many *Uncle Tom's Cabins* in American culture, and even a single one could elicit wildly different responses according to the viewer's perspective. A single production could— and did—warm the heart of one abolitionist, offend another for making slavery seem like a pretty good state, and incense a supporter of slavery for depicting the institution as barbaric and cruel. Despite this ambiguity, however, dramatizations of *Uncle Tom's Cabin* were a major force in turning the North against slavery, not only through their denunciatory depictions of slavery but also through their sympathetic and respectful representations of the enslaved. Indeed, pro-slavery publications recognized the deep influence of the *Uncle Tom's Cabin* plays in building anti-slavery sentiment. In March 1854 the pro-slavery *Spirit of the Times* cautioned that sympathy generated by the play was influencing American politics by "ma[king] converts to the abolition doctrine many persons . . . who have never examined the subject, and know nothing of its merits. Well represented sufferings and wrongs, whether fabulous or not, create sympathy, and that sentiment grows into advocacy."[20] Many white

Americans had never given much thought to those enslaved in the South. By provoking sympathy for their plight, the *Uncle Tom's Cabin* plays spread a new recognition of slavery's injustice, recognition that could be the first step toward more concrete political advocacy.

"The Strongest Anti-Slavery Impression": George L. Aiken's Uncle Tom's Cabin

Although a few brief dramatic riffs on Stowe's novel appeared in the summer of 1852, the George L. Aiken play that first made *Uncle Tom's Cabin* a national theatrical sensation premiered that September at the Troy Museum in Troy, New York, playing for a record seventy-nine nights.[21] For a town with a population of 30,000, this was an astounding run. When Aiken first scripted his play for his cousin George Howard, he hewed to Stowe's novel quite closely, often taking long passages of dialogue from the novel verbatim. But he stopped two thirds of the way into the novel with Eva's death and did not follow the Uncle Tom plot to Legree's plantation. Focusing mostly on the Eliza and George plot and the Christian love between Uncle Tom and Little Eva, this script demonstrated that slavery pulls apart families and that black people can be heroic and virtuous, but stopped short of representing the institution's violence. But when Troy audiences clamored to see the rest of Stowe's novel dramatized, Aiken quickly composed a new play, "The Death of Uncle Tom," which opened at the end of October and played for several weeks on its own before Aiken joined the two parts together into a single six-act drama. In adapting the last third of the novel, Aiken relied less on its text and more on nineteenth-century theater conventions, introducing a comic marriage plotline for Ophelia and incorporating additional character types already familiar to theatergoers. Chief among these was Gumption Cute, a Yankee con artist who tries to exploit his distant relationship to Ophelia (his second cousin married her niece) for financial gain and in the process tries to drive away both Topsy and Ophelia's prospective suitor, Deacon Perry. Ultimately, however, Ophelia, Deacon Perry, and Topsy form a happy family, offering a satisfying resolution that contrasts with the two deaths (of Uncle Tom and of Simon Legree, who is killed by the lawyer, Marks) that end Aiken's play.

Despite the tremendous length of the full drama, the Howard production was so successful that, after a brief stop in Albany, it moved to Purdy's National Theatre in New York City. Premiering on July 18, 1853, to immediate and extraordinary success, the production ran for an unheard-of three hundred performances. This was not, however, the first performance of an *Uncle Tom's Cabin* theatrical adaptation in New York City. Another play, by the Purdy's actor Charles Western Taylor, had appeared the previous August, running for a respectable but hardly exceptional eleven nights.[22] With neither an Eva nor a Topsy in the cast and Uncle Tom playing just a minor role, Taylor's version focused on the slave-traders' pursuit of the George and Eliza characters and concluded with them, Uncle Tom, and Aunt Chloe all free but living happily back on the old plantation.[23] It also included multiple scenes of slaves dancing and singing in minstrel numbers such as "Nigga in de Cornfield," "Kentucky Breakdown Dance," and "We Darkies Hoe the Corn."[24] But such scenes of plantation dancing and singing did not necessarily efface a performance's anti-slavery sentiment. Indeed, the response to this early performance of *Uncle Tom's Cabin* indicates just how heavily a viewer's politics influenced her interpretation of the play. Even without the cruelty of Simon Legree or the death of Uncle Tom, Taylor's play infuriated the strongly pro-slavery New York *Herald*, which described it as "an insult to the South—an exaggerated mockery of Southern institutions—and calculated, more than any other expedient of agitation, to poison the minds of our youth with the pestilent principles of abolitionism."[25] According to the critic, the play featured "the most extravagant exhibitions of the imaginary horrors of Southern slavery. The Negro traders, with their long whips, cut and slash their poor slaves about the stage for mere pastime. . . . Uncle Tom is scourged by the trader, who has bought him, for 'whining' at his bad luck." Because no other publication appears to have covered the Taylor play at the National, it is not possible to corroborate the *Herald*'s report. Even so, such vehement antipathy underscores the difficulty of assigning a firm political stance to a given version of *Uncle Tom's Cabin*. Although the plot synopsis might suggest that the dramatization softened the anti-slavery politics of Stowe's novel, the *Herald* clearly read Taylor's adaptation as a strong attack on the institution.

Taylor's adaptation advanced another attack on slavery through its humane characterizations of the enslaved. When the script was staged in

Cleveland, *The Plain Dealer* gave it a generally favorable review but objected to the acting of those who played the slave characters, and especially Uncle Tom. As with all black characters on nineteenth-century American stages, whether comic minstrel types or Shakespeare's Othello, white actors in blackface took these roles. (Blackface, a common feature of the minstrel stage, represented not just black Americans but a variety of races and ethnicities, including Irish and German; dialect, rather than color, indicated a character's racial or ethnic group.)[26] In Taylor's *Uncle Tom's Cabin*, complained *The Plain Dealer*'s critic, "the negroes talk too like those pedagogues who pride themselves on their complete mastery of Noah Webster. Now Uncle Tom, in the book, is an intelligent, but illiterate, old negro; the play makes him discourse like a divine. Mr. Ellser should give his language a bit of the negro 'brogue.'"[27] Apparently acted without the use of dialect, Ellser's Uncle Tom was far more dignified and well spoken than the typical blackface character—perhaps even more so than Stowe had written him.

Indeed, from the beginning, performances of *Uncle Tom's Cabin* offered unusually dignified portrayals of black characters. The surprise was that audiences were so ready to accept them. It was one thing for Stowe's work to touch the hearts of the relatively genteel literate class in mid-nineteenth-century America; it was quite another to imagine that it would find a welcoming reception from the rowdy audiences at Bowery theaters. This was the class of men who had, not so long before, formed mobs to attack anti-slavery meetings. Purdy's theater in particular had a violent past when it came to abolitionism. In 1834, when the building was a chapel owned by the American Anti-Slavery Society leaders Arthur and Lewis Tappan, it was booked for a racially integrated anti-slavery meeting, but when neighborhood roughs heard about this, they became so infuriated that they gathered into a two- or three-thousand-person mob, broke into the chapel (where the abolitionists, forewarned of the mob's plans, never appeared), and passed resolutions in favor of Negro deportation. For eight days the mob rioted against abolitionists, destroying Lewis Tappan's home, the Bowery Theatre, abolitionist meeting halls, and black homes and churches throughout the city.[28]

Two decades later, the Bowery, like most American theaters, remained racially segregated both onstage and off. Theaters hired white actors only and relegated black patrons to segregated seating—when they allowed them inside at all. When Aiken's version of *Uncle Tom's Cabin* made its New York City debut at the Bowery's National Theater, the venue had a reputation for being particularly squalid even compared to its neighbors in the Bowery, where gangs prowled the streets and prostitutes solicited clients inside theaters. Aiken's play, however, brought a new respectability to the neighborhood, and particularly to the National. Alongside the usual crowd of rowdy theatergoers, the production attracted an audience of leading citizens and devout Christians, many of whom were entering a theater for the first time.[29] The theater's manager, A. H. Purdy, recognized that Aiken's play could expand his audience and decided to revamp the venue to accommodate more respectable patrons. He decorated the lobby with scriptural texts and commissioned a painting of himself with a Bible in one hand and *Uncle Tom's Cabin* in the other, as if these were the two foundational texts of American morals.[30] To sweep vice from the balconies, he extended the ban on "ladies unaccompanied by gentlemen"—code for prostitutes—from the lower floor to the entire theater. To complete this transformation of his theater into what he now called "The Temple of the Moral Drama," Purdy also added a matinee, at the time an unusual feature, in order to attract women and children who might not want to visit Five Points at night.[31]

With Aiken's *Uncle Tom's Cabin*, the National became a rare site of cross-class exchange: rough young men who had never stepped foot in a church eagerly listened to Christian anti-slavery rhetoric alongside New York's "better classes," who now packed the cars of the new stage lines running through Chatham Street.[32] As one newspaper reported, "[t]he National, until recently the Bowery headquarters and the great peanut mart, has come into notice, and is now patronized by the elite and the 'white kids.' . . . [I]t has now become quite the thing to go to the National."[33] Among those crowds of elites was a young Henry James, who attended so many different versions of the plays that they formed what he later remembered as his first critical corpus.[34]

While area theaters were generally considered too seedy to be given notice by New York newspapers, soon after Aiken's play opened at the National, a correspondent for the *New York Times* attended a performance, expecting that the Bowery B'hoys would laugh and jeer at Uncle Tom rather than sympathize with his plight. After all, the critic wrote, "[t]hese low theatres are usually the places where coarseness and lewdness are bred, and where the better thoughts are only expressed to be parodied."[35] As he expected, when Uncle Tom spoke his first words on the National's stage, a laugh came from the theater's pit. Because black dialect was virtually always associated with comedy, audiences were accustomed to laughing at black characters. But in this case, the laughter quickly died. For the rest of the show, the audience watched Uncle Tom with "the deepest stillness—almost solemnity." A critic for the *New York Atlas* reported a similar feeling of surprise when he attended *Uncle Tom's Cabin* at the National. At the dramatic moment of Eliza's escape, the entire theater had gone silent; a glance around the theater revealed a whole audience, even the roughest men, in tears.[36]

In provoking the sympathy of the lower classes for American slaves, Aiken's *Uncle Tom's Cabin* seemed to have miraculous powers. It heralded what the *New York Times* called "a new era of dramatic representation in this country," bringing piety and morality into the theater and introducing "the great ideas of Brotherhood, Equality, and religious responsibility" to area roughs.[37] A New York correspondent for Garrison's *Liberator* marveled at the play's power to bring the highest of virtues to the lowest of audiences. "If the shrewdest abolitionist amongst us had prepared the drama with a view to make the strongest anti-slavery impression," he wrote, "he could scarcely have done the work better. O, it was a sight worth seeing those ragged, coatless men and boys in the pit (the very *material* of which mobs are made) cheering the strongest and the sublimest anti-slavery sentiments!"[38] Aiken's script had not, of course, been written by a "shrewd abolitionist" looking "to make the strongest anti-slavery impression." Nevertheless, a play that censured slavery and featured dignified, sympathetic black characters was such a stark departure from dramatic precedent that even the most fervent abolitionists celebrated it.

"A New Type"

In line with Stowe's precedent, Aiken's dignified Uncle Tom was a major innovation in the representation of blacks on the American stage. Before *Uncle Tom's Cabin*, according to Robert Toll, the few black characters in American dramas were generally minor, and almost always comic.[39] (An important exception on the American stage was Shakespeare's *Othello*, which was the rare serious blackface role.) As one veteran actor explained, "up to that time the only type of negro man ever seen on stage was the 'Jim Crow' darkey, and the appearance of an actor made up for a 'nigger' was the signal for shrieks of laughter."[40] The actor who first played Uncle Tom in Aiken's play, Green Germon, at first refused the role because he assumed it would be a comic one and he considered himself a serious actor. But George Howard prevailed upon him to take the part by explaining "that *Uncle Tom* was a new type, demanding the ability of a leading man to bring out the sweetness and pathos of the character, and that to cast a 'nigger actor' for the part would ruin the play."[41] Germon finally consented.[42]

Aiken's Uncle Tom is, like Stowe's, a model of Christian virtue and strength. Before Tom appears on stage, Shelby describes him in an early conversation with the slave trader, Haley, as "an uncommon fellow" in both labor and morals: "steady, honest, capable, manages my whole farm like a clock" (1.2).[43] According to Shelby, ever since Tom "got religion," he has been "a good, steady, sensible, pious fellow" who can be trusted with anything. Physically, he is "a behemoth" (2.1), according to the Marie St. Clare of both Stowe and Aiken. But Aiken's original script gives Uncle Tom no moment of brave physical action; here his rescue of Eva after she falls from the steamer is recounted by St. Clare rather than dramatized. Whether or not the rescue occurs on stage, however, St. Clare is so impressed by Tom's bravery that, using dialogue that never appears in Stowe's novel, he calls him "my modern Hannibal" (ibid.). This allusion to the ancient Carthaginian general famous for his superb military strategy positions Uncle Tom in a line of exceptional African heroes.

Undoubtedly, Tom is devoted to his two kind masters, Shelby and St. Clare, but as in Stowe's novel, his true commitment is to God. Aiken's characterization emphasizes Tom's Christian virtues and knowledge, advancing his faith as a form of power. At the St. Clare estate in New Orleans, Tom is a respected spiritual advisor to both Eva and her father. Eva tells St. Clare that she loves listening to Uncle Tom sing hymns, and she recounts a mutual exegetical process in which "I read to him in my Bible, and he explains what it means" (2.2). Even though Tom is illiterate, his theological wisdom and leadership is profound. Indeed, he takes it upon himself to preach to St. Clare, urging him to take better care of both body and soul. The unsolicited guidance is effective, or at least it seems to be: touched by Uncle

Tom's concern, St. Clare twice pledges to stop drinking. As Tom exits their conversation, St. Clare says to himself, "I'll keep my faith with him, too" (3.1).

Uncle Tom's piety mandates servitude to God, not man. Although Tom will not run away from the Shelby plantation with Eliza, he affirms, "Let Eliza go—it's her right" (1.3). Nor does Tom's Christianity conflict with his own fervent desire for freedom. When St. Clare points out to Tom that he's probably materially better off now, as a slave, than he would be if liberated, the script retains his crucial assertion of his desire for freedom. Repeating dialogue from Stowe's novel, Uncle Tom insists that his freedom is worth more to him than any material riches. When he offers to stay and take care of St. Clare, Tom's sense of Christian service takes precedence over his personal desire for liberty. Believing that St. Clare is on the verge of Christian conversion, Tom realizes the great things that could come of this, not just for St. Clare's soul but also in the larger world: "Why, even a poor fellow like me has a work; and Mas'r St. Clare, that has larnin', and riches, and friends, how much he might do for the Lord" (4.2). St. Clare, with all of his social and financial power, could do more as a Christian than can a humble man like Uncle Tom.

What is less clear in Aiken's script is why Uncle Tom doesn't try to escape from the Legree plantation. Whether for reasons of length or politics, several scenes that explain Uncle Tom's decision not to accompany Cassy and Emmeline in their escape were cut from the last act of Aiken's original 1852 script, which was already less nuanced about Tom's reasons for staying than is Stowe's novel. In the original Aiken script, Cassy asks Tom to help her and Emmeline murder Legree. Tom begs her not to, and ultimately suggests that, because the two women cannot stand the difficulties of the Legree plantation, they should try to escape. "Try it," he tells Cassy. "I'll pray with all my might for you."[44] He won't escape with them, he explains, because he can stand it. Unlike in the novel, however, Tom does not say anything about having work to do among the people. Instead, he offers that explanation earlier in the play, when he refuses to escape with Eliza. This gives these words a less noble meaning, since the Shelby slaves are treated well and are not degraded, as the slaves on Legree's plantation are. But Uncle Tom's decision to remain on the Legree plantation serves no real purpose in Aiken's play.[45]

The absence of any explanation for Tom's staying with Legree is a meaningful deviation from Stowe's novel and as such sheds some light on how

Uncle Tom became known as a man who advocates submission to whites above all. But there's no mistaking Uncle Tom for a race traitor. In the play just as in the novel, Tom sacrifices himself to save the Shelby plantation and all the slaves on it. Echoing Stowe's novel, he refuses Eliza's suggestion that he escape with her by explaining that "If I must be sold, or all the people on the place, and everything go to rack, why, let me be sold. I s'pose I can bar it as well as any one" (1.3). At Legree's plantation, too, Aiken's Tom sacrifices himself for his fellow slaves. In what became a key scene in the *Uncle Tom's Cabin* stage tradition, when Legree commands him to whip Emmeline, Tom bravely refuses, making it clear that God, and not his master, guides his decisions. "My soul a'nt yours, mas'r," he tells Legree; "you haven't bought it—ye can't buy it; it's been bought and paid for by one that is able to keep it, and you can't harm it!" Admitting that he knows something about their escape, he refuses to divulge any information even though he knows his silence will likely mean his death.

In Aiken's play, as Les Harrison rightly suggests, "Tom's passive martyrdom earns him a place in Eva's heaven," rather than any real-world change.[46] While in Stowe's novel Tom's death provokes the young George Shelby to vow to do what one man can to end slavery, Aiken's script ends with Tom's triumphant dying words, making heaven his ultimate victory. The final tableau is similarly heaven-bound: before a background of "gorgeous clouds, tinted with sunlight," a white-robed Eva appears "on the back of a milk-white dove, with expanded wings, as if just soaring upward" (6.6). Her hands extend in benediction over a kneeling Uncle Tom and St. Clare, who gaze up at her. Then the curtain falls, the plot tied neatly with Legree already dead and Tom glorying at the gates of heaven alongside Eva. This lack of urgency about further earthly action is part of a broader tendency in Aiken's script to minimize the importance of life on earth. Throughout, numerous characters express a preference for death over enslavement under a hard master, including Chloe, George, Eliza, and Emmeline. Even St. Clare has little attachment to this world once he has lost his daughter. Jeffrey D. Mason criticizes the play's ending for allowing the audience to "enjoy the sensation, however illusory, of having achieved what the play implies is morally right, but without having to make any efforts or take any initiative."[47] Indeed, in the Aiken play only St. Clare imagines the possibility of Tom's freedom, and even Topsy, who ends the play alive and free, does not get an independent future. When

Ophelia asks her if she wants liberty, Topsy doesn't even know what it is. Unprepared for independence, she will live with Ophelia in Vermont.

Regardless of the compromises to Stowe's novel in Aiken's play—and indeed, regardless of the compromises in Stowe's novel itself—its endowment of Tom with dignity provides a powerful suggestion of the true injustice of slavery. Dignity, according to Kant, gives all human beings intrinsic, unconditional value by virtue of their capacity for morality. This capacity not only separates human beings from the rest of the natural world but also requires a commensurate mode of behavior, in which all human beings must recognize this value in each other. Dignity makes it immoral to treat human beings as means rather than ends and is thus incompatible with slavery.[48] Ultimately the plays did not need to demand a specific action to have a large effect on the nation's attitude toward slavery; their power was rooted in their ability to spread the radical idea that slaves were human beings, too, and that slavery, in denying this, was unjust.

Conway's Uncle Tom's Cabin *on P. T. Barnum's Stage*

While Aiken's *Uncle Tom's Cabin* drew nightly hordes to the National, two hundred miles to the north an adaptation scripted by H. J. Conway for the Boston Museum was finding similar success. For many years, the lack of an extant Conway script encouraged scholars to rely on incomplete newspaper coverage and a playbill plot synopsis to conclude that Conway's play is pro-slavery, or at least conciliatory to Southerners. With the recent exception of David Reynolds, who in a brief discussion of the play emphasizes its subversive elements, the discovery of a partial script in the 1990s has tempered the assessment instead of changing it.[49] Perhaps its New York City production by Phineas T. Barnum, a showman known for his commodifying displays of racial, ethnic, and physical "others," has made the pro-slavery interpretation seem even more likely. But contemporaneous accounts do not support a pro-slavery interpretation of Conway's play.

When Conway's adaptation premiered at the Boston Museum in 1852, audiences generally greeted the production as a faithful adaptation of Stowe's anti-slavery novel. William Lloyd Garrison, who attended and enjoyed both the Conway version at the Boston Museum and the Aiken play at the

National, wrote to his wife that in some respects he preferred the Conway version.[50] (Unfortunately, the letter is brief and doesn't explain why.) Conway's adaptation did, however, receive one mixed review from an anti-slavery critic, who found that "[t]he slang conversation of the negroes and the Ethiopian 'break-downs,' seemed to seriously mar the otherwise favorable impression the drama was producing."[51] The objection to minstrelsy, a primarily working-class theatrical form, may have been as much about its jarring difference from the more respectable genre of the reform melodrama as its racial characterizations. Despite these limitations, however, the critic identified a departure from minstrel conventions in the role of "'Uncle Tom,' the hero of the piece": "The faithful, devoted, pious old negro was capitally delineated—a *real* character, and not one of fiction." Indeed, Conway's Uncle Tom is a significant departure from the minstrel "aged darkey" figure both physically and intellectually. Haley describes Tom as "broadchested, strong as a horse," with a high forehead that shows he's "calculating."[52] This strength and quick-wittedness come on display when Tom courageously rescues Eva after her fall from the boat's deck, an event that Aiken's original script narrates but does not dramatize. Conway's Tom is also literate, as we find out when he reads aloud a letter from his family to Eva. This literacy distinguishes him from most people enslaved in the South, where in many places it was illegal to teach a slave to read.

To pro- and anti-slavery spectators alike, the production made a strong anti-slavery statement. When abolitionist Parker Pillsbury attended, he reported that, in a theater "almost literally crammed nearly an hour before the rising of the curtain," the five-hundred-person audience loudly applauded the play's "most radical sentiments," including the moment when the slave-catchers chasing George Harris and Eliza were shot dead.[53] Pillsbury was delighted to witness an audience cheering the black man and woman breaking the law rather than the white men pursuing their legal property. "*Vive la agitation!* [*sic*]," he concluded. A pro-slavery spectator also recognized the anti-slavery power of the Boston Museum's *Uncle Tom's Cabin*, condemning it as "a slander upon the slaveholding community" that reached the level of "treason."[54]

After seeing the hordes drawn to the National every night to see Aiken's *Uncle Tom's Cabin* and hearing about the success of his longtime friend and collaborator Moses Kimball with Conway's adaptation, the showman

Phineas T. Barnum—himself no stranger to productions that keyed into American uncertainties about race[55]—decided to mount his own competing version at his American Museum in New York City.[56] There is little reason to think that Barnum made significant changes to the play when he brought it to the American Museum.[57] Barnum was sympathetic to many reform movements, including temperance (he was a fervent teetotaler), women's rights, and abolition and black civil rights.[58] But as he was the first to admit, his primary interest was making money, not political statements—though the latter could at times aid the former. By staging the Conway script at the American Museum, a theater located just a few blocks from the National, Barnum planned to divert some of A. H. Purdy's profits into his own pocket.

Opening on November 7, 1853, Barnum's production of Conway's *Uncle Tom's Cabin* sparked initial resistance from the Republican *New York Tribune*. One week into the show's run, a *Tribune* review charged Barnum's production with "destroy[ing] the point and moral of the story of Uncle Tom" and transforming Stowe's novel into "a play to which no apologist for Slavery could object," one that came perilously close to "a mere burlesque negro performance."[59] The worst parts were the weak characterizations (especially of Eva and Topsy); the light tone of the slave auction scene, which ended with a "ridiculous squabble" that transformed any moral seriousness into comedy; and the ending, in which, instead of dying, "Uncle Tom is allowed to run with flying colors, after having had a pretty good time, so far as is seen or represented, throughout his entire pilgrimage." This last was perhaps an exaggeration. In the Conway script's final act, Legree strikes Tom with a whip, and the stage directions call for the removal of Tom's jacket, "showing to audience his back very bloody" (5.3). But at the end of the play, Legree is dead, killed by supernatural forces, and Tom, his wife, and his children are alive and free. Rather than dying and ascending to heaven with Little Eva, as he does in Aiken's play, Tom receives a gift of money for "a lot of good land down East" where he and his family will live in freedom.

Responding to the *Tribune*'s criticism with a revamp of his advertising, Barnum defended his production's departures from Stowe's novel as dramatic interventions rather than political ones. The American Museum's first week of advertisements had made no reference to the production's politics, instead emphasizing its continuity with Stowe's novel and its magnificent scenery.[60]

Now, Barnum's ad directly addressed politics, insisting that the play *was* an anti-slavery work and that it offered a true picture of the horrors of slavery, "represent[ing] Southern Negro SLAVERY AS IT IS, Exposing all its abhorrent deformities, its cruelties and barbarities."[61] Quoting Othello's final speech, in which he asks all who are present to write about him as he is, with neither excuse nor cruelty, Barnum's ad maintained that his production did "nothing extenuate or set down aught in malice." This allusion situated the American Museum's *Uncle Tom's Cabin* in *Othello's* more serious American blackface tradition.

At the same time, Barnum conceded that there was a difference between his version and the one at the National, which the *Tribune* evidently preferred. His advertisement asserted that his production did not make light of slavery but did offer a different—and, according to Barnum, more realistic—representation of the slaves themselves: "It does not foolishly and unjustly elevate the negro above the white man in intellect or morals. It exhibits a true picture of Negro life in the South, instead of absurdly representing the ignorant slave as possessed of all the polish of the drawing-room, and the refinement of the educated whites." Challenging Stowe's novel, Aiken's adaptation, or both, the ad critiqued the notion that black slaves could match and even exceed whites in intelligence, morality, and respectability. The advertisement further held that the play's happy ending had nothing to do with politics; this change to Stowe's plot was done simply to accommodate the "dramatic taste" of "having Virtue triumphant at last." The movement from page to stage demanded a different set of conventions; heavenly reward might be a satisfying conclusion to a novel, but a theatrical audience needed to see vice punished on earth.

Not long after, the paper accepted Barnum's invitation to take a second look at the show and published a more favorable review, reporting that "a successful effort has been made to make the play conform to the spirit of the original story."[62] Most of the offensive parts of the play had been excised or toned down, including the auction scene, which was now "rendered in a much more suitable and impressive manner." Did Barnum significantly change Conway's play from the Boston Museum's version initially and then return it to its original politics? The progression of the *Tribune's* responses to Barnum's production illustrates just how slippery the play's political stance

could be. It was difficult to be certain about the politics of something so dynamic as a theatrical performance.

Indeed, Conway's play offers its own attack on slavery in the clear-headed
reasoning of a character he introduced to *Uncle Tom's Cabin*, the Connecticut
traveler Penetrate Partyside. At first glance, Penetrate seems to be roughly the
equivalent of the Aiken adaptation's Gumption Cute: a typical stage Yankee
who makes the audience laugh and extends the narrative arc of the Ophelia
character. But Penetrate, a New Englander who is traveling in the South with
his eyes and his notebook wide open, goes far beyond the comic diversion
of Aiken's Gumption Cute. The aptly named character introduces a mood
of penetrating, nonpartisan engagement with the issue of slavery. Indeed, a
pro-slavery reading of Conway's play works only if one views Penetrate as an
insignificant figure. But Penetrate is fundamental to both the plot and the
anti-slavery argument of Conway's play. His innocent questions and logi-
cal conclusions, which begin the moment he appears on stage in the second
act, highlight the ethical problems of slavery. Constantly comparing things
"ginerally" and "particlarly," Penetrate is preoccupied with matching principles and actions. And in his view, slavery violates both Christian values and
America's basic principle of freedom.[63] That Penetrate ultimately searches
law books to help free Tom rather than turning to moral suasion or violence
is telling. For Penetrate, and for Conway's play as a whole, the solution to an
injustice as huge as slavery lies in creating and obeying ethical laws. Where
Aiken's *Uncle Tom's Cabin* envisions heaven as the site of ultimate justice, the
Conway script is invested in legal solutions to social wrongs.

Yet the secular tone of Conway's adaptation weakens the religious power
of Tom's characterization. Although he is a dignified Christian, Conway's
Tom is more devoted to his masters (at least those who are kind) than is
Stowe's or Aiken's. Shelby offers the same words of praise for Tom's piousness
as in Stowe and Aiken, calling him a "good sensible pious fellow" who "got
religion at a camp-meeting four years ago" (1.2) in a conversation with Haley.
But here Tom's Christianity is largely a means for him to serve his masters,
not God—at least until he encounters the evil demands of Legree. At the
beginning of Conway's play, Tom's birthday wishes for the young George
Shelby include a prayer that "heaven [may] grant me length of days to serve
you as faithfully as I have [your parents]" (1.1), a hope that makes slavery

sound more like a privileged service position than a denial of humanity. And Tom reassures Mr. Shelby that he will not run off by asking, "[H]ave I ever broken word to you, or gone contrary to your desire, especially since I have become a Christian?" (1.3). The question implies that Tom's interpretation of Christianity mandates not only honesty and fidelity but also obedience.

Nevertheless, just as in Stowe and Aiken, on the Legree plantation Conway's Tom is heroic and devoted to his fellow slaves. He resolutely refuses Legree's demand that he whip an old woman for failing to pick enough cotton. When Legree tells Cassy that Tom must apologize for refusing to follow this command, Cassy rightly insists that Tom won't do it—"Because he has done right, and won't do, or say, he has done wrong." And just as Cassy predicted, Tom, "with deference but firmly" (5.3), refuses Legree's command again. Echoing Stowe's dialogue, he promises to be "a true and faithful servant to you" and "give you all the work of my hands, all my time, all my strength, but my soul I won't give up to mortal man." Distinguishing between legal and moral rights, Tom asserts that Legree may lay claim only to his body, but not to his soul. Knowing that Legree intends to kill him, he nevertheless insists "quietly but firmly" that he would rather die than do a cruel thing.

Even so, the play's happy ending for Uncle Tom continued to rankle the Tribune's critic even after the newspaper amended its harsh assessment of P. T. Barnum's production. If only Barnum would change the ending to more accurately reflect Stowe's novel, the production would receive the paper's complete approval: "Now let him kill Uncle Tom and all will be right."[64] For critics who castigate Stowe for her inability to imagine a racially integrated nation—after all, the novel concludes with Uncle Tom's death and the emigration of all other major black and mulatto characters—this sense of the necessity of Tom's death might seem surprising.[65] Aiken's script, which concludes with both Tom and Legree dead, falls short even more because it skips over the young George Shelby's crucial vow to "do *what one man can* to drive out this curse of slavery from my land!" (Stowe's italics) and his final decision to free his slaves.[66] Aiken's play concludes with sympathy for Uncle Tom—a radical feeling in an era when black humanity was still widely questioned—but without compulsion to act.

Conway's adaptation goes beyond Stowe in imagining a future for freed slaves in the United States. For Stowe, Tom's death is both a spiritual victory and a spur for action; her investment in the rewards of heaven does not stop her from advocating major civil reform. In her concluding remarks to the novel, she writes that the will of Christ shall "be done on earth as it is in heaven" and warns that the day of vengeance will come to a nation that harbors slavery.[67] The complicity of Christian clergy in this injustice is, she writes, what motivated her to write *Uncle Tom's Cabin*. This call for a change to the nation's laws goes beyond Aiken's adaptation but does not picture a racially integrated nation in which emancipated slaves can develop meaningful lives away from their former masters. Instead, Stowe describes a temporary period of education for freedmen before they are sent to Africa as Christian missionaries. In Conway's *Uncle Tom's Cabin*, however, Tom finds freedom in the United States. Early on, the young George Shelby envisions Tom's liberty; instead of vowing to buy Tom back (as he does in Stowe's novel and attempts to do at the conclusion of Aiken's play), the boy vehemently commits to the slave's freedom: "As there is a heaven above us and one who hears and sees all, I promise if I live you shall be free" (1.2). This urgent promise, which the kneeling boy reiterates three times as his last dying wish, launches the play's movement toward Tom's emancipation long before the scenes of Legree's cruelty. Young George does not explain why Uncle Tom must be freed, but his pledge complements Tom's later response to the news that his wife is working to buy his freedom: it is the culmination of his prayers.

Conway's play is most progressive in its final scene. Pro-slavery dramas of the 1850s allowed their enslaved protagonists to live but never to be free; after depicting a fugitive's miseries under freedom in the North, the plays would conclude with a joyful return to the former master. Conway could have ended his play by sending Tom back to the Shelby plantation, even as a free man. Moreover, once Tom and his family are free, Penetrate could simply keep the money that he and Aunty Vermont (Conway's name for Stowe's Aunt Ophelia character) have scrimped and saved to purchase Tom's freedom. After all, he begins the play as a speculator whose initial romantic interest in Aunty Vermont is based entirely on the supposition that she might be rich. Instead of keeping his money, Penetrate enthusiastically invests in Tom's future in the United States, offering funds to Tom to purchase "a lot of good land down East" (5.3) (for New Englanders, the term refers to the eastern coast of Maine[68]) where he can build a cabin for himself and his family. Ultimately,

Conway's play understands that investment in the freed people's futures is as necessary as emancipation.

Penetrate concludes the play by telling the audience to stand in support of Uncle Tom's freedom and to offer their best wishes and hopes "that his life may be happy though it be life among the lowly—Uncle Tom's Cabin" (ibid.). This call to rise demands the audience's physical support for Tom's future. To be sure, Penetrate's unquestioning acceptance of the notion that Tom must live "among the lowly" even once he is free is deeply problematic from a contemporary perspective. Moreover, the play's vision of a nation that includes freed slaves comes at the cost of some of the black characters: while Conway's Uncle Tom is a dignified, well-spoken Christian, many of his minor characters are purely comic and lack the nuance of Stowe's characterizations. But those who object to Uncle Tom's death in Stowe's novel may well appreciate that Conway's script imagines that there is indeed a place for free blacks in the nation. In an era when even many abolitionists embraced colonization, Conway's play advanced a potentially progressive alternative to Stowe's anti-slavery vision.

Uncle Tom and the Civil War

The Barnum and Howard productions were among many adaptations of *Uncle Tom's Cabin* staged during the 1850s. In New York City alone, five versions ran concurrently, including a Bowery Theatre show starring T. D. Rice, the famous originator of the Jim Crow act, as Uncle Tom. The most salient feature of *Uncle Tom's Cabin* dramatizations might be their variation of a common set of characters, plots, and themes. This variety shined vividly in the memory of Henry James, who in his memoir *A Small Boy and Others* (1913) recalled enjoying many different versions of *Uncle Tom's Cabin*, including those at the National Theatre and Barnum's Museum, during his youth in 1850s New York City. "I must have partaken thoroughly of the feast to have left the various aftertastes so separate and so strong," he wrote.[69] What struck James most about *Uncle Tom's Cabin* was its expansiveness. He famously described it as "a wonderful 'leaping' fish" that "simply sat down wherever it lighted and made itself, so to speak, at home," drawing crowds wherever it went.[70] James' "leaping fish" metaphor points to the unique combination of stability and flexibility in Stowe's creation; somehow it retained its own singular power and identity while appealing to people from every walk of life—"save indeed for Northern as differing from Southern," James reflected, though there is evidence that some Southerners did read the novel and attend the plays. This was no ordinary book, to be picked up and read and then put down. Stowe's novel was, James wrote, "much less a book than a state of vision, of feeling and of consciousness, in which [people] didn't sit and read and appraise and pass the time, but walked and talked and laughed and cried and, in a manner of which Mrs. Stowe was the irresistible cause, generally conducted themselves."[71]

James' description of *Uncle Tom's Cabin* as "a wonderful 'leaping' fish" certainly holds true in the historical archive, for dramatizations sprang up all over the country. Without the protection that copyright laws would eventually afford, the plays multiplied informally. For example, a Cincinnati theater manager attended an early show at the National, wrote down an outline, filled it in from memory, and staged *Uncle Tom's Cabin* in his hometown, all within a few months of seeing it.[72] The play attracted overflowing houses as far west as San Francisco and as far south as New Orleans, "swe[eping] across America in . . . prairie-fire fashion."[73] Each production of the play adapted to its surroundings. Some versions were anti-slavery, others were pro-slavery, and still others tried to capitalize on the popularity of *Uncle Tom's Cabin* by using similar titles but had virtually no connection to Stowe's work.

However a contemporary audience might respond to the nineteenth-century Uncle Tom, in the majority of the accounts of nineteenth-century drama critics, Uncle Tom is described as a virtuous and dignified character, a figure of pathos and piety rather than ridicule. Green Germon, the actor initially reluctant to take the role of Uncle Tom because he assumed that it would be a comic one, was praised for his rich portrayal of an earnest man whose triumphant faith revealed "the grand truths of immortality and of religion."[74] According to another critic, Germon's performance as Uncle Tom in a Cleveland production revealed the character's "mild and equable temper, his homely but sterling religious mind, his yielding nature when encountering the necessities of the bondsman's lot, and his unconquerable will and calm heroism when facing the tyranny and brutal violence of Legree."[75] One review of an 1858 Howard production of *Uncle Tom's Cabin* on Broadway reported that the actor who played Uncle Tom had done a satisfactory job, "although the people more noisily rejoice in his comic negro representations," a comment that indicates a significant difference between Uncle Tom and comic stage characters.[76]

Moreover, the role broke a major convention of blackface by failing to make Uncle Tom's race his most salient feature. According to a Cleveland theater critic in 1854, Uncle Tom was a "truly upright man, one who would be an honor to any race if acted in reality."[77] Some of the actors who blacked up to play Uncle Tom had major Shakespearean roles to their credit. After taking the title role in *Hamlet* and playing Iago in *Othello* during the 1840s, George Ryer appeared as Uncle Tom in the 1850s and 1860s.[78] A Washington, DC, critic called the role "one of the most difficult on the stage, and we have seen it in the hands of masters, where it stood, as a piece of acting, by the side of Lear."[79] In Albany, a veteran actor performed the role of Uncle Tom "in a style which for pathos and truthfulness cannot be surpassed."[80]

Of course, there were also minstrel versions of *Uncle Tom's Cabin*. In the North, where minstrelsy was already a popular and well-defined theatrical tradition, these capitalized on the fame of Stowe's story while upholding the genre's conventions. Minstrel versions of *Uncle Tom's Cabin* ran the political gamut in the 1850s, and their positions on slavery, as Sarah Meer suggests, "were neither uniform nor predictable."[81] No scripts survive, but extant playbills suggest that the shows simply repurposed Stowe's title and characters for existing material. Christy's Minstrels, for example, had always included a third section of Southern plantation specialties in their shows, but once *Uncle Tom's Cabin* became ubiquitous on the American stage, this section was retitled "Life among the Happy," a revision of the novel's subtitle, "Life among the Lowly." Even when "Life among the Happy" was extended into a full-length "opera" in 1854, its attention to Stowe's plot was nominal, staging typical minstrel scenes with characters newly named Uncle Tom, Eliza, George, and Topsy. According to the synopsis from an 1855 playbill, in the first scene Uncle Tom, recently returned from a revival meeting, criticizes "free Darkies" and describes his "preference for Old Kentuck." In another scene, George Harris serenades Eliza, followed by a duet from Topsey [*sic*] and "Lame Jake." In the last act, George and Eliza are married in a wedding complete with "jumping the broomstick," and the entertainment concludes with a "Grand Characteristic Dance, 'Pop goes the weazle.c[82] If the names had been changed, nothing about "Life among the Happy" would have suggested Stowe's novel; *Uncle Tom's Cabin* was merely a new idea to wrap around minstrel traditions.

Indeed, some minstrel Uncle Tom skits had nothing more in common with Stowe's novel than the single name "Uncle Tom." Frank Brower's "Happy Uncle Tom," which appeared as early as 1854, resembled Stowe's story in name only. The short skit, a prelude to a "Happy Uncle Tom dance," depicts a young man, Jeff, attempting to tell an old man named Uncle Tom about his banjo, a typical minstrel instrument. With his extravagant description of his banjo—he claims that it cost sixty dollars and is made of steel and brass, both expensive materials at the time—Jeff is obviously not telling the truth. But because Uncle Tom is hard of hearing, Jeff has to repeat himself over and over again. In this skit, Uncle Tom is essentially the straight man to Jeff's comic bragging.[83]

Overall, the *Uncle Tom's Cabin* adaptations had an enormous role in moving the American masses to sympathy for enslaved people and opposition to slavery. As various productions sprang up all over the North and Midwest, observers consistently noted their surprise at the responsiveness of even the roughest audiences to the plight of the slaves. An attendant at an 1853 performance in Philadelphia marveled that the "purely abolition" play could impart sympathy for the slaves to all classes, even the lowest, "who have heretofore been ignorant and cruelly bitter in their prejudices against color."[84] The audience cheered sympathetically "at the expression of the sentiments of love of liberty and equality of rights, (among men, whatever be their color) and also at those parts wherein the slave is assisted and rescued, and the slave hunter and dealer foiled." In an era in which many black men and women were legally considered property, this acknowledgment of the humanity and rights of people of all colors was significant. In effect, the plays advocated a higher law over American law. They inspired audiences to root for lawbreakers over law followers, to cheer for fugitive slaves and those illegally helping them rather than the lawful slave-catchers.

This sympathy did not lose its power when audiences left the theater. One writer predicted that the enthusiasm of the working class audiences at the Bowery Theatre's 1854 rendition of *Uncle Tom's Cabin* would translate into real change in the nation's slavery policy, which had recently taken a southward turn with Senator Stephen A. Douglas' proposal of the Kansas-Nebraska Act. The act would repeal the 1820 Missouri Compromise and allow the spread of slavery into new American territories. According to an Ohio newspaper, the play's effect "upon the unthinking, unreasoning masses who will derive their notions of its justice from the representations they see, is not hard to foretell. We are inclined to think it will not be long before Douglas' Nebraska bill will be very unpopular with the New York b'hoys, and on them his chances for the succession depend."[85] (The act passed in 1854 regardless, but the Civil War followed not far behind.)

Where contemporary critics have read the proliferation of *Uncle Tom's Cabin* adaptations and merchandise as diluting Stowe's anti-slavery message, some nineteenth-century critics embraced them as welcome contributions to growing anti-slavery sentiment. A piece published in *Frederick Douglass' Paper* in 1865 celebrated the massive penetration of Stowe's anti-slavery text into virtually every cultural realm and form:

> The time was, when banks, tariffs and internal improvements were the subjects which engrossed the thoughts of the people. Now, the anti-slavery question is the order of the day. It shakes the country from centre to circumference. The people read anti-slavery books, sing anti-slavery songs, dance anti-slavery dances, drink tea and coffee from anti-slavery cups and saucers, and after [illegible] attend the anti-slavery drama and then go home with the determination that their homes shall also be anti-slavery.[86]

Uncle Tom's Cabin adaptations and merchandise changed the political attitudes of American families by humanizing a formerly ignored group of people. If the injustice of slavery had not previously been on their minds, it was now. Indeed, supporters of slavery felt threatened by the way that the plays generated sympathy for the plight of the enslaved. Southern playwrights came up with their own anti-*Uncle Tom's Cabin* stage productions, with titles referencing the falseness of the original *Uncle Tom's Cabin*. Augmenting the happy portrayal of plantation life often seen in minstrel shows with central conflicts and resolutions that mirrored those of the anti-Tom novels, these plays claimed to correct Stowe's misinformation by presenting "Uncle Tom as he is."[87]

To pro-slavery critics, the Uncle Tom of Stowe's novel and the Northern stage adaptations was particularly objectionable because of his dignified
persona, with its alarming suggestion that a slave could be so clearly equal
and even superior to whites. In "Uncle Tom's Cabin in Louisiana," a popular production in New Orleans and one of three different pro-slavery Tom
shows that appeared in that city in 1854 alone, Stowe's Uncle Tom was replaced with a happy, comic figure.[88] In "The Old Plantation, or Uncle Tom
as He Is," the writer and actor George Jamison created his own version of
Uncle Tom as an offset for Stowe's representations; rather than staging the
play "merely to amuse and excite laughter," Jamison, according to the New
Orleans *Picayune*, "holds up to view the radical error that lies at the heart
of Abolitionism."[89] In 1860, Jamison's show appeared in New York, advertised as an entertainment for "everybody who wishes to understand the true
(and not fancied) condition of THE SOUTHERN NEGRO."[90] The story
had little in common with Stowe's novel other than the name of its title
character; following a typical pro-slavery plot, the play depicted the decep-
tion of slaves by evil abolitionists, who spin tales of gold in the streets of
the North but exploit the helpless fugitives when they arrive in the North.
The only cruel slaveholder is "Scoerum, a foreigner to the South," who is
"reprimanded for his inhumanity, by a real Southerner."[91] When an evil
abolitionist kidnaps an unwilling slave named Daisy, Uncle Tom, an "aged,
faithful servant; a perfect type of Southern negro," accompanies his master
to New York (where he is "disgusted with the climate") to rescue her. After
searching all over the city to find Daisy and encountering myriad unhappy
fugitives in the process, Uncle Tom discovers her lying senseless in the street
and saves her just in the nick of time. When the group returns to the plantation, they rejoice in song and dance, and Uncle Tom concludes the play
by expressing his "delight in getting back to de Bressed Old Souf."[92] According to pro-slavery Southerners, this representation was far more in line
with reality than Stowe's. A Louisiana newspaper approved of this change
in the character, reporting that "Mrs. Beecher Stowe's beau-ideal of African
intelligence, piety and respectability, has been stripped of the false gilding of
romance and humbug, and clothed in the true attire of the 'cullud population'
as they are"—as if only white people could be intelligent, pious, and respectable. In the pro-slavery version, the character was "put on the stage as a fact,

not a fiction; just such a fellow as exists and can be met with in our streets daily, full of fun, good humor, and contentment."[93] Stowe's Uncle Tom and the many versions of him on stage threatened a notion crucial to the system of slavery: that all black people were happy and fun-loving because of the care of benevolent whites.

Ultimately, however, the pro-slavery plays could not efface the nation's rising anti-slavery sentiment. With the April 12, 1861, Confederate firing on Fort Sumter, the United States of America entered a Civil War. Having helped spread anti-slavery feeling, the Uncle Tom dramas were now propelled by it. With the nation transfixed by "the negro question," the Negro was, as *The Philadelphia Inquirer* reflected, "a first-rate 'paying card.'"[94] Many different productions of *Uncle Tom's Cabin* continued to draw large houses across the North during the war years. In 1862, the *Lowell Daily Citizen* commented that it was clear why four different productions of *Uncle Tom's Cabin* could play in New York at the same time successfully (actually, it was five): "The events of the past year have evidently not added to the popular admiration for the system of human bondage. The straws indicate which way the wind blows."[95] A Philadelphia critic explained that "[f]ew dramas ever written have so entirely enlisted the sympathies of humanity as this, and from being slandered and abused, it has grown into more favor until it is recognized as the most eloquent appeal ever written on behalf of a down-trodden race."[96] Audiences attended *Uncle Tom's Cabin* for entertainment, but also to confirm the rightness of the war.

Stowe's novel and its theatrical adaptations had galvanized the North against slavery by representing the institution of slavery as unjust and promoting a compelling picture of Uncle Tom and his family as sympathetic and respectable human beings. In 1862, a *Tribune* writer argued that these humanizing stage portrayals were fundamental to the immense political power of *Uncle Tom's Cabin*, which had penetrated the nation "from the great city mansion to the humblest village home."[97]

Its effects were seen prominently in the fact that a dramatization of Negro character as contained in it—not the wretched caricature at which fools had always laughed—but presenting it under the aspect of human capabilities, aspirations, and rights, became possible in our theatres, and not only possible, but popular. The men who were hitherto ready to mob, burn, and destroy everything that bore the name of Abolition . . . began to find in the theatrical version of *Uncle Tom's Cabin*, new ideas. They discovered that the slave was a man.

In both fictional and dramatic forms, *Uncle Tom's Cabin* had shown Americans the humanity of a race previously represented only in foolish caricature. And this humanity, they knew, entitled blacks to the rights guaranteed to all Americans by the U.S. Constitution. Even if Abraham Lincoln's famous comment that Stowe's novel "started this great war" was apocryphal, many Americans across the political spectrum shared the belief that Stowe's novel and its dramatizations were key forces in provoking the Civil War and bringing about emancipation. Whether *Uncle Tom's Cabin* was to be blamed or celebrated for this, however, was a matter of one's political perspective.

CHAPTER 3

UNCLE TOM AND JIM CROW

WITH THE RATIFICATION of the Thirteenth Amendment in December of 1865, the United States formally abolished slavery, bringing to fruition the major goal of Stowe's novel. Yet the end of slavery left many unanswered questions and also raised some new ones. What would happen to the freed people? How would the South navigate what was supposed to be a new political and social order? How would the nation reconcile bitter divisions and come together as the United States of America? During the antebellum era, *Uncle Tom's Cabin* had given Americans a common framework and vocabulary for debating race and slavery. Now, as the tenuously reunited nation sketched out its future without slavery, Stowe's story proved just as culturally useful. For millions of Americans, Stowe's character was still the most prominent conception of an American slave. Whether in the novel, its dramatic adaptations, or Uncle Tom merchandise, *Uncle Tom's Cabin*, as Leslie Fiedler has argued, essentially "invented American Blacks for the imagination of the whole world. Before *Uncle Tom's Cabin*, they existed as historical, demographic, economic facts, their existence acknowledged but not felt with the passion and intensity we accord what moves through our dreams as well as our waking lives."[1] During the nineteenth century, the figure of Uncle Tom largely remained tied to *Uncle Tom's Cabin*, but the name of this still-controversial character also became a generic term in the American vernacular for Southern blacks born under slavery. Now, with both blacks and whites

describing the era of slavery as "the days of Uncle Tom," the nation debated
how the future of "Uncle Tom" and his descendants would look: would he
get the vote?[2] Would he vote in his own interest?[3] What exactly was that
interest, anyway? Straddling history and fiction, Uncle Tom was both an accepted symbol of the nation's many liberated slaves and a character whose
closeness to reality was frequently contested. This slippage gave *Uncle Tom's
Cabin* enormous symbolic resonance, making the novel and the plays enduring cultural touchstones in American debates about the legacy of slavery and
the future of black Americans.

In the years after the Civil War, Uncle Tom's Christian perfection was
still the most controversial thing about him. Famously describing *Uncle Tom's
Cabin* as the nearest prospect for a "Great American Novel," John William
DeForest wrote in 1868 that the novel's major flaw was its idealized portrayal of "a black man painted whiter than angels": "the impeccable Uncle
Tom—uncle of no extant nephews, so far as we know."[4] If DeForest, a
Connecticut-born former Union Army captain, saw Uncle Tom's unrealis-
tic idealization as a mark against the novel's literary excellence, many white
Democrats posited far more destructive effects from this character. Insisting
that the South would have ended slavery peaceably, they blamed the allegedly
false characterizations of Stowe's novel and its stage adaptations for sparking
what they insisted was an unnecessary war. A writer for the *Chicago Tribune*
lamented that Northerners who mistakenly took Stowe's fictional character as fact had become "too apt to look upon the plantation negro as that
large-affectioned, generous-natured, great-brained being of whom Uncle
Tom is the type."[5] By making Americans believe in the possibility of such a
character, Stowe had done the nation a great harm. Some white Democrats
argued that Stowe's flawed characterizations provided the shaky foundation
for Reconstruction-era policies. *Pomeroy's Democrat* asserted that Stowe's er-
roneously "sentimental" characters—"which gave about as accurate an idea of
the race as Fenimore Cooper's novels did of the Indian"—were to blame for
Negro suffrage and the other "mischief" of Reconstruction; no one who lived
in the South could believe that giving freed people the vote was a good idea.[6]

During Reconstruction, the most common strategy among whites for
counteracting the power of the Uncle Tom character was insisting that there
had never been a Negro so virtuous and intelligent. Thomas Nelson Page,

the prolific author of fiction steeped in the Lost Cause mythology, held that although abolition was, all in all, a positive development for the nation, slavery had been a blessing to black Americans. "Uncle Tom was not a negro in any of his characteristics except his color," Page wrote in the Baltimore *Sunday Herald*. "He belonged to a far higher race, the race of his creator, who endowed him with the richest virtues, feeling and sensibilities of his own race."[7] Identifying Christian virtue and feeling as markers of whiteness, Page argued that the inaccurate characterization of Uncle Tom was "the vice of 'Uncle Tom's Cabin' as a picture of slavery." At the same time that white Democrats insisted that a black man like Uncle Tom could never exist, however, they incorporated him into their criticism of Reconstruction. Forced by the Fifteenth Amendment to "g[i]ve up the fight on the nigger and politically recognize[] 'Uncle Tom' as a 'man and a brother,'" they soon charged that Republican mishandling (or "Radical misrule") had resulted in a net loss for black Americans.[8] In a refrain that came up several times during the 1870s and 1880s, political critics quipped that Uncle Tom was now "without a cabin."[9] Under this view of Reconstruction, black educational progress was no progress at all: it diverted energy away from the industrious labor to which the race had a "peculiar adaptability" and toward professions in which black people could never hope to be successful.

As Americans fought over the political future of "Uncle Tom," many also continued to read Stowe's novel and attend its dramatic adaptations. Despite its antebellum origin and subject, *Uncle Tom's Cabin* acclimated to the postbellum era with remarkable facility, at least in the North and West, where both the novel and the dramas were extremely popular after the Civil War. According to a *Publishers Weekly* survey, Stowe's novel was one of the most salable novels of 1876.[10] For the remainder of the nineteenth century, libraries and booksellers regularly reported that Stowe's novel was one of the most favored books among patrons. In 1895, New York City's free library society noted that its twenty-nine copies were checked out far more than any other book: a total of 666 times.[11] (In comparison, the second most popular book, Jules Verne's *Around the World in Eighty Days*, was borrowed 282 times.)

Meanwhile, dramatic adaptations of Stowe's novel spread across the nation. Staged in productions large and small, by actors of all levels of ability, *Uncle Tom's Cabin* was an elastic drama, one no less popular now that slavery was abolished.[12] Over the decades, they appeared in nearly every conceivable form, including moral drama, opera, variety, burlesque, and vaudeville, nimbly incorporating new theatrical trends—fountains flowing with real water for the St. Clare estate, live mastiffs for Eliza's flight across the ice—even while holding to a familiar set of characters and tropes.[13] These dramas are commonly described as embracing the worst of American racial views, their "anti-abolitionist and ostensibly anti-black representations" mirroring the "racial attitudes that manifested themselves in the Black Codes of the Reconstruction era and the Jim Crow legislation that followed."[14] Yet as I shall show, Stowe's anti-slavery message stubbornly clung to the *Uncle Tom's Cabin* dramas, and nineteenth-century Americans understood a wide assortment of these adaptations as part of the same ideological tradition as the novel. Moreover, the contentious status of these dramas figured prominently in national debates over the memory of the antebellum South and the reasons for the Civil War, debates which held heavy repercussions for what race would mean in a nation without slavery.

Uncle Tom's Cabin *on the Postbellum Stage*

In 1867, a critic for a Salt Lake City newspaper described *Uncle Tom's Cabin* as a "mixed play."[15] To this critic, the mixed nature of the play came from its combination of "fun, sentiment, tragedy and the tightest sort of religion"; these elements would, he wrote, "afford satisfaction to a very mixed assembly." This idea of a "mixed play" is also useful in thinking about the politics of the *Uncle Tom's Cabin* shows. Both within and among the many versions that were performed, the politics of the plays embraced a persistent doubleness for decades after the Civil War. Like Stowe's novel, dramatizations of *Uncle Tom's Cabin* were both agents of progressive politics and reflections of their era. While performances of *Uncle Tom's Cabin* dramas during the late nineteenth century varied considerably according to the location, the resources of the company, and the quirks of any given group of producers and performers, most of them followed some version of the Aiken script, making Eliza's flight across the ice, George and Eliza's defense, Eva's deathbed, and Tom's futile resistance to Legree into indispensable components. As the nineteenth century continued, the most common changes to the plays were innovations that heightened spectacle and comedy, including live animals, elaborate "plantation scenes" featuring a roster of black singers and dancers, and the doubling of the two most comic characters, Topsy and Marks. Nevertheless, the *Uncle Tom's Cabin* plays continued to be forces of social reform into the twentieth century.

The characterization of Uncle Tom in the late nineteenth-century adaptations was largely constant: the typical Uncle Tom stage character was old, white-haired, and balding, quoting scripture and singing hymns in dialect. Among hundreds of nineteenth-century descriptions of the Uncle Tom stage character, newspapers and periodicals most frequently described him as faithful, pious, and serious: "the staid and religious old slave," "the ebony hero," "pious and devoted," "the faithful, scripture-quoting, hymn-singing, old slave," "the religious and patriarchal character."[16] As the former minstrel comedian George Kunkel played the role, for example, Uncle Tom was "a solid mass of goodness done in black cork."[17] Even in the *Uncle Tom's Cabin* shows that emphasized comedy as much as pathos, Uncle Tom was the emotional center. In one poster, titled "Uncle Tom Leaving Home," a sorrowful Uncle Tom embraces his grieving wife and children as Loker looks on, grasping a whip (see figure 3.1).

In the postbellum plays, Uncle Tom's pathos worked hand in hand with the character's dignity and manliness, both also key terms in descriptions of Uncle Tom. For example, an account of an 1888 Boston production describes the actor who played Uncle Tom as giving the character "a personation of quiet dignity."[18] An actor in an 1894 production had "a fine conception of the part, and portrays it in a manly, dignified manner," while a report the same year of a performance of *Uncle Tom's Cabin* starring the famous black boxer Peter Jackson as Uncle Tom praised his "quiet, manly, unassuming impersonation of the old slave."[19] This seriousness persisted even when the surrounding roles were comic. In the production by Al. W. Martin's Uncle Tom's Cabin Company (see figures 3.2 and 3.3), a Minneapolis critic observed, "Pathetic little Eva, sublime Uncle Tom, stand out like beautiful statues around which a motley aggregation of farce comedy people perform and make merry."[20] Indeed, across the many different extant *Uncle Tom's Cabin* scripts and playbills from the nineteenth and early twentieth centuries, Tom's refusal to flog another slave is a consistently important scene, enduring no matter how many light-hearted interpolations.

Figure 3.1. "Uncle Tom Leaving Home," color lithograph poster for stage production of *Uncle Tom's Cabin*, Erie Lithograph Company, New York and Erie, Pennsylvania. Harriet Beecher Stowe Center, Hartford, CT.

Figure 3.2. "Characters That Will Live Forever," lithograph poster for Al. W. Martin's Mammoth Production of *Uncle Tom's Cabin*, U.S. Printing Co., ca. 1899. Theatrical poster collection, Prints & Photographs Division, Library of Congress POS-TH-1899. U53, no. 10.

Figure 3.3. "Scenes from Al. W. Martin's Mammoth Production of *Uncle Tom's Cabin*," lithograph poster, U.S. Printing Co., ca. 1899. Theatrical poster collection, Prints & Photographs Division, Library of Congress POS-TH-1899.U53, no. 9.

In George Fawcett Rowe's 1878 adaptation, Uncle Tom refuses to act as slave driver ("I'd rather be driven myself than drive these poor critters in de field"), to tell where the runaways have gone ("I *could*, Mas'r, but I won't"), and to flog another slave ("No, Mas'r, I can't. You may kill me, but I'll raise no finger agin any helpless critter here").[21] Likewise, both an 1889 adaptation composed for traveling troupes and William A. Brady's lavish 1901 revival highlight Tom's refusal to flog Emmeline even after Legree whips him three times, or to tell where Cassy and Emmeline have gone even though he knows he will die as a consequence.[22] This is not to say, of course, that the Uncle Tom of the post-bellum stage was wholly or universally dignified. Sometimes the character was a foolish, contented slave. During Reconstruction, the minstrel performer Sam Sanford reframed the traditional last act of his minstrel shows, traditionally a plantation scene, as one from *Uncle Tom's Cabin*. Here, Sanford's "Happy Uncle Tom" and his family enjoy plantation life, and no one gets sold.[23] Sanford's performance was, according to an 1865 account, "one of the happiest pictures of the old plantation darkey that has ever been witnessed upon the stage."[24] To be sure, even the most seemingly dignified representations would almost certainly offend if replicated today.

Even so, some white Americans insisted that the characters in both Stowe's novel and its stage adaptations were dangerously inaccurate. In 1869, *Pomeroy's Democrat* bitterly attacked a local Chicago adaptation for its allegedly topsy-turvy racial hierarchy, snidely suggesting that this production, which portrayed Southerners as "a set of yawhoos" and "Southern niggers" as "brevet angels disguised with lamp-black," would appeal to "all who believe the nigger is greatly superior to white trash."[25] The dramas did not need to suggest that all black characters were better than all whites in order to cause offense; simply the implication that some black characters were superior to "white trash" was incendiary. Moreover, if Stowe's novel was responsible for the Civil War, so were the stage adaptations. "Both the play and book undoubtedly had as much to do with bringing on the war, by arousing the feeling of the Northern people, as any other effort made in that direction," wrote one Southerner upon attending a Jarrett & Palmer production of *Uncle Tom's Cabin* in 1881.[26] Arguing that both the novel and the plays unfairly depicted slave-owners as brutal and made black characters—especially Uncle

Tom—impossibly virtuous, he took particular objection to the actor who performed the role of Uncle Tom, George Kunkel:

> The individual who took the part of Uncle Tom had no more conception of the negro character than an Esquimaux [sic] would have. Anyone from the South would have been amused at his idea of the old-fashioned negro character. Instead of the simple, credulous and true style of the old-time darky, he tried to make the character of Uncle Tom similar to Richelieu, Virginius, Lear, Spartacus and Brutus, as played by Booth, McCullough and Barrett.[27]

For white Southerners, there was little distinction between Stowe's hero and the Uncle Tom of the stage. In comparing Uncle Tom to a list of some of the strongest and most powerful characters in the Western theatrical canon, this critic revealed the continuing threat of such a representation. A system of white supremacy relied upon an inherent racial hierarchy, and an image of a brave and intelligent Uncle Tom, as Kunkel played the role in 1878, called that hierarchy into question.

George Kunkel's Uncle Tom had itself changed considerably from his minstrel days, a development that shows just how flexible *Uncle Tom's Cabin* could be. In the 1850s, his Nightingale Opera Troupe produced a Southern revision of Stowe's novel, *Uncle Tom's Cabin, or Freedom at the North and Service at the South*, that showed a fugitive's misery among Northern abolitionists and voluntary return to slavery.[28] In the mid-1870s, however, Kunkel's performance took on a new moral and sentimental seriousness, as the former comic minstrel brought a persona of manliness and dignity to the role of Uncle Tom. Kunkel was "a most gentlemanly *Uncle Tom*," according to a critic of an 1878 New York production, and he gave the character "a certain stateliness and manly quality which is very pleasant to see, and which, we suppose, is as Mrs. Stowe intended to represent the old gentleman," according to an 1876 account of a production in Boston.[29] After beginning his Uncle Tom career arguing *for* slavery, Kunkel's acting and singing now made a powerful case against it.[30] Indeed, the role had a way of eliciting surprising performances from actors usually pigeon-holed as minstrels. When Cool White took the role in 1879, a Northeast periodical marveled that "that veteran Ethiopian delineator ... could take so solemn a part!"[31] Likewise, the role was a major change for the black performer Sam Lucas, who "suddenly developed from a first-class comedian into a rare emotional actor."[32]

Ultimately, the meaning of the stage Uncle Tom during the nineteenth century came as much from the social and political reputation of *Uncle Tom's Cabin* as from any individual performance. American audiences generally perceived the plays as anti-slavery works with significant implications for Jim Crow. This is what made them both appealing to black audiences and threatening to the Southerners who increasingly organized against them in the post-Reconstruction era, insisting that Southern slavery had not been so bad after all. At the turn of the twentieth century, the Lost Cause ideology that glorified the Old South and minimized the importance of slavery in the Civil War would be expressed more forcefully in protests *against* the plays than in the plays themselves.

Accounts from the postbellum era convincingly document black participation in and attendance and appreciation of the *Uncle Tom's Cabin* plays. Just as black Americans kept reading Stowe's novel, black theater groups staged adaptations. An amateur company in Saginaw, Michigan, staged *Uncle Tom's Cabin* in 1871, and others followed suit.[33] In 1884, H. T. Eubanks, a prominent black Clevelander and future member of the Ohio legislature, portrayed Uncle Tom in a production at the city's Euclid Avenue Opera House.[34] In addition to attending performances put on by amateur theater groups, black audiences enthusiastically attended the shows produced by white companies, from a packed show put on by the New York Standard Uncle Tom's Cabin Company in Martin's Ferry, Ohio, to a Cincinnati show headlined by the minstrel comedian Sam Sanford, where "[q]uite a number of the audience were colored people."[35] For an 1878 show in Stockbridge, Massachusetts, "a colored woman, eighty years old and obliged to walk with two canes, trudged nearly a mile through the pouring rain to see *Uncle Tom's Cabin* . . . , it being the first play she had ever witnessed."[36] These audiences continued for the rest of the nineteenth century and beyond. "Uncle Tom's Cabin showed here recently," the *Indianapolis Freeman* reported to its readers in 1895. "Uncle Tom will live as long as this Republic remains."[37]

Given the reputation of these plays among contemporary critics, this attendance is perhaps surprising. Why did black Americans attend the plays? What were they looking for when they purchased a ticket? While during this time the growing number of black newspapers generally did not print extensive theater reviews, instead focusing on current events, their responses to the shows later in the century suggest that part of the work's appeal came from its widely acknowledged role in bringing on the abolition of slavery and its unique depiction of slavery and race: *Uncle Tom's Cabin* was the rare popular American work that presented negative images of slavery and positive images of black people. To Bob Cole, a member of the prominent black songwriting team that included the brothers Rosamond and James Weldon Johnson, *Uncle Tom's Cabin* was one of the few dramas in which the American Negro was characterized in a "humane manner"; for this, Cole wrote in a 1902 article on "The Negro and the Stage" for *The Colored American Magazine*, "the Negro race will ever be indebted. . . . More good has been wrought to the American people by the advent of 'Uncle Tom's Cabin' on the literary and dramatic horizon than volumes could record."[38] For Cole, Stowe's novel and the stage adaptations operated in the same humanizing vein.

Another draw of the *Uncle Tom's Cabin* shows was the opportunity they provided to talented black artists who were awakening Americans to the richness of black performance. Beginning in the mid-1870s, elaborate plantation scenes featuring large casts of black singers, dancers, and musicians performing a variety of numbers, including jubilee singing, banjo melodies, and cakewalks, became an expected part of the *Uncle Tom's Cabin* shows. Featuring black (rather than black*face*) performers, these scenes developed as a result of the earlier success of the Fisk Jubilee Singers, a traveling performance group formed to raise money for Fisk University in its efforts to educate newly freed slaves. As the singers toured the eastern United States and Europe performing spirituals and anti-slavery songs, they not only raised hundreds of thousands of dollars for Fisk, thus ensuring the institution's survival, but also introduced black spirituals to white audiences, giving many white Americans "their first lesson in African American culture, the promise of emancipation, and the meaning of the Civil War."[39] The complex politics of these performances gestured backward to slavery and forward to the products of African American education, offering evidence of the progress that had and would continue to be made by former slaves.[40] American audiences, used to seeing blackfaced performers on stage, became eager to attend performances by black artists. The success of the Fisk group spawned so many imitators that jubilee singing became probably the most common employment among black entertainers of the 1870s and 1880s.[41]

Although the *Uncle Tom's Cabin* dramas certainly limited black artists to a narrative and visual frame of slavery, the extent to which they encouraged a widespread appreciation of black performance arts should not be underestimated. Jubilee singers and other plantation-scene performers often received multiple rounds of encores. Even if the play itself was a little tired after more than two decades, critics noted, the plantation scenes alone were more than worth the price of the ticket.[42] A typical response from a Philadelphia critic pronounced an 1877 plantation scene "a triumph of the theatrical art."[43] For the first time, the nation at large was interested in watching black performers in serious artistic forms. As David Reynolds notes, these plays were the mechanism through which many Americans discovered the Negro spirituals, which W. E. B. Du Bois, among others, believed would promote the full recognition of the race.[44] In the twentieth century, some elites would protest jubilee singing as culturally regressive, arguing that depictions of an unjust position of the past were harmful to racial progress. (Hattie McDaniel, of course, later rejected this argument, famously announcing that she'd rather make $700 a week playing the role of a maid in a film than $7 a week actually being one.) Nevertheless, the incorporation of black performers into the plays may have also opened the door for black actors to take roles previously reserved for white actors in blackface. In 1878, Sam Lucas became the first black actor to take the role of Uncle Tom in a white production, and a number of others followed in his wake: by 1883 there were enough groups, black and white, with a black Uncle Tom that the *Cleveland Gazette* identified an actor named John Howard as "the greatest colored personator of Uncle Tom."[45] With *Uncle Tom's Cabin* bringing so many black performers onto American stages, it is perhaps no surprise that *The Cleveland Gazette* and the Indianapolis *Freeman* regularly published updates from cast members of the traveling *Uncle Tom's Cabin* companies. "Mr. Samuel Chrismond, of Syracuse, joined Draper's Uncle Tom company as leading man, here, last week, and gave THE GAZETTE office a most pleasant call," reported the *Gazette* in a typical report from 1885. "Success to you, Mr. Chrismond."[46]

Perhaps there was also something valuable in the way that *Uncle Tom's Cabin* represented "the bright as well as the dark side of slavery," as a 1917 short story by a black American writer described the allure of the play to the younger generations.[47] Writing in 1902, Bob Cole suggested that some black folks avoided the *Uncle Tom's Cabin* dramas because recalling slavery felt demeaning. "Most feel somewhat belittled," he wrote, "when they watch the chase of the bloodhounds, the heartless slave sale, the inhuman whipping post, the murder of Uncle Tom by the heartless Legree."[48] Indeed, Legree's violence against Uncle Tom was such a key feature of the plays that it was often depicted on the posters that advertised touring productions. (See figures 3.4 and 3.5.) If the *Uncle Tom's Cabin* plays had portrayed slavery as a wholly degrading experience, to which there was no sufficient response besides escape, they might not have been appealing to ex-slaves and their descendants. After the Civil War, as William L. Andrews has documented, slave narratives turned away from the antebellum tradition of depicting slavery as a state of utter deprivation. Instead, they pragmatically emphasized the ways that experiences in slavery had built "credentials that the new industrial-capitalist order might respect," helping construct "a usable American past on which [black Americans] could build."[49] Similarly, the *Uncle Tom's Cabin* plays' plantation scenes (see figure 3.6), with their dazzling performances, could augment depictions of the horrors of slavery with the notion that the experiences of slavery—and particularly the musical traditions that emerged within it—could produce something valuable for the era of freedom.

Uncle Tom's Cabin *in the South*

Uncle Tom's Cabin became particularly germane to the racial situation in the South after Reconstruction, as new laws systematically stripped away black rights and opportunities. With slavery abolished, white leaders tried to create a caste system as close as possible to the old civil and socioeconomic order. In an effort to prevent blacks from voting, white Southerners instituted poll taxes, literacy requirements, "understanding" clauses, and "grandfather" clauses. From 1887 to 1891, the South passed a series of Jim Crow laws, giving an official stamp of approval to discriminatory practices already in place in schools and railroads.[50] In the North, blacks maintained political rights, at least on paper, but unofficial rules and customs increasingly mandated segregation. The U.S. Supreme Court's 1896 *Plessy v. Ferguson* decision, which

Figure 3.4. "Legree Whipping Uncle Tom," color lithograph poster for Shipman's *Uncle Tom's Cabin*, Erie Lithograph Company, New York and Erie, Pennsylvania. Harriet Beecher Stowe Center, Hartford, CT.

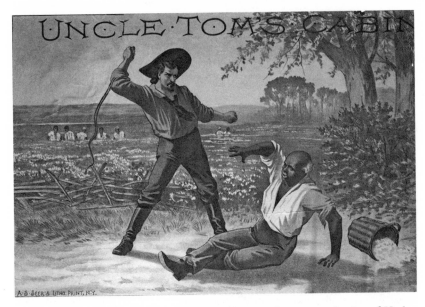

Figure 3.5. "Uncle Tom's Cabin," color lithograph poster for stage production of *Uncle Tom's Cabin*, A. S. Seer's Litho. Print, New York. Harriet Beecher Stowe Center, Hartford, CT.

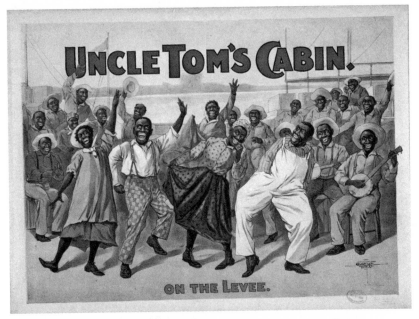

Figure 3.6. "On the Levee," *Uncle Tom's Cabin* color lithograph poster, Courier Lithograph Company, ca. 1899. Theatrical poster collection, Prints & Photographs Division, Library of Congress POS-TH-1899.U53, no. 3.

introduced the paradoxical category of "separate but equal" to American jurisprudence, further encouraged the spread and intensification of Jim Crow laws in the decades to come. As the Ku Klux Klan rose in power, so did the extralegal violence of lynching, increasingly targeted at black men.

Efforts to maintain a social and economic order that closely resembled slavery went hand in hand with a growing national romanticization of slavery. As David Blight and Nina Silber have shown, after Reconstruction an increasingly lavish and cheerful vision of the antebellum South gained cultural dominance across the nation, dramatically reorienting American memory of the causes of the Civil War and the realities of slavery.[51] According to this Lost Cause ideology, the Old South was a place of grand chivalry and romance, populated by benevolent plantation owners and their loyal, devoted black "servants." Among these, the "black mammy" became a particularly celebrated cultural icon.[52] To some extent, *Uncle Tom's Cabin* plays participated in this romantic vision of the antebellum South because their elaborate plantation scenes included a mixture of high-spirited performances and sorrowful songs. Yet with the end Reconstruction, defenders of the Lost Cause would increasingly target *Uncle Tom's Cabin* dramas as a grave threat to the region's tenuous peace.

How audiences felt about slavery often determined how they interpreted the play. Consider Jarrett & Palmer's 1878 production, with its "grand plantation scene" and "WONDERFUL CONGREGATION OF HAPPY SLAVES / Illustrating by characteristic songs and dance the bright side of life among the lowly in Dixie's land twenty years ago."[53] It introduced a stage full of hundreds of black performers of every hue—a classified job listing for the show solicited "100 octoroons, 100 quadroons, 100 mulattoes and 100 decided black men, women, and children capable of singing slave choruses"—in "slave dress, bandanas, handkerchiefs."[54] Politically, their songs ranged from the anti-slavery song "Mother, Is Massa Goin' to Sell Us Tomorrow?" to the pro-slavery song "The Old Home Ain't What It Used to Be," in which a former slave yearns for the happiness of slavery days. They also sang hymns such as "Sweet By and By." Not surprisingly, the show made a variety of conflicting impressions. To one critic, it made slavery look pretty cheerful: "If it were not for the goody goody figure of Uncle Tom himself, and the extremity of his misery, one would imagine from this performance that the colored population of the South did nothing but sing and dance in the ante-bellum times."[55] For this critic, only the virtuous Uncle Tom's tragic story suggested the misery of slavery. A couple of years later, however, when Jarrett & Palmer's combination returned to New York from its successful European tour, some bemoaned the production's harsh representation of slavery. After seeing the company's production at the Booth Theatre in New York, one Southerner wrote to an Atlanta newspaper that he was "astonished no longer at the effect it has had on the anti-slavery sentiment":

> A more unfair and yet vivid statement of a case can not be imagined. The air was rent during all the play with the hissing of slave whips and the shrieks of slaves. Mothers were sold away from their children, and husbands from their wives. Blood-hounds were put on the track of dying women and children. . . . There was no hint on the stage of the real ante-bellum life of the South that made the old plantation darkey the happiest labor in all the earth. No touch of the strange tenderness that bound the old slave to his old "massa" and "missus," in a bondage softer and yet stronger than slavery.[56]

With its scenes of slave auctions, fugitive-chasing bloodhounds, and the whipping of slaves, *Uncle Tom's Cabin* vividly challenged this Southerner's happy vision of antebellum life, in which slaves and masters felt nothing but tender devotion to one another. The play showed just how little Northerners understood about antebellum plantation life, but its representations of the horrors of slavery would be hard for inexperienced audiences to resist.

Southerners hadn't been quite so antagonistic to *Uncle Tom's Cabin* during Reconstruction, when the dramas appeared in the South largely without serious objection. While some newspapers expressed disgust at the appearance of the plays, at first they recommended nothing more than refraining from attending.[57] Some of this receptivity likely came from the managers who staged adaptations "purged, as far as possible, of obnoxious sentiments."[58] But even "Southern" versions of the play, which sometimes ended with Little Eva's death and skipped the Legree scenes altogether, could not always snuff out the play's radical politics. Reception across the region varied: reports that an 1873 touring production was meeting success in New Orleans inspired some commentators to feel optimistic about developing sectional harmony but provoked shame in an Arkansas critic who felt "sicken[ed] with disgust at the thought that gentlemen of Louisiana have become so low, craven, and debased as to take their wives and children to witness a vile play that scandalizes southern society, defames southern women, and is designed to imbue the minds of southern youths with a loathing for their own people and section, and a hatred of the heroes who fell in the cause of the confederacy."[59] Because *Uncle Tom's Cabin* showed the cruelty of slavery, it could be interpreted as an attack on everything the white South considered sacred.

After the withdrawal of federal troops from the South, emboldened Southerners began to direct increasing social and legal fire at performances of *Uncle Tom's Cabin*. Emerging gradually over several decades, with some audiences continuing to enjoy the play even as others barred it from their towns, Southern protests were at once community-building displays of recalcitrant sectional identity and resistance to the social and political changes that might be inspired in the play's enthusiastic black audiences. The first instance of violence against an *Uncle Tom's Cabin* show occurred in 1881 in Griffin, Georgia, during a performance by the Chicago Ideal Uncle Tom's Cabin Company. Earlier in the year, the same company packed theaters in Georgia, Kentucky, and Tennessee, reportedly drawing tears from the most stoic of men.[60] The show was a "great curiosity for everybody here south," *The Atlanta Constitution* commented, and was surprisingly unobjectionable: "Strange to say, while the drama is a plea against slavery, it sets rather the character of the southern planter under a favorable light, and all the villains in the piece are [Y]ankees."[61] There was "one unpleasant feature" of the group's performance in Atlanta, however: the unseemly boldness of the many black people who packed the galleries and "seemed to have an idea that it was their show from the interest they took in the performance."[62] That the idea of black audiences viewing *Uncle Tom's Cabin* as "their show" gave this critic such displeasure suggests the play's continuing threat to the Southern racial order. If black Southerners witnessed a show that called attention to the injustices of slavery, they might be reminded of ongoing injustices. In that case, there was no telling what might happen.

When the Chicago Ideal Uncle Tom's Cabin Company headed to Griffin, a town not far from Atlanta, citizens had already made up their minds against the drama. During the first act, members of the audience

hurled eggs at the black members of the cast, including the one who played
Uncle Tom. They succeeded in driving the group from the stage and then
from the town.[63] Many Georgians rallied around this anti-*Uncle Tom's Cabin*
sentiment, claiming that the drama unnecessarily revived negative feeling
against the South. Slavery, wrote one writer for the *Constitution*, was "a dead
issue, and if there were wrongs committed during its existence, it is not right
now to stir up popular prejudice by taunting us with 'Uncle Tom's Cabin.'"[64]
Even those who claimed to be "thoroughly reconstructed" insisted that, after
all that Stowe's novel had done to "prejudice the people of the North against
slavery," the plays could never be received with anything but antagonism
in the South: "[T]he sentiment of the drama can never be stuffed into the
Southern people. It may be modified and toned down to certain extent to
meet Southern audiences, but—it might as well be said as thought—we hate
the book from the bottom of our souls."[65]

This opposition to *Uncle Tom's Cabin* reflected a stubborn refusal to acknowledge any significant truths in Stowe's portrayal of slavery. Even if
abolition was in the end a good thing, it was not for any of the reasons suggested by Stowe's novel, which had aroused Northern minds to "needless
rage and fury on the subject of slavery," "made John Brown's raid possible,"
and was yet responsible for "much of the sectional prejudice against the
South."[66] While Southern opposition was premised on avoiding sectional
tensions, it in fact clung fast to sectionalism, uniting the South around a
common enemy: *Uncle Tom's Cabin*. Protesting the dramas as "a cruel slander
of Southern civilization"[67] was a way of asserting sectional solidarity and revising the national memory of slavery into one in which whips and shackles
did not figure.

At the turn of the century, the Lost Cause ideology would be expressed
more forcefully in protests against the plays than in the plays themselves.
Surfacing intermittently during the 1880s, Southern efforts against *Uncle
Tom's Cabin* renewed in the 1890s and intensified early in the new century,
even spreading to pockets of the North. In 1903, New York City's superintendent of schools banned Stowe's novel from school libraries, prompted
by the desire to avoid discussion of slavery. "Mrs. Stowe's story," the superintendent explained, "does not belong to to-day, but to an unhappy period
of the country's history, the memory of which it is not well to revive in our

children."[68] This decision provoked criticism from the St. Paul, Minnesota, black newspaper *The Appeal*, which saw the ban as a new low in American racial politics. "As things now seem to be going," the paper lamented, "we will soon need another Harriet Beecher Stowe, another John Brown, and another Lincoln to get us out of our impending disasters more dreadful than they were 'befo' de wah.'"[69]

For those who protested *Uncle Tom's Cabin*, the problem wasn't just the purported misrepresentations; if that was all, Southerners might simply have ignored it. Ultimately, what motivated them to mobilize against the play were its radical political implications for black audiences who saw the parallels between the injustices of slavery and the deterioration of black rights and opportunities under Jim Crow. When citizens of a town in Brazos County, Texas, saw posters advertising Griswold's *Uncle Tom's Cabin* in 1892, they convinced the opera house proprietor to cancel the booking because it was "liable to renew old ill-feelings."[70] (The company's manager moved to a different venue, where attendance was low.)[71] The withdrawal of federal troops from the state had already begun the process of restoring Texas to white leadership—Brazos County had just elected a white Congressman for the first time in years—and some white Texans worried that *Uncle Tom's Cabin* would inspire resistance to this new political climate among black residents. In a district "very evenly divided between the Negroes and the whites," whites had managed to hold the county government "only by the most careful and judicious management."[72] While the *Austin Statesman* deemed the protest "silly and childish" because the issues the play addressed were long settled, this did not stop the spread of numerous protests across the state and region in the following months.

The radical power of *Uncle Tom's Cabin* reached beyond the imaginations of white Americans; for black Americans, the scene of Legree's violence against Uncle Tom could be harnessed to protest contemporary racial injustices. In the wake of a brutal lynching in Paris, Texas, the black composer Will Marion Cook planned to stage an operatic adaptation of *Uncle Tom's Cabin* with an all-black cast at the 1893 Chicago World's Fair. Several prominent black leaders, including Frederick Douglass, endorsed the idea.[73] It was rumored that Cook's opera would stage Uncle Tom's deathbed scene as a re-creation of the recent lynching, in which a white mob had brutally burned a black man at the stake without even investigating the charges against him. By drawing a connection between the death of the innocent Uncle Tom at the hands of Legree and the lynching of a black man by a white mob, Cook's opera reoriented Stowe's anti-slavery narrative toward the contemporary problem of racially motivated lynching. When Southern Democrats heard about this scene, they mobilized against the production, arguing that Cook's opera would perpetuate the "slanders on American slavery and on the southern people that are embodied in 'Uncle Tom's Cabin.'"[74] In the end, Cook's full opera was never staged at the fair; its only appearance was in a few musical selections performed at the ceremony for "Colored People's Day."[75] And there was no lynching scene. The enduring social and political power of Tom's murder would be at the heart of Southern antagonism toward both the novel and the play.

Avenging Southern Honor

As the twentieth century arrived, Tom's onstage suffering at the hands of Legree was still a provocation to some ex-Confederates and their descendants. Early in 1901, a white Southerner named Thomas Dixon attended a performance of *Uncle Tom's Cabin* in New York. What he saw onstage filled him with sorrow and anger. As he later recalled, the play inflicted "unspeakable shame" on "my mother and father and all my people of the Southland. . . . I leaned over on the seat in front of me and burst into tears. Then and there I promised Almighty God that if life gave me strength that I would tell the story of my own silent people."[76] Like many Southerners of his time, Dixon believed that false depictions of both slave-owners and slaves were responsible for postbellum racial friction. Believing that it was past time to repair the damage done by *Uncle Tom's Cabin* to the "silent" South, Dixon began writing a refutation of Stowe's novel and the plays it had inspired. Before long, Dixon's novel, *The Leopard's Spots* (1902), and its sequel, *The Clansman* (1905), would inspire the most viciously anti-black film in American history, D. W. Griffith's *Birth of a Nation* (1915).

Many fictional refutations of *Uncle Tom's Cabin* were published before Dixon's, especially in the years leading up to the Civil War. Yet none had achieved nearly the cultural impact of Stowe's novel. Dixon was probably not the first person anyone expected to write the one that finally did. Born to a slave-owning family in North Carolina at the tail end of the Civil War, Dixon grew up amid the chaos of Reconstruction. He was a man of peripatetic interests and seemingly unlimited energy: by his late thirties, he had already spent time as a legislator (he was elected to the North Carolina Senate before he was old enough to vote), a lawyer, a Baptist clergyman, an actor, and an orator. After attending that 1901 performance of *Uncle Tom's Cabin* in New York, however, Dixon decided to make his first stab at fiction, writing a novel about a post–Civil War Simon Legree who becomes an opportunistic exploiter of the black vote.

Initially, Dixon planned to directly refute *Uncle Tom's Cabin* by titling his first novel "The Rise of Simon Legree," but Dixon and his publisher ultimately chose a title, *The Leopard's Spots* (1902), that suggested the intractable inferiority of black people and the impossibility of a black man as virtuous as Uncle Tom. The novel is prefaced by a quotation from Jeremiah that would at first glance seem to give Biblical credence to Dixon's notion of a fixed racial hierarchy: "Can the Ethiopian change his skin or the leopard his spots?" (Jeremiah 13:23). But Dixon's former experience as a minister did not make him a particularly sensitive exegete. In the passage from which the novel gets its title, the prophet Jeremiah excoriates the people of Jerusalem for their sins. Telling them that a coming invasion is a deserved punishment from God, he asks, "Can the Ethiopian change his skin, or the leopard his spots?" Out of context, the answer to these questions would seem to be no, and indeed, early Christian commentators interpreted this passage as an indication of man's inherent sinfulness. But the later and more frequent interpretations suggest that the answer to Jeremiah's questions is, perhaps counterintuitively, yes: as Jeremiah observes, through submission to God, the Ethiopian *can* change his skin, and a leopard *can* change his spots.[77] Rather than supporting a fixed racial hierarchy, then, the Biblical passage to which Dixon alludes actually opposes it, suggesting that the power of God's grace can change human beings both inside and out.

But Dixon, of course, did not see it this way. *The Leopard's Spots*, which sold a million copies, and the two novels that completed the trilogy, *The Clansman* (1905) and *The Traitor* (1907), was as much a challenge to the development of a younger generation not born in slavery as it was to *Uncle Tom's Cabin*. Challenging the possibility of a virtuous black man like Uncle Tom, it proposed the inevitability of black savagery without the controls of slavery. Imagining

Emancipation as a social turn in which black people transform from well-governed chattel into uncontrollable beasts, the trilogy portrays the demise of the faithful servants of the old order and the rise of a new generation of black men with animalistic desires for white women.[78] Dixon's novels elaborate the same racial crisis—in W. E. B. Du Bois' incisive summary: "There's a black man who thinks himself a man and is a man; kill him before he marries your daughter!"[79] Unlike Stowe's novel, which aligned black men with white feminine virtue through the relationship between Uncle Tom and Eva, *The Leopard's Spots* dramatized the threat of black men to white women. Dixon's suffering Tom is not Stowe's virtuous slave but the poor white Tom Camp, whose two daughters are sexually assaulted by black men.

When *The Leopard's Spots* came out, it provoked controversy among both blacks and whites for stirring up racial antagonism, but even white criticism of the novel tended to agree that the racial characterizations of Stowe's *Uncle Tom's Cabin* had needed correction.[80] A *New York Times* review charged Dixon with taking "the most gloomy view possible" of Southern blacks and "creat[ing] monsters that he may make war upon them," but conceded that "the negro is not as Mrs. Stowe imagined him, an Anglo-Saxon bound in black."[81] While Dixon's novel went too far, the *Times* argued, Stowe's characterizations were just as problematic in imagining that the differences between whites and blacks were only skin deep. Some months later, Dixon declared that *The Leopard's Spots* was a refutation of Uncle Tom, and not just *Uncle Tom's Cabin*. Writing in *The New York Times Saturday Review of Books and Art*, he defended his novel as an "authentic human document" that corrected "the prejudices of those who have idealized or worshipped the negro as canonized in Uncle Tom. Is it not time they heard the whole truth? They have heard only one side for forty years."[82] For Dixon, Uncle Tom's saintly virtues were precisely the problem, for such an "idealized" representation prevented Northerners from understanding what he saw as the South's need to limit black rights. His fiction, he hoped, would give the North the full picture. And with the adaptation of *The Leopard's Spots* and its sequel into a drama in 1905, Dixon strengthened his rebuttal of Stowe's representations. "At last," the New Orleans *Times-Picayune* rejoiced, "the South has an Uncle Tom of its own"; Dixon's play was "a complete answer" to *Uncle Tom's Cabin* and the first to do "justice to the white side of the race question."[83]

While Dixon chose to "answer" *Uncle Tom's Cabin* with his own fiction and drama, other Southerners simply refused to allow it entrance into their region, alleging that the plays could disrupt the power dynamic of Jim Crow. Efforts against *Uncle Tom's Cabin* became more organized in the twentieth century. During the fall of 1901, a Lexington, Kentucky, citizen who had heard that the city would soon be "afflicted" with another *Uncle Tom's Cabin* play published an article in the *Lexington Herald* warning that the play, "a gross exaggeration of the worst episodes in the slave-life of the old South," would threaten the city's alleged racial harmony, in which each race was "contented to be left in sole possession" of "its own churches, own schools, own society."[84] Finally free of the federal forces that had occupied the state during Reconstruction, some acutely felt the tenuousness of white control in a county in which 37 percent of residents were black, one of the highest percentages in the state.[85] By "arous[ing] the hatred of the negro toward the white man," the plays were "against all public policy, peace and prosperity."[86]

This concern about what black citizens would do if they attended the play soon activated a formal campaign against the *Uncle Tom's Cabin* plays by the Lexington branch of the United Daughters of the Confederacy (UDC). In 1902, the UDC petitioned the proprietor of Lexington's Opera House to stop booking the traveling troupes that brought the play to the city. At the time, *Uncle Tom's Cabin* was "unquestionably the premiere popular-price attraction" in the city, drawing large numbers of whites and blacks when it came to town once or twice a year.[87] It was so attractive to black audiences that the Opera House significantly expanded the seats available to black patrons when *Uncle Tom's Cabin* came to town.[88] But the UDC claimed that the play hurt the community by misrepresenting a relationship between master and slave that had really been "on the whole . . . kindly and mutually beneficial."[89] That the group viewed *Uncle Tom's Cabin* as a depiction of history and not just a work of imagination was unsurprising. After the Civil War, Stowe's text and its adaptations were often framed as a lesson in American history, one that authentically depicted the antebellum South.[90] If the historical frame had the potential to diminish the radical potential of Stowe's story by implying that there was no further racial injustice once slavery was abolished,[91] it also made *Uncle Tom's Cabin* more contentious. One feature of the plays that particularly bothered the UDC was the street parade often put on by traveling productions to build excitement for upcoming shows. In their petition, the women expressed concern that, at a recent parade, local students had witnessed "two immense blood-hounds, and a life size statue of an old negro in chains"—presumably Uncle Tom.[92] Presenting a brutal representation of slavery threatened Jim Crow from two directions. First, the UDC women alleged, white youngsters would get a wrongly negative impression of their ancestors, one that would color how they thought about themselves and their relationships to black people in the future. Second, the plays would have "a tendency to inflame race prejudice among the large class of our negro citizens."[93] Here, "race prejudice" was a code for black resentment that could be "inflamed" into resistance, or even violence, against whites who sought to keep political, social, and economic conditions as close as possible to those of antebellum days.

Given the previous popularity of *Uncle Tom's Cabin* plays, the Lexington Opera House's manager initially resisted the women's protest; his sharp response to the petition informed them that "the war has been over about 36 years."[94] But what his initial refusal didn't take into account was that even though the military battles were long finished, the war was still being fought—and one of the places it was fought most fiercely was *Uncle Tom's Cabin*. For white Southerners, the question of whether or not Stowe's novel and its adaptations would be tolerated was a question of whether or not slavery had been a cruel injustice. In order for the Jim Crow social order to be legitimate, slavery had to be remembered as a benevolent, natural arrangement between kind (and inherently superior) masters and their contented, inherently childlike slaves. The representation of a virtuous man like Uncle Tom being cruelly beaten offered a powerful challenge to the revised memory of slavery proposed by Confederate groups.

Despite initial resistance from the Bluegrass State's legislators, who suggested that sectional feeling was already a thing of the past, the Lexington women's protest against *Uncle Tom's Cabin* convinced other Daughters of the Confederacy groups, the Confederate Veterans' Association, and city councils all over the region to follow suit.[95] The play began to meet resistance across the South. A black member of E. F. Davis' Uncle Tom's Cabin Company reported from Clarksville, Tennessee, that the group had not been able to put on the show "owing to agitation, mostly 'hot air' of indignant citizens in imitation of the Blue Grass populace."[96] In 1903, Howard County, Missouri, effectively banned *Uncle Tom's Cabin* plays through enormous additional taxes: while ordinary theatrical performances were charged five to ten dollars a day and entire circuses were charged fifty, Uncle Tom shows had to pay two hundred dollars daily.[97] According to one account, the taxes were predicated on the theory "that the negroes of Howard—and they are quite numerous—always show a little less respect to the white for a few days after they have witnessed a 'Tom' entertainment."[98] The same year, in Worcester County, Maryland, a theatrical company scheduled to stage *Uncle Tom's Cabin* had its performance license revoked because of fear that it would spark black resistance. After all, a recent performance of the play had "produced considerable excitement and disorder among the negroes," and the people of the Eastern Shore were already "greatly inflamed" about the recent lynching of a black man in Delaware.[99] Officials explained that "it would not contribute to the peace and good order of the Maryland counties, where the negro populations are so large, to permit the presentation of such a play as 'Uncle Tom's Cabin' at this time."[100] With its potential to connect past and present injustices, the play might set fire to already-heated racial tensions. Ultimately these protests led to the 1906 passage in Kentucky of what became known as the Uncle Tom's Cabin Law, which banned "any play that is based upon antagonism alleged formerly to exist, between master and slave, or that excites race prejudice."[101] Violators of the law, which was not repealed until 1974, would be fined between $100 and $500 and sentenced to prison for one to three months. After the bill's passage, women from all over the South wrote to the Lexington chapter of the UDC to find out how they might be able to pass similar legislation in their own states.[102]

While white ex-Confederates found the image of violence against Uncle Tom dangerous, some black Americans felt that this scene held deep relevance for contemporary racial injustices. "With the peonage cases of Georgia and Alabama, a stench in the nostrils of all decent people, and numerous lynchings, including burnings at the stake, staring the American people in the face," *The Cleveland Gazette* commented in response to the Kentucky controversy, "it strikes us that it takes a northerner or southerner with an unlimited amount of gall to counsel the forgetting of Harriet Beecher Stowe's greatest work, 'Uncle Tom's Cabin.'"[103] Of course, Stowe didn't write the stage adaptations, but the *Gazette*, like those who agitated against the plays, understood the novel and the plays as operating in a similar political vein. And as long as exploitive peonage systems and lynchings were an accepted part of American race relations, *Uncle Tom's Cabin* was still important, and possibly even necessary. As they always had, attitudes toward *Uncle Tom's Cabin* were shaped by the network of representations of slavery and black Americans also appearing on American stages. The Baltimore *Afro-American* didn't mind losing *Uncle Tom's Cabin* if the vicious *Clansman* could be eliminated from some American stages.[104] But others worried that Dixon's play was undoing the good work of *Uncle Tom's Cabin*. In 1908, the black Indianapolis newspaper *The Freeman* complained that *The Clansman* had bred such race hatred that sometimes blacks were not even allowed to play the slave roles in *Uncle Tom's Cabin*, "rob[bing] the public of the good side of what they should see of the Negro in a true picture of the South."[105] The implication was that black actors who took slave roles had a positive effect on racial opinion that white actors in blackface simply could not have.

While black folks condemned the notion that *Uncle Tom's Cabin* exaggerated the wrongs of slavery, they disagreed on the play's ideal fate. In 1902, *The Freeman* published two different perspectives on the plays. One contributor insisted that *Uncle Tom's Cabin* was a crucial record of slavery's injustices and that, contrary to the arguments of the UDC, the younger generation needed to see these injustices in order to avoid their perpetuation in the future. It was "time the Southern children were becoming ashamed of the records of the[ir] slaveowning ancestors. . . . Long live Uncle Tom's Cabin!"[106] In contrast, another contributor to *The Freeman* reflected that although slavery had been a monstrous evil, it was over and should not be represented on the stage. "It is not the period for dragging forth those hideous skeletons of the past to affright those of to-day," the contributor asserted.[107] This question of whether or not the cruelties of the slavery past needed to be represented would become more contentious in the coming decades. As American culture romanticized the antebellum South and the race struggled to move forward despite the restrictions of Jim Crow, black Americans would increasingly challenge the wisdom of representing slavery at all.

CHAPTER 4

WRITING THE OLD NEGRO

IN 1915, the Baldwin-Melville stock company arrived in Atlanta ready to stage *Uncle Tom's Cabin* at the Atlanta Theater. But the local chapter of the United Daughters of the Confederacy, like their compatriots in Kentucky a decade earlier, quickly gathered with representatives of several other Confederate women's groups (including Mrs. E. L. Connally, vice president of the Uncle Remus Memorial Association) to pass resolutions against the play. In a meeting with the theater and stock company managers, the women claimed that because "the very name of 'Uncle Tom's Cabin'" held "suggestions that are filled with injustice and misrepresentation towards the south and her people," the production would "be inimical to the growing spirit of unity and peace which is desired between the two sections of our country by all Christian people."[1] During the meeting, the managers decided that, instead of cancelling the play altogether, the company would "cut out a number of lines and scenes," including the whipping scene, and, "as a final concession," change the name to "Old Plantation Days."[2] Instead of banning *Uncle Tom's Cabin*, they would try to defang it.

As news of the change spread around the nation, some black public voices protested.[3] In an editorial for *The New York Age*, James Weldon Johnson protested that a theatrical company "had been forbidden to play the usual version of 'Uncle Tom's Cabin'" and had instead transformed it into a show in which "the offensive parts were expurgated, Simon Legree was transformed into a sort of benevolent patriarch, Uncle Tom was made into a happy old darkey who greatly enjoyed being a slave and who ultimately died of too much good treatment."[4] And so, he continued sarcastically, "a performance was given that was no doubt a great success and offended nobody's sensibilities." Holding on to the anti-slavery meaning of *Uncle Tom's Cabin*, the next year Johnson memorialized Sam Lucas, the first black actor to play Uncle Tom in a major production (see figures 4.1 and 4.2), for his "fine and sympathetic portrayal of the gentle 'Uncle Tom.'"[5] For Johnson, there was more at stake in *Uncle Tom's Cabin* than the memory of slavery. Believing that both the work and its hero remained relevant to continuing oppression, Johnson would soon write his own adaptation. In his 1917 text, which I discuss later in this chapter, he features Uncle Tom as a model of spiritual strength in the face of racial violence.

What makes a "good" literary character? Do the aesthetic criteria change when a character influences a group or political movement? Recognition of the moral and social function of literary characters goes back to Aristotle, whose *Poetics* advocates a specific set of attributes for characters in a tragedy.[6] The contours of "good" characters have varied significantly over time and geography, responding to a complex set of cultural norms, political goals, and aesthetic standards. Accordingly, changing ideals and theories of literary characterization have shaped Uncle Tom's meaning in American culture, transforming the same character from a model of politically effective, emotionally powerful characterization to, eventually, a political and aesthetic travesty.

With the publication of *Uncle Tom's Cabin*, the Uncle Tom character was quickly incorporated into American culture as both a social type found in the South and a character type found in literature and drama. While nineteenth-century African Americans saw the social type and the character type as one and the same, during the early twentieth century these two categories diverged into two distinct cultural narratives of Uncle Tom. One referenced a historical type endemic to slavery, an old-fashioned black identity that might have been necessary in the past but would, as I suggest in the next chapter, become deeply dangerous to the quest for equal rights when perpetuated in the present day. In the second, Uncle Tom was an "Old Negro" character who was often though not always tied to Stowe's novel and its stage and film adaptations; he was not only a representation of the historical type but also a potential model

Figure 4.1. "Sam Lucas, Colored Comedian," color lithograph poster for C. H. Smith's Double Mammoth Uncle Tom's Cabin Co. Historical Society of Pennsylvania Theater Posters Collection [V06], Historical Society of Pennsylvania.

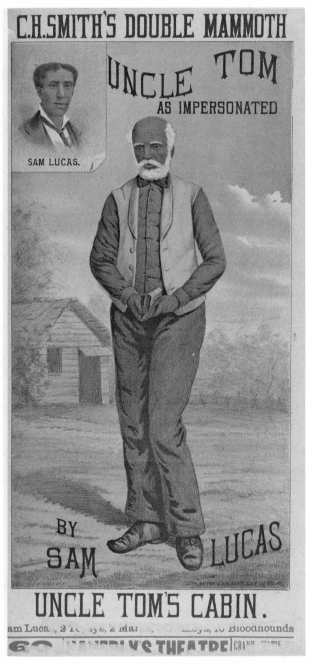

Figure 4.2. "Uncle Tom as Impersonated by Sam Lucas," color lithograph poster for C. H. Smith's Double Mammoth *Uncle Tom's Cabin*. Historical Society of Pennsylvania Theater Posters Collection [V06], Historical Society of Pennsylvania.

of characterization for African American writers seeking to effect the kind of transformational social and political change Stowe's novel had achieved.

Responses to the Uncle Tom character addressed four issues: historical influence (had the novel played a role in the abolition of slavery, and how did the character of Uncle Tom figure into that?), historical accuracy (had it accurately represented black life in the antebellum South?), aesthetics (how skillful were Stowe's methods of characterization according to the critic's standards, and how much did this matter?), and contemporary relevance (what kind of social or political impact did the novel have in the present moment?). In the case of Uncle Tom, Stowe's sentimental characterization maintained a perhaps surprisingly long hold on American literary aesthetics, especially for black writers. Until the Harlem Renaissance brought the first significant wave of censure for Stowe's novel among black critics, writers praised Uncle Tom as a model of literary characterization. Viewing feelings as the foundation of the novel's historical influence, writers and critics commended the emotion Stowe's characters sparked in readers. Yet by the time of the Harlem Renaissance, James Weldon Johnson would be unusual among his contemporaries in suggesting the importance of Stowe's protagonist even in a new era. Increasing calls for American literature to address modern black life would challenge and finally topple black critical appreciation of Uncle Tom and *Uncle Tom's Cabin*.

Weeping with Uncle Tom

While many Americans approached *Uncle Tom's Cabin* as a work of history, activist writers paid attention to its literary qualities, concluding that it might have features worth emulating. Among these was the character of Uncle Tom. To those who endorsed the literary and political value of reformist fiction, *Uncle Tom's Cabin* was in many ways a model text. How could contemporary black literature serve the changing needs of the race? Both Charles Chesnutt, one of the first prominent African American fiction writers, and Mary Church Terrell, a deeply committed "race woman" who devoted her life to promoting positive images of black Americans and decrying American racial injustices, believed that Stowe's novel had achieved its enormous cultural effect through the emotional power of its characters.[7] For Chesnutt and Terrell, sentimental characterization could be revolutionary because, at its best, it evoked such strong emotion in the reader that it changed her thoughts and actions. Most characters could produce a strong emotional response only momentarily, if at all; only a master of fiction could create a character as enduringly vital as Uncle Tom.

Terrell's support for *Uncle Tom's Cabin* and Harriet Beecher Stowe was a pillar of her lifelong activism. Born in Memphis, Tennessee, near the close of the Civil War to light-skinned, formerly enslaved parents, Terrell grew up wealthy, in a home environment that prioritized education and encouraged her ambitions.[8] As a brilliant student at Oberlin, at the time one of the few white institutions that accepted black students, she chose the classical course of study, traditionally a "gentleman's course," and impressed a visiting Matthew Arnold with her pronunciation of Greek. After receiving bachelor's and master's degrees from Oberlin, she continued her education in Europe, where she became fluent in French, German, and Italian, proficiencies that later dazzled the audiences of her European speaking engagements. Even after her marriage to Robert Terrell, the first black municipal court judge in Washington, DC, and while raising her two daughters, she was active in civic and political organizations to an extent that few women of her time equaled. Like many other black elites at the turn of the twentieth century, Terrell embraced a civilizationist outlook on racial advancement, one that relied on a narrative of cultural progress from humble origins to respectability and minimized intraracial divisions. Her many speeches and articles continually returned to four related rhetorical purposes: instilling racial pride, promoting positive black images, spreading awareness of racial injustice, and praising Harriet Beecher Stowe and *Uncle Tom's Cabin*.

Recognizing as early as 1904 that fiction was more potent than nonfiction ever could be, Terrell dreamed of a modern-day *Uncle Tom's Cabin* that would liberate the race from its twentieth-century shackles.[9] In the eyes of a woman who believed that it was her duty to promote the welfare of her race but struggled with the constraints of gender, Stowe was an inspiration. Speaking about Stowe was, Terrell wrote in her 1940 autobiography, "truly a labor of love," and she "poured out [her] soul" when doing so.[10] For the one-hundredth anniversary of Stowe's birth, Terrell garnered the support of other black women and spearheaded a national celebration of the author, complete with a commemorative pamphlet.[11] *Harriet Beecher Stowe: An Appreciation* offered aesthetic and political praise for the feminine sentiment of Stowe's major novel, describing the author as "a woman in the completest and broadest sense of that word" whose literary genius came from her union of the head and the heart.[12] In Terrell's view, Stowe's womanly sentiment accounted for the literary and sociopolitical success of *Uncle Tom's Cabin*, a novel that "throbbed with the beats of a woman's heart, wailed with her cry of anguish, trembled with her sympathy and was wet with her tears."[13] According to Terrell's sentimental aesthetic, the greatest artists were those whose full and vital creations provoked deep emotions. She predicted that Stowe, "whose creations are so complete, whose types are so vivid, whose situations are so touching and original," would one day be "written in the annals of American authors the foremost artist of them all."[14] In other words, Terrell believed that *Uncle Tom's Cabin* was great art not in spite of its characters but because of them.

Praising Stowe's Uncle Tom for his character traits as well as the embodied sympathy he provoked in readers, Terrell asked, "Who has not wept with Uncle Tom, who, though a slave in body, was a philosopher in mind, a saint at heart, and a martyr in death?"[15] Terrell's description of *Uncle Tom's Cabin* assumed the reader's full-body immersion in the world of the novel. The reader would "*stand* with Mrs. Stowe at the auction block, *witness* the agony of the mother torn from her child, *see* the despair of the wife" who will never see her husband again, "*hear* the cries that are wrung from the broken hearts crushed by the master hand without one pang of remorse," "*blush* with shame and pale with horror" at Emmeline's sale to Legree, and give "a *sigh* of relief" when Lucy, whose only remaining child was stolen, disappears into the waters of the Mississippi (my emphasis).[16] The most effective characters pulled the reader into a deeply felt imaginary world, provoking sympathetic identification. Whether or not Uncle Tom was a realistic character or a desirable role model for the twentieth century was not a question that mattered to Terrell. She admired Tom as a finely wrought character whose Christian virtue and philosophy had made so many Americans *feel* the injustice of slavery. An idealized character like Uncle Tom became real by moving readers to tears.

The work of Stowe's novel was not finished, of course. "Everybody knows what *Uncle Tom's Cabin* did for the slave," *The Chicago Defender* observed in 1920. "Yet Eliza's grandchildren are still crossing the ice."[17] Terrell believed that a more complete freedom required the circulation of "a modern version of *Uncle Tom's Cabin*" that picked up where Stowe left off, "showing the shackles by which colored people are bound today, though nominally free, as the original *Uncle Tom's Cabin* bared the cruelties perpetrated upon them, when they were legally enslaved."[18] Terrell's call for a contemporary equivalent to Stowe's novel was rooted in her twin convictions that literature was a crucial agent of social and political change and that sympathy was the central mechanism of its power. Unfortunately, the publication of a modern *Uncle Tom's Cabin* required the cooperation of white publishers. And as a general rule, American publishers and periodicals would print nothing having to do with the Negro, W. E. B. Du Bois observed, "unless it takes the form of caricature or bitter attack, or is so thoroughly innocuous as to have no literary flavor."[19]

At a 1916 luncheon, Terrell asked one of the editors of *The American Magazine*, the former muckraking journalist Ray Stannard Baker, if he thought any leading American periodical would accept a work of fiction as well written as Stowe's novel but showing present injustices to black Americans. The work she envisioned would be set in the contemporary moment but would use the sentimental strategies of *Uncle Tom's Cabin*, showing the "assault and battery constantly committed upon [black Americans'] hearts, their sensibilities and their feelings." After debating the question with other editors, the group of journalists "finally admitted that, in their opinion, no periodical in the country would publish any such story at that time"; this conclusion, Terrell recalled, "sounded my literary death knell," convincing her that trying to publish her own stories was a hopeless cause.[20] White editors wanted only "ridiculous or criminal" black characters and reserved sympathetic representation to white characters. Far from objecting to the characterizations of *Uncle Tom's Cabin*, Terrell saw them as a productive model—if only a white publisher would accept them.

The Uncle Tom Type

Fifteen years before that luncheon, Charles Chesnutt published a novel that he intended to be a modern *Uncle Tom's Cabin*. As he wrote to his publisher, Chesnutt hoped that *The Marrow of Tradition* (1901), a fictionalized account of the organized massacre of black residents of Wilmington, North Carolina, in 1898, would "become lodged in the popular mind as the legitimate successor of 'Uncle Tom's Cabin' and 'Fool's Errand' as depicting an epoch in our national history."[21] Both Albion Tourgée's *A Fool's Errand* (1879), a lightly fictionalized narrative of the dismantling of Reconstruction, and *Uncle Tom's Cabin*, a novel of life under slavery, were critically acclaimed best-sellers about the drama of race in America.[22] Being the "legitimate successor" to these novels meant alerting the nation to the racial injustices of a historical moment by creating a vivid and truthful picture of them. Later in the twentieth century, black fiction writers would try to overthrow Stowe's novel, but Chesnutt wanted *Marrow* to continue its project in a new era.[23] Indeed, at the turn of the twentieth century, black fiction writers and critics were more likely to want to continue Stowe's project for the modern era than to refute it. Approaching Stowe's novel as the great historical precursor to more recent literature of black life in America, Albon Lewis Holsey's review of Du Bois' *The Quest of the Silver Fleece* (1911) for the *Baltimore Afro-American* suggested that Du Bois' novel of the post-Reconstruction South was the "remarkable sequel" to *Uncle Tom's Cabin* and that both should be required reading for future generations of black children.[24] Spanning a long history of black life in the South, the two worked in tandem to form a cohesive literary narrative of African American life.[25] For many black Americans, *Uncle Tom's Cabin* was not just a great influence *on* the race's history but also an important chronicle *of* that history, providing essential information about black life in the antebellum era.[26] Readers assumed that the novel's settings and characters could be found in real life. According to a 1920 issue of *The Crisis*, for example, one could find the "real site" of Eliza's crossing of the ice as well as "the first home of Uncle Tom" in Kentucky.[27]

Where Terrell celebrated the sympathy *Uncle Tom's Cabin* embodied in its readers, Chesnutt located Stowe's achievement in her truthful, purpose-driven representation of a variety of social types, including Uncle Tom. For Chesnutt, literature was both a document of human life and a force that acted on the feelings, thoughts, and behavior of living people. In his estimation, nearly every great work of literature came from a "worthy motive": the Hebrew scriptures, the Greek orators and poets, and the works of Dumas, Balzac, and Stowe provided a few of his examples.[28] Characters, "perhaps the most important element in a work of creative imagination," were crucial to a novel's purpose. The greatest ones were "more real, more convincing than . . .

even the men and women whom we see around us" and thus had the capacity to change how readers thought, felt, and behaved.[29] A novel's power came from its ability to evoke deep emotional recognition of its characters.

In writing fictional characters, Chesnutt combined a romantic commitment to sentiment with an embrace of the concept of literary and sociological "type." While William Dean Howells praised Chesnutt as a realist writer, the latter's aesthetic was just as romantic as it was realist, his characters often idealized, his plots frequently reliant on highly unlikely coincidences.[30] When it came to literary characters, Chesnutt wrote in the romantic realist tradition of Honoré de Balzac, whose *Avant-propos* to the *Comédie humaine* invokes two different concepts of type: a romantic type that "incarnate[s] ontological energies of fate and failure" and a scientific type "concerned with the representation of the many by the one."[31] Reflecting his commitment to both of these types, in a 1916 speech Chesnutt praised *Uncle Tom's Cabin* for its accurate representation of "all types of colored people": Uncle Tom, "a model of fidelity and self-sacrifice," "the inimitable Topsy," "the unworthy Sambo and Quimbo," and the fair-skinned Eliza and George. Stowe's characters, he reflected, were "all well drawn and true to nature."[32] Chesnutt believed that writing authentic characters required an author's close study of a group. It is "obvious," he told an audience in 1916, that "to draw any true picture of the life of a race or class of men, or of types of any race or class, it is necessary to know the race or class or type thoroughly."[33] With such study, literary characters could accurately represent biological or sociological categories.

Just as Balzac's *Comédie humaine* was an attempt "to depict the two or three thousand conspicuous types of a period," Chesnutt strove in his novels to expand what he repeatedly pointed out was a very limited set of American Negro literary types, including the "bad Negro," the buffoon, the wastrel, and the "faithful servant," of which Uncle Tom was a prototype.[34] By expanding literary representation of the Negro to more fully match social reality, authors could combat the racial prejudice that lumped the whole race into one unit and failed to distinguish classes. Rather than contradicting the accuracy of such types—he thought they were "true enough so far as they went"—Chesnutt wanted to expand their variety.[35] Indeed, he admitted that the Old Negro type, "a common expedient among short story writers," could be found in his own conjure tales.[36]

WRITING THE OLD NEGRO

To Chesnutt, who grew up in Fayetteville, North Carolina, "a community a hundred years behind the times," the Old Negro provided an opportunity for both documentary and imaginative work. But, curiously, the new types that Chesnutt called for did not necessarily require new aesthetics. Chesnutt's literary models were the nineteenth-century reformist novels that combined the romantic with the real. Near the end of his life, as the Harlem Renaissance brought unprecedented attention to black writers and topics, Chesnutt suggested that while the situation and characters of *Uncle Tom's Cabin* no longer existed, its literary methods remained useful. The novel's portrayal of the effects of the institution of slavery on the individual lives of its varied types "stirred the heart and conscience of the nation and was perhaps the most powerful influence in the abolition of slavery," he suggested in a 1929 speech to Oberlin students on "The Negro in Present Fiction." In Chesnutt's view, sentiment was a gateway to the real:

> *Uncle Tom's Cabin* registered because it dealt with deep-seated, funda-
> mental realities, things which exist in all men, regardless of worldly
> station—the relations of husband and wife, parent and child, the right to
> the fruits of one's toil—the freedom of one's own person,—and indeed of
> one's own soul.[37]

Chesnutt believed that feelings—romantic, familial, spiritual—were the "fundamental reality" that joined all human beings. Stowe, by making the suffering of the novel's characters universal, had convinced millions of Americans that slavery was a violation of the natural rights the nation held so dear. This didn't mean that Chesnutt wanted American writers to rehash the same old stories of the plantation and rural Southern black life. After all, Uncle Tom was by no means a representative of the entire race. Like Mary Church Terrell, Chesnutt believed that the sentimental techniques used so effectively in Stowe's novel should be applied to modern subjects. In this way, a literary character could not only provoke sympathy but also raise awareness of the existence of what Chesnutt called the "better types" of the race. Readers who encountered well-mannered doctors, lawyers, and clerks in literature would, he thought, develop a picture of the American Negro that was both more relatable and more fully "representative" of the race's variety of types. Chesnutt shed no tears for the "old Uncle Tom type" that seemed to be disappearing from modern black literature. Yet he suggested that modern writers would do well "to analyze the reasons for [*Uncle Tom's Cabin's*] success."[38]

As for Uncle Tom, Chesnutt thought he was "a likable old fellow, almost too good to be true," and viewed the character with more amusement than concern. He even joked about the many old Negroes who claimed to be the man upon whom Stowe based her great novel: "[W]e cherish a pleasant memory of him, and always read with interest any item identifying the original Uncle Tom, of which there would seem to be almost as many as there are pieces of the true cross in Catholic countries."[39] Uncle Tom was a relic of the past, old-fashioned but essentially harmless. With the newer types emerging on the page and in American culture, the figure was no more threatening than an old piece of wood in a church basement.

Remembering Uncle Tom

Terrell's and Chesnutt's praise for Uncle Tom and *Uncle Tom's Cabin* was shaped by a literary and social climate that usually remembered slavery as a beneficent institution and then proceeded to use that memory to justify continued racial oppression. Stowe's graphic representations of the cruelties of slavery still stood out markedly from the sanitized image that dominated both cultural representations of the antebellum South and American historical scholarship. During the 1870s and 1880s, a literary vogue for "local color" writing combined with an undercurrent of resistance to black progress to produce charming stories of the South by writers such as Joel Chandler Harris and Thomas Nelson Page. Validated on the pages of national magazines such as *Scribner's, Century, Harper's,* and *The Atlantic Monthly,* a mythology of gentle masters and contented slaves became a common feature of American fiction. As Sterling Brown observed in his 1937 essay "The Negro in American Fiction," the stereotype of the happy, foolish slave arose in response to Reconstruction, "so that slavery could be resurrected in practice though not in name."[40] Writers such as Page, who had "lavish praise for the 'old time darky'" and "virulent disgust at the 'new issue,' ruined by emancipation," used fiction to justify efforts to restrict black rights.[41] This tradition continued in the early twentieth century, as "a legion of writers wept over the vanished glory of the old plantation and presented Negroes of extreme devotedness to their masters."[42]

At the turn of the century, in the political atmosphere of national reunion that Chesnutt sarcastically called "the modern era of harmony and good feeling," *Uncle Tom's Cabin* was still controversial because it portrayed slavery as an immoral system. This perspective violated the consensus over which the North and South had finally reunited after the Civil War. After Reconstruction, the divided nation began to put aside sectional animosities by reuniting around a romanticized vision of the antebellum South and a defanged narrative of the Civil War that did not condemn the South. Under this ideology of national reconciliation, the memory of slavery, the emancipation cause, and indeed any political conflict at all were muted in favor of celebrating the valor of both Union and Confederate soldiers.[43] Becoming an implicit but powerful force against black progress, the reconciliation ideology also involved a complementary reimagining of antebellum Southern life. Under what Nina Silber has called the "romance of reunion," the nation came together over romantic fictions of aristocratic Southern plantation life that denied the horrors of slavery and instead "stressed the loyalty and devotion of the old black servant to the southern family."[44] Although not as vicious as much of the nation's political rhetoric against blacks, romantic visions of Southern plantation life could be just as pernicious, folding an argument for an immutable racial hierarchy into a happy plantation story. Noting the crucial role of these narratives in reuniting the nation, Chesnutt observed, "So warm has become the *rapprochement* between North and South, that slavery is almost regarded in some quarters as a beneficent patriarchal institution, which *Uncle Tom's Cabin* grossly slandered, and which, but for its influence on free labor, it might have been well to perpetuate indefinitely."[45] That *Uncle Tom's Cabin* still provided the likeliest candidate for the slander of slavery indicates the extent to which the rosy narrative of slavery dominated American literature and culture.

White American historians of the 1890s affirmed the literary romance of the antebellum South by "reassess[ing] the history of slavery and [finding] a system characterized by intimacy and loyalty."[46] According to historians, slaves were contented, dutiful, and devoted to their kind masters and cruelty was rare.[47] Influential scholarship by historian William Dunning argued that the rights granted to blacks during the Reconstruction era had been a disaster for the South and for the nation, and the "Dunning school" of historians he trained continued this ideological trajectory. In *American Negro Slavery* (1918) and *Life and Labor in the Old South* (1928), Ulrich Bonnell Phillips asserted that slavery had been a benevolent system of civilization for Africans, not the harsh institution abolitionists had claimed it to be. Phillips and Dunning dominated American understanding of antebellum Southern life and Reconstruction through at least World War II.[48] To recall the horrors of slavery was to "wave the bloody shirt" and work against the nation's sectional reunion.[49]

Accordingly, white Southerners more hotly contested the novel's accuracy about slavery than did black critics, who came to the novel's defense. Responding in 1921 to the persistent charges that *Uncle Tom's Cabin* was "a piece of propaganda that gave an overdrawn picture of Southern conditions," the black critic and author Benjamin Brawley insisted that Stowe "had abundant proof for her incidents."[50] This defense was part of an ongoing debate about race that was often focalized through Stowe's novel and its adaptations. White Southerners were the most vociferous in their attacks on *Uncle Tom's Cabin*, but Northern libraries and schools sometimes followed suit. In 1903, New York City's superintendent of schools banned Stowe's novel from school libraries. "Mrs. Stowe's story," the superintendent explained, "does not belong to to-day, but to an unhappy period of the country's history, the memory of which it is not well to revive in our children."[51] While sometimes *Uncle Tom's Cabin* was banned outright, other times it was reinterpreted or amended to be friendlier to conservative white interests. Among those who tried to reinterpret Stowe's novel as, in the end, a work that supported slavery, Joel Chandler Harris revised Stowe's hero into the less religious Uncle Remus. He wrote in his 1880 introduction to *Uncle Remus: His Songs and Sayings* that Stowe's novel was "a wonderful defense of slavery as it existed in the South"—at least in the parts in which she wasn't inventing and "attack[ing] the possibilities of slavery with all the eloquence of genius."[52] Francis Shoup, reflecting on "Uncle Tom's Cabin Forty Years After," wrote that Stowe's novel contained the best defense of slavery in the character of Uncle Tom. "[P]erhaps the most remarkable thing," he wrote, "about this most remarkable book is that, when rightly read,"—which certainly meant selectively—"the very citadel and ground of defence [*sic*] of the Southern people is to be found in the pages of this true story of the not uncommon character, Uncle Tom. He was all he was, by virtue of his condition as a slave."[53] Where many white Southerners claimed that Uncle Tom was far too virtuous to be realistic, here his character was possible only in the confines of slavery. Indeed, some argued that slavery was a far better molding mechanism of black character than were freedom, education, and civil and political rights. Beyond reinterpreting *Uncle Tom's Cabin*, post-Reconstruction poets and fiction writers including Irwin Russell and Joel Chandler Harris also created their own warped versions of Stowe's "old Negro" character: old, gentle, religious, and unconditionally devoted to their white master and his descendants.

As the glorified mythology of the South saturated American culture, black Americans increasingly questioned the value of recalling slavery in any fashion, accurate or not. That is why even those who admired Stowe's novel called for American literature to create modern representations of the race. In *A Voice From the South* (1892), Anna Julia Cooper asserted that the spiritual qualities of actual American slaves provided the inspiration for the fictional *Uncle Tom's Cabin*. But freedom had produced great changes in the race, and now the nation needed a more current account of black life and character: "an authentic portrait, at once aesthetic and true to life, presenting the black man as a free American citizen, not the humble slave of *Uncle Tom's Cabin*."[54] Such a portrait would reflect the changed circumstances of freedom and showcase a new black identity far removed from the "humble slave." Believing that literary representation of the modern Negro could play a central role in the race's future advancement, Benjamin Brawley called for American writers not to "remain forever content to embalm old types and work over outworn ideas. Rather they should sift the present and forecast the future."[55] "Why," he asked, "should we not occasionally attempt to paint the Negro of the new day—intelligent, ambitious, thrifty, manly?"[56] Chesnutt had already stopped writing his "conjure tales." Following the early death of Paul Laurence Dunbar, author of numerous dialect poems, the "Old Negro" lost traction in African American literature. Rather than producing more accurate accounts of slavery, black writers of the early twentieth century often embraced a respectable, middle-class orientation that focused on the present moment.[57] In doing so, however, this body of work left in place the powerful stereotypes of Page, Harris, and others writing in the plantation tradition.

James Weldon Johnson's Uncle Tom

While Alain Locke and other critics of the Harlem Renaissance would position the New Negro against an Old Negro best forgotten, James Weldon
Johnson understood the necessity of both figures in African American literature. In his 1912 novel *The Autobiography of an Ex–Colored Man*, he portrays
the attractions and perils of accepting seemingly benign white-authored narratives of the Old Negro, telling the story of a man who, from his early years,
uses literature to understand himself and the world around him. Reading
Uncle Tom's Cabin, the ex–colored man is quick to accept Uncle Tom as a
historical truth and to reject the character as a personal model. In what was
up to that time the most extensive discussion of Stowe's novel and its protagonist within black literature, the ex–colored man describes a deep personal
identification with this novel. "*Uncle Tom's Cabin*," he asserts, "opened my
eyes to who and what I was and what my country considered me; in fact, it
gave me my bearing."[58] Endorsing the accuracy of *Uncle Tom's Cabin* at the
level of both system and character, the ex–colored man situates Uncle Tom in
what he calls the novel's "fair and truthful panorama of slavery" and further
describes the character as representative not only of "lots of old Negroes"
in American history but also of their descendants living in the South. The
ex–colored man's problem arises from his refusal to identify with this portion
of the race even as he travels the South collecting folk songs that he plans to
adapt for his own musical compositions. After witnessing a shocking lynching, he is forced to acknowledge his own impotence against robust external
forces that classify the entire race into a single, victimized group. As a result,
he decides to live the rest of his life as a white man. Unable or unwilling to
contradict white characterizations of the Old Negro, Johnson's narrator fails
to imagine the full humanity of the lynched man and ultimately leaves behind the very cultural tradition that could have helped him do so.

In *Autobiography*, Johnson suggests that without access to alternative depictions of enslaved ancestors and folk communities, black readers are likely
to accept white-authored fictions as truth. But Johnson believed that instead
of ignoring or refuting Uncle Tom and the Old Negro, black artists should
build on this figure for their own purposes. And he did so himself in writing a 1917 stage adaptation of *Uncle Tom's Cabin*, an operatic cantata with

orchestral accompaniment.[59] It is not clear whether the surviving hand-written notes and detailed nine-page synopsis were ever fully scripted or performed, but the fact of their composition illuminates Johnson's relationship to the figure of the Old Negro in general and to Stowe's novel and its stage adaptations in particular. Bringing together selections from the plot and characters of Stowe's novel, the music of the spirituals, and the operatic form, Johnson's adaptation not only suggested that Stowe's story should be interpreted as a testament to black strength but also exemplified how black literature could mobilize the Old Negro literary tradition for new challenges. Drawing a straight line from Simon Legree's violence against Uncle Tom to twentieth-century lynch mobs, the adaptation portrays the persistence of both American racial violence and black spiritual strength. In this work, Johnson emphasizes the imperviousness of Tom's soul to Legree's physical attacks, seriously and sympathetically refashioning *Uncle Tom's Cabin* as a defiant cry against the racial violence of the Jim Crow era.

The cantata reflects Johnson's involvement in the National Association for the Advancement of Colored People's anti-lynching campaign. After becoming the NAACP's field secretary in 1915, he spent his first year in the position traveling from Richmond, Virginia, to Tampa, Florida, and back again, building a Southern membership for the fledgling organization. Lynching was a key issue for the NAACP at the time. In the summer of 1917, Johnson traveled to Memphis, Tennessee, to investigate the murder of Ell Persons, a black man gruesomely burned alive under an unsupported accusation of murder. Arriving in Memphis, Johnson visited the pile of ashes and charred wood where the lynching had recently taken place. As he later recalled in his autobiography, *Along This Way* (1933), the bones were all gone, "scrambled for as souvenirs by the mobs."[60] At the site, Johnson "reassembled the picture" of the lynching in his mind, imagining "a lone Negro in the hands of his accusers, who for the time are no longer human; he is chained to a stake, wood is piled under and around him," and five thousand men, women, and children "look on with pitiless anticipation, with sadistic satisfaction, while he is baptized with gasoline and set afire."[61] Envisioning the murder of Ell Persons as a martyr's baptism by blood, Johnson challenges the power dynamic of slavery. "I tried to balance the sufferings of the miserable victim against the moral degradation of Memphis," he recalls, "and the truth flashed over me that in large measure the race question involves the saving of black America's body and white America's soul."[62] The loss of black life brings with it a grave moral and spiritual loss to white America.

In the months after this experience in Memphis, Johnson looked to *Uncle Tom's Cabin*, and particularly to the character of Uncle Tom, for spiritual sustenance. The theme of his operatic cantata, typed on the cover page of his synopsis, closely echoed his realization at the lynching site: "Theme of the work—Those who persecute and oppress the Negro may harm him physically, but they cannot crush him so long as they cannot crush his soul." This theme defuses some of the power of the oppressor, stressing the humanity that even the most extreme violence can never take away. Unlike the refutations of Stowe's work that would begin to appear in African American literature during the late 1930s and 1940s, Johnson rewrites Stowe's novel as African American literature: told from a black perspective and woven with the emotional expression of the spirituals, this is a story about the depth of black romantic love and the spiritual endurance of black Americans in the face of oppression. If *The Autobiography of an Ex–Colored Man* (1912) anticipates the aesthetics of modernism,[63] Johnson's *Uncle Tom's Cabin* looks back to the melodramatic mode, calling on us to sympathize with the suffering of the virtuous Uncle Tom. In staging Legree's attack on Uncle Tom, Johnson's script departs from an emerging realist tradition of lynching dramas.[64] In the black-authored lynching plays of the 1910s and 1920s, violence is often left offstage; the practice's communal damage is the focus.[65] Johnson, however, uses the individual body as an emblem of the community, embracing Stowe's hero as a figure of comfort and strength during an era of racial violence.

Johnson began working on his adaptation from the novel's rich stage tradition rather than Stowe's novel. His preparatory notes largely follow the plot and structure of George L. Aiken's influential 1852 adaptation of *Uncle Tom's Cabin*, incorporating nearly the full panoply of Aiken's characters as well as a conclusion in which Marks, as he did in many of the stage productions, shoots Legree. But by the time Johnson marked up a cheap printed copy of Aiken's script, his focus tightened on a small set of scenes. In the three-part synopsis that he ultimately created, Johnson reorients the attention of Stowe's story toward its black characters. Eliminating almost all of the white characters (the only ones are Legree and a slave auctioneer) as well as Topsy, Johnson focuses on the woes and joys of Eliza and George, Cassy and Emmeline, and Uncle Tom. The synopsis also features slave chorus numbers throughout, underscoring the relevance of the Old Negro and his musical traditions. This music, which Johnson indicates should be based on jubilee songs, suggests a variety of experiences under slavery, from "joyful" singing on the Shelby plantation to a "slow and mournful, weird and solemn" rendition of the spiritual "Go Down, Moses" in the slave market scene.

One might expect Johnson's *Uncle Tom's Cabin* to tell the story of the defiant fugitive George Harris rather than the martyred Uncle Tom. But Johnson's synopsis, which in the first part lingers on the "passionate love" between Eliza and George, makes George's role primarily romantic; there is no scene of the freedmen's defense. Even so, this scene is radical, coming at a time when black romantic love was essentially absent from any U.S. performance for a white audience. ("Negroes were supposed to mate in a more primeval manner," Johnson later reflected.)[66] Opening on the Shelby plantation at daybreak, the first part of the cantata begins with Tom summoning the other slaves from their cabins and sending them off to work. They exit, singing joyfully. The action turns to Eliza, whose song about her happy love for her husband and child is interrupted by a visit from George, who reports that his cruel master has demanded that he forsake Eliza and take a new wife on the master's plantation. Because of this, he intends to escape to Canada and work to purchase Eliza and their son Harry from the Shelbys. The two say goodbye in a "Passionate love farewell." That evening, Eliza visits Tom's cabin and tells him that Shelby has sold both him and her child to a slave trader. Here, unlike Stowe's novel, Tom at first tries to dissuade Eliza from running away, but he then concedes that she should go. However, he won't go with her. With his total Christian submission to God, he thinks that it's God's will for him to go down the river. After Eliza exits, Tom sings "Down River, Down River" and then breaks down sobbing, his sorrow contrasting with the joyful singing and dancing of the slaves back in their quarters.

Following a musical interlude in which Eliza crosses the ice, the second part of the cantata takes place in the slave market where Uncle Tom is now confined and waiting with Emmeline and others to be auctioned off by the slave-trader, Skeggs. The scene begins with the slaves singing "full chorus pleading for deliverance." Skeggs then "commands the slaves to cease

their mournful noise, to get jolly and come out." Legree buys Tom as well
as Emmeline, who is torn from her mother. In an important departure from
the variety of performances by black singers and dancers in the plantation
scenes staged by the many *Uncle Tom's Cabin* companies, Johnson's auction
mart features only sorrowful singing, a choice that underscores the spiritual
and emotional damage of slavery.

Unlike the black-authored lynching plays that shied away from representing violence against black bodies on stage, the third part of Johnson's
Uncle Tom's Cabin transforms Legree's assault on Uncle Tom into a scene of
spiritual victory. Set on Legree's Red River plantation, the third part begins
with a chorus of slaves. Arriving with Tom and Emmeline, Legree tells them
that they cannot escape, for he owns all the land as far as the eye can see.
Having established the slim possibility of escape to Tom and Emmeline as
well as to the audience, Legree tells Tom he will be an overseer—and that
"he wants none of his psalm singing or [B]ible business." He also informs
Emmeline that she will be his mistress. Cassy, now the spurned mistress,
confronts and threatens Legree. When Emmeline resists Legree's advances,
he calls for Tom and commands him to flog her. But Tom refuses, and Johnson's tense account of the struggle between Legree and Tom stresses the
immense power of the slave's Christian faith:

> Legree is furious. He demands, "Do as I command you. Are you not
> mine in body and soul?" Tom answers, "My body belongs to you, but my
> soul belongs to God." Tom stands serene in God's strength. The devil
> in Legree quails before the God in Tom. Legree knows he can rule and
> injure Tom's body, but he is infuriated because he wants to rule and injure
> his soul and sees that he cannot, <u>showing that whatever the enemies of
> the Negro may do, they cannot crush him so long as they cannot crush
> his soul</u>. Tom refuses to take the cowhide which Legree hands him.
> Legree, in a paroxism [*sic*] of rage, strikes Tom over the head with the
> butt of the lash, felling him to the ground. He is then seized with a
> panicky fear of the good in Tom. He cannot look at him lying there. He
> hides his eyes from the sight shrieking, "He has conquered! I could not
> crush his soul." In his frenzy he turns on Emmeline, seizes her roughly
> and says, "I could not conquer his soul, but I shall conquer his body." As

he drags Emmeline towards [the] house Cassy walks stealthily out and down the steps, and uttering a curse in French, plunges a dagger into Legree's heart. He falls. Cassy goes to Tom and takes his head on her lap. Slaves gather around.

Curtain.

Johnson's scene inverts Legree's power over Tom, so that the faithful Christian spiritually triumphs despite Legree's physical dominance. Tom's faith and virtue provoke terror in Legree, whose exclamation that he "could not crush his soul" makes Tom's supremacy explicit. At the end, Cassy defends Emmeline by plunging a dagger into Legree's heart, killing him. But it is Tom who has shown, as the script emphatically underlines, that the black soul is stronger than any physical violence. Like Stowe's novel, Johnson's *Uncle Tom's Cabin* turns righteous suffering into a form of power, one fortified rather than undermined by Uncle Tom's Christian submission. Instead of advocating a particular strategy of protest, this theme reapportions power, suggesting that, whatever whites might do to black bodies, the black spiritual self will not be crushed. Injured and perhaps dying at the end of the script, Tom does not model effective political action, but his Christian fortitude is a source of defiant comfort and ultimate triumph, a tragedy for the black body but a victory for the black soul.

It would not be so for long. Johnson's operatic protest against lynching takes on a much less aggressive tone than Claude McKay's instantly famous anti-lynching poem "If We Must Die," written and published just two years later during the death and destruction of the Red Summer of 1919. McKay's poem accords with Johnson's script in suggesting that victory is a matter of attitude more than outcome, that death is inevitable and triumph comes through something internal rather than the achievement of a political or social goal. But where Johnson's Uncle Tom finds triumph in his faith, the speaker of McKay's poem celebrates manly self-assertion. In "If We Must Die," death is assumed from the very title, and the only question is whether blacks will die "like men" or "like hogs / Hunted and penned in an inglorious spot." Here, the losers are not those who die but those who respond in "cowardly" ways. In empowering the men who "face the murderous, cowardly pack, / Pressed to the wall, dying, but fighting back!" the poem also denigrates those who do not.

Unlike many of his contemporaries, Johnson was reluctant to abandon the Old Negro types. In his 1928 essay "The Dilemma of the Negro Author," he reflected on the limited artistic conception of the Negro in American literature. Ninety-nine percent of the black characters white Americans encountered were a variation on two types. One was the simple, devoted servant, "picturesque beside his log cabin and in the snowy fields of cotton," "a singing, dancing, laughing, weeping child," and "faithful, ever-smiling and genuflecting old servitor to the white folks of quality"; the second was the "impulsive, irrational, passionate savage, reluctantly wearing a thin coat of culture, sullenly hating the white man, but holding an innate and unescapable belief in the white man's superiority . . . a figure casting a sinister shadow across the future of the country."[67] Yet Johnson is quick to point out that his issue is not with whether or not these characters should be created or whether they can provide the material for great literature, but rather with the lack of freedom black authors confront when writing characters for a racially divided audience. White readers would accept only the worn stencils of these character types, he wrote, and black readers did not want them used at all. "There are certain phases of life that [the Negro author] dare not touch, certain subjects that he dare not critically discuss, certain manners of treatment that he dare not use" (480), Johnson observed. Yet Johnson hoped for a day in which black authors could write freely, without fear of upsetting white America or arousing the censure of black America. And he believed that black writers could find something valuable in the characters and literary modes of the past, even those by white writers. Neither embracing nor rejecting the old Negro created by white fiction, Johnson suggested that black writers should not ignore this figure; they needed to rewrite him. For several decades, few would take on this challenge.

CHAPTER 5

UNCLE TOMS AND NEW NEGROES

"A TERRIBLE MORTALITY has set in among the original 'Uncle Tom,' the hero of Mrs. Stowe's novel," a Chicago newspaper reported in 1877, "and he is dying with fearful and unprecedented rapidity all over the country."[1] When a Kentucky man who claimed to be the inspiration for Stowe's Uncle Tom died in 1903, the black newspaper *Washington Bee* offered a similar joke, wryly observing, "This makes about the two hundred and third 'original' Uncle Tom who has died within the past 45 years."[2] Although a white woman created the character of Uncle Tom and whites produced most representations of him in nineteenth-century popular culture, quite a few former slaves and their descendants were more than happy to claim him as their own. So many claimed to be the "original Uncle Tom" that Stowe, despite partially attributing the character to Josiah Henson in the 1850s, ended up repeatedly releasing statements for the next several decades insisting that Uncle Tom was not based on any single individual.[3] Henson, for his part, took Stowe's endorsement and ran with it, revising his previously published autobiography to follow the novel more closely (the new title was *Truth Is Stranger Than Fiction*) and making tours of the United States and England as "the real Uncle Tom" and "the original Uncle Tom" for the rest of his life.[4] The 1876 London edition of Henson's autobiography was titled *Uncle Tom's Story of His Life* (see figure 5.1).

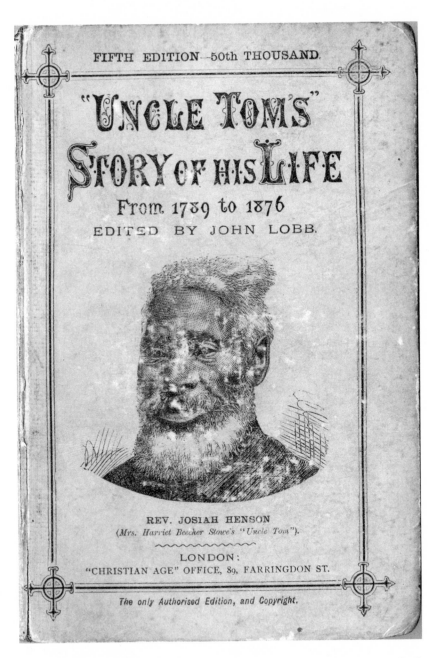

Figure 5.1. Uncle Tom's Story of His Life: From 1789 to 1876, by Rev. Josiah Henson, edited by John Lobb (London: "Christian Age" Office, 1877). Courtesy Department of Special Collections, Stanford University Libraries.

But by the 1920s, no black man wanted to be called "Uncle Tom." A hero of the nineteenth century had become a danger to the race. Although critics have almost universally assumed that Uncle Tom developed a derogatory meaning thanks to racist adaptations of *Uncle Tom's Cabin* for the American stage, Uncle Tom first became a derogatory slur not in the theater but in politics. Black protests against *Uncle Tom's Cabin* did not arise until the late 1930s, but the figure's pejorative meaning developed during the 1910s. Amid Jim Crow's retightening of many of the social, economic, and political shackles of the antebellum era, a new generation of African Americans challenged the race's old political attitudes and strategies by invoking Uncle Tom.

How and why did this figure remain useful? After the Civil War, the continued reach of Stowe's novel as well as its many adaptations for the stage kept *Uncle Tom's Cabin* the nation's most visible image of slavery and Uncle Tom the most famous slave. The novel and its characters did not just influence how whites saw blacks but also, as I shall suggest, how blacks saw themselves and their history. In the late-nineteenth-century rhetoric of both blacks and whites, the era of slavery was often called "the days of Uncle Tom," and Uncle Tom generally signified an antebellum slave.[5] This lasting slave status was fundamental to his transformation into a derogatory slur. In both politics and art, Uncle Tom became a problem when the past was seen neither as the building block of future progress nor as something that could be safely ignored but as a powerful contemporary adversary. This situation required a group of potentially influential people large enough that intraracial tensions became unavoidable. Black Americans arrived at this moment earlier in politics than in creative culture. During the first two decades of the twentieth century black Americans controlled the production of the race's political leaders far more than its cultural images. Certainly, white political and financial power influenced black politics, but neither as visibly nor to the same extent that whites produced literary, visual, theatrical, radio, and cinematic representations of the race. As such, the pool of available alternatives to Uncle Tom looked quite different in politics than it did in cultural production. Black literary culture would not acknowledge the contemporary danger of the Uncle Tom character until the late 1930s and early 1940s, as the Uncle Tom type proliferated in popular culture despite the optimistic claims and predictions of the Harlem Renaissance.

As a perpetual slave, Uncle Tom held an increasingly fraught cultural meaning for African Americans after Emancipation. On the one hand, *Uncle Tom's Cabin* deserved praise for its virtually unquestioned role in the abolition of American chattel slavery and for its path-breaking portrayal of black humanity, dignity, and virtue. On the other hand, amid the South's pervasive arguments that blacks were unfit for civil rights, its increasing legal and extralegal efforts to create a socioeconomic order as close as possible to slavery, and Northern assent to these attitudes and policies, there was a powerful onus on black Americans to prove just how far from "the days of Uncle Tom"—and from Uncle Tom himself—the race had progressed.

Moreover, the Christ-like qualities that made this character a hero in Stowe's novel and to many nineteenth-century Americans, black and white, became increasingly unappealing to a new generation that embraced a more assertive understanding of masculinity and were less interested in heaven's salvation than in earthly progress. This turn-of-the-century transformation in cultural values set the stage for a more pointed political critique of Uncle Tom in the 1910s, a decade of great turmoil in the black community. In addition to the rise of racial violence and the spread of segregation and disfranchisement, major educational, political, and geographical shifts within the race sparked new restraints on black Americans and produced contentious disagreements within the black community. First, the widespread success of black education provoked pushback from white supremacists across the nation and heightened the divide between the rising educated classes and their elders. It also encouraged a Lost Cause nostalgia among Southern whites for the antebellum Negro, a figured imagined never to have held the "New Negro's" pretensions of social and economic advancement. As this nostalgia blanketed the nation, a younger generation of black Americans more insistently rejected their predecessors. Second, a new set of protest strategies shaped by more aggressive understandings of masculinity increasingly dominated black politics. In a time of frequent lynchings, Christ's model of turning the other cheek seemed less and less viable. A third shift in black American life was the Great Migration, a mass movement from the rural South to Northern urban centers that created new political and representational challenges for black elites. Amid these shifts within the race, Uncle Tom, the ubiquitous figure of the old Southern slave, became a frequent foil both for more assertive and educated younger folks looking to attack the older generation and for Northerners anxious that Southern migrants were encouraging the replication of Southern racial practices. By the end of the decade, in the racial violence of the Red Summer of 1919, the figure developed a cogent identity in black politics as a submissive race traitor.

The Old Negro

Given how variable Uncle Tom's meaning was, even within a single newspaper, it might seem surprising that he was invoked at all outside of discussions of *Uncle Tom's Cabin*. How useful a metaphor could he be when he meant everything from spineless to brave? Shaped by the nation's shifting values, these different meanings reflect the many assorted Uncle Toms that existed in American culture even beyond literature and theater. In the late nineteenth century, Uncle Tom's name was persistently invoked in American conversations about slavery and racial difference. As we have seen, from the moment *Uncle Tom's Cabin* was published, white Southerners claimed that Stowe's novel perpetuated a dangerously inaccurate vision of black character. At its root, this criticism of Stowe's novel was an attempt to restrict black political and civil rights. For example, during the 1890 debates over the Federal Election bill, which would have guaranteed blacks the right to vote in the South had it not been successfully filibustered in the Senate, one white Southerner argued that Stowe's inaccurate portrayals of blacks were to blame for such wrong-headed legislation. *Uncle Tom's Cabin*, he charged, had made Northerners view Southern blacks as "a legion of political Uncle Toms who scarcely need dissolution to convert them into angels of light."[6] This "political Uncle Tom" was an allegedly fictional man of impossible virtue who was capable of voting responsibly.

Even while some Americans condemned Stowe for her allegedly wrong representations of blacks, others revised or co-opted Stowe's hero in the service of a romanticized vision of the Old South that became an implicit but powerful force against black progress. As Southern whites confronted a rising educated class of African Americans, a group they knew would challenge the racial order, some recalled the antebellum slave with growing fondness. In an attempt to neutralize the threat of the New Negro, the South increasingly championed the antebellum slave, and occasionally a refurbished interpretation of Uncle Tom. While some white Southerners continued to criticize Stowe for what they charged was an unrealistically virtuous and dignified representation of black character, others presented Uncle Tom as evidence of slavery's positive—and unfinished—effects on black character. They argued that emancipation and enfranchisement had been premature: slavery had begun a process of "civilizing" Africans that was not yet complete when slavery was abolished, and it was only within the beneficent and patriarchal "tutelage of slavery" that the Negro could properly be readied for civil rights. Blaming Stowe's novel for spreading inflated expectations of black character, in 1886 one Louisianan charged that Stowe had ignored the "fact" that "the negro . . . came here a savage, and he could only be prepared for freedom through the tutelage of slavery. . . . He is certainly not yet the equal of the white man, and legislative enactments are powerless as the most glowing pages of over-wrought fiction to change his status in that regard."[7] Alongside the growing national romanticization of the antebellum plantation, this notion of slavery as a civilizing process for Africans helped justify a postbellum racial order that closely followed the social infrastructure of slavery.

Uncle Tom transformed from an unthreatening old slave to an active danger to the race alongside the shifting rhetoric of the New Negro. A generation after Emancipation, black leaders began to distinguish themselves from the older generation of former slaves by calling themselves "New Negroes," a term that allowed rising leaders to define their values and strategies against those of a previous generation. (Alain Locke's New Negro movement of the 1920s is the most well-known use of the term, but it was just one among many, coming some three decades after "New Negro" entered black rhetoric.)[8] Over the years, this term took on a variety of celebratory meanings, in the 1920s becoming identified with political radicalism and creative expression. Whatever the New Negro's signification, he was almost always positioned against a dynamic Old Negro figure that also took on a variety of cultural and political identities. While the Old Negro was influenced by the many literary and visual images of black Americans circulating during the nineteenth century, it was as much a product of black discourse as of images produced by whites.[9] This figure served a crucial rhetorical function over decades of racial protest, embodying the race's past as well as a new generation's rejected values.

As American culture and black political exigencies changed, so, too, did the perpetual Old Negro, Uncle Tom. During the late nineteenth century, the Old Negro was generally described as the simple, uncivilized foil for an educated and refined "New Negro," a figure championed at length by Booker T. Washington and his associates in *A New Negro for a New Century* (1900). Here, the old became new by diligent acquisition of formal education and culture. Washingtonian New Negroes used the figure of Uncle Tom to describe an old-fashioned but decent representative of the antebellum South, one who resembled plenty of older folks. While they did not see Uncle Tom as a particularly desirable model, as long as he remained a figure of a fast-receding past he did not seem especially dangerous to those who did not want to emulate him.

When Washington and his compatriots described themselves as New Negroes, they confronted a relatively small black leadership pool, in which no one had yet seriously challenged Washington's position. Early in the twentieth century, however, the rhetoric of a younger generation of leaders turned the Washingtonian New Negroes into Old Negroes whose Southern slave mentality was an active threat to the race's progress. Now the New Negro defined himself not by the acquisition of civilization but by self-assertion, and the value of education came less from promoting cultivation than from encouraging resistance. To a generation struggling against previous leadership, Uncle Tom, the perpetual Old Negro, was not a slave of the past. Rather, he was a dangerously old-fashioned leader who reproduced the dynamics of slavery.

Reflecting nineteenth-century American ideals of hard work and self-sacrifice, black political leaders of the late nineteenth century championed self-improvement as the best means of racial progress. Living in a society in which leading scientists argued that black people occupied a separate place on the human evolutionary chain, black Americans made the case for their equality using existing terms and values. As Gail Bederman has shown, white Americans of the late nineteenth century defined their own civilization against what they imagined as black savagery or barbarism.[10] Yet civilization was also a key term for many black elites of the Progressive era. In Washington's writings and speeches, civilization and progress were nearly interchangeable terms.[11] Alexander Crummell likewise proclaimed that civilization was "the primal need of the race."[12] To a great extent, these leaders believed that the race would prove itself worthy of rights and respect through its assiduous progress toward civilization. They rooted their appeals for racial equality in a narrative of racial progress in which a morally degraded and primitive African advanced, by education and training, toward ever-rising levels of civilization, arguing that the Negro, although hampered by the experiences of slavery and perhaps not yet at the same level of civilization as the Anglo-Saxon, had made remarkable progress in a single generation.

The casualty of this "civilizationist" discourse was the image and memory of slaves themselves. Black elites consistently described the enslaved as lacking not just the trappings of respectability but also morals—as if they had indeed been lesser beings than whites. In the late nineteenth century, as David Blight has noted, black Americans often referred to the days of slavery "as a kind of historical void, a long dark night of denial and futility."[13] In an 1893 speech to the Congress on Representative Women, the women's club activist Fannie Barrier Williams tracked the "intellectual progress" of black women since Emancipation, describing emancipated slaves as "children of darkness," with "inherited inaptitudes for the moralities," for whom "there was no definition . . . of such precious terms as marriage, wife, family, and home."[14] To Williams, the race's "students of freedom and civilization" would progress by replacing the slave's cabin and the old religious superstitions with the homemaker's neatly appointed home and "a more godly and cultivated ministry."[15] While civilizationist black women located their progress in the domestic sphere, civilizationist men found it in the spirit. For Frederick Douglass, the "order of progress" began with "barbarism," represented by "physical force," and moved toward a higher civilization represented by "spiritual power."[16] Indeed, despite his ardent condemnation of the Lost Cause ideology, Douglass often characterized slavery as a state of ignorance and moral degradation, a two-hundred-year setback from which the race had to begin its journey toward civilization.

How black Americans defined civilization differed (for Williams, Douglass, and Washington, it was modernity and Christian morality, while for Crummell, it was high culture). But these definitions all emphasized a process of mental and moral acquisition rather than a defining physical action. The civilizationist understanding of progress placed responsibility on the individual to "better" himself. Civilization could not be grabbed or demanded from others; it had to be developed in oneself through sustained effort. In Reverend W. E. C. Wright's 1894 narrative of "The New Negro," for example, slavery had made blacks ignorant and illiterate, and the Old Negro had been plagued with "inveterate unthrift and dependence."[17] But through rigorous education, a younger generation was producing teachers and scholars, entrepreneurs and professionals. These forces were even transforming black Christianity from a practice of spiritual intuition that relied on the physical body to one that helped discipline and control the body. Formal Bible study in schools was, Wright observed, "changing the old-time religion of emotion into a religion that concerns the intelligence and the conduct as well as the feelings. We are making a new Negro."[18] Indeed, for Wright and many other black leaders of his day, the new Negro wasn't simply born; he was *made*— through rigorous civil, educational, and moral cultivation.[19]

The South's Uncle Tom

For some civilizationists, progress required not just personal cultivation but also geographical and social movement away from the rural South and what Fannie Barrier Williams described as its "non-progressive peasants."[20] To locate the New Negro, one had to travel the long distance from "the humble, one-room log cabin" to the major cities of the South or the North.[21] Because many Americans viewed Uncle Tom as the archetypal Southern slave, how one felt about this figure had a lot to do with one's relationship to the slavery past and vision of the way forward. For those who thought the circumstances and mentality of slavery were certain to fade away with the passage of time, an antebellum figure like Uncle Tom did not pose a threat, even if he wasn't to be emulated. In the post-Reconstruction era, black Americans most frequently invoked Uncle Tom to represent an enslaved older generation. Yet the figure had an unstable cultural meaning, sometimes designating a generic slave, sometimes a submissive response to injustice rooted in an old-fashioned version of Christianity, and sometimes a folksy example of the old Negro.

Mixed with other, positive references to the figure, objections to Uncle Tom appeared very rarely in black rhetoric, usually functioning as a means of distancing oneself from the attitudes and policies of slavery. The prolific black poet and preacher Albery Whitman, for example, positioned himself as a "progressive negro" by recalling Stowe's characters as approximations of formerly enslaved people. In the preface to his 1884 epic poem, *The Rape of Florida*, Whitman asserted that he refused to ask for any special allowances on account of his "previous condition" as a slave and argued that heroism was the product of endurance through adversity.[22] Announcing that "[t]he time has come when all 'Uncle Toms' and 'Topsies' ought to die," Whitman expressed a desire to shed the influences of slavery and move toward a future of agency and action.

Another rare, negative late-nineteenth-century reference to Uncle Tom fit squarely into the civilizationist narrative of progression from an uneducated Old Negro to a cultivated New Negro. In an 1883 address to the Bethel Historical and Literary Society in Washington, DC, Walter G. Christopher, a black New York lawyer, spoke about the challenges posed to racial progress by the unavoidable realities of skin color.[23] Responding to widespread eagerness for higher education among black Americans, Christopher recommended patience. For the present time, he argued, the race should not seek admission to universities; higher education would only prepare young folks for jobs not open to them and make them too proud to take the only employment they could get. Although he appreciated the position of those who insisted on pursuing higher education, he advocated achieving a "middle ground of general industry and comparative [financial] strength" before proceeding to higher education. Unlike the freed Roman slaves and Russian serfs of earlier eras, who had quickly been able to integrate into the larger society, "[t]he mark of former servitude rests upon us in the guise of a black skin, and wherever a black man is seen, the mind of a white man very naturally reverts to slavery and its former victims."[24] Black skin didn't just signify difference or inferiority to many white Americans—it signified slavery. And in Christopher's estimation, the psychological chasm between enslavement and university education was too wide to bridge in a single generation. This didn't mean that he wanted the race to remain in the conditions of slavery. Making sure to establish his philosophical distance from the Old Negro, he insisted:

Of course no one wishes to revive the "Uncle Tom" type of manhood; I despise that as heartily as any one: but a man who will kick up a row when he knows that he can't win is a fool, and for us, 6,000,000, to raise

a disturbance with the odds of 44,000,000 against us, is the height of ab-
surdity. Rather let us mask our feelings behind prudent and conservative
action, never forgetting however to seize the opportunity to get square,
when the time comes.[25]

Christopher's counsel of patience in political and educational progress not
only serves as an example of the late-nineteenth century meaning of Uncle
Tom but also exemplifies the cautious and patient stance by which the New
Negroes of his era would become the Old Negroes of the early twentieth
century. For Christopher, "the 'Uncle Tom' type of manhood" was that of the
patient, uneducated slave, but his counsel of "mask[ing] our feelings behind
prudent and conservative action" was hardly a challenge to the Uncle Tom
model of behavior.[26] By calling for black Americans to wear a metaphorical
mask, he was suggesting that they perform a racial identity unthreatening to whites. As such, he raised the possibility of not just *being* an Uncle
Tom by virtue of one's age, region, and personality but also of playing one
strategically.

At the turn of the century, negative and positive uses of the Uncle Tom
figure could coexist within the pages of the same newspaper in the space
of a single month. This instability reflected the jagged cultural shift from
a masculinist rhetoric of civilization to one of self-assertion. Consider the
Indianapolis *Freeman*. Founded by Edwin E. Cooper in 1888 as a staunchly
independent publication that attacked black subservience to the Republican
Party, the newspaper was purchased in 1892 by the successful barber, public school and A.M.E. church organizer, and Republican leader, George L.
Knox.[27] Although some charged Knox with sharply shifting the paper's tone
to support the Republican Party, on November 11, 1893, an article appeared
in *The Freeman* criticizing a local man, a "leading colored citizen," for refusing to run for a political office because he didn't want to jeopardize a white
Republican's chances of winning.[28] In appreciation of his loyalty, whites had
rewarded the man with a low-wage janitor position. To *The Freeman*, the fact
that the man was willing to accept this job added insult to injury. Indeed, *The
Freeman* continued, "[t]he trouble with the Negro has been, and is to-day,
he's got too much 'Uncle Tom,' good 'humble darkey' stock in his rank; and
not enough of the Nat Turner blood, without which he need not look to

be respected or go forward." Reflecting the emergence of a new American notion of masculinity, progress in this account depended not on cultivation but on resistance. Too many leaders, it seemed, humbly assented to white demands. *The Freeman* also called such individuals "URIAH HEAP 'niggers,'" referencing the falsely humble character from Charles Dickens' *David Copperfield*. Uncle Tom's humility wasn't despicable or conniving like Uriah Heap's—not yet, anyway—but he was an inadequate model for the race's progress in the present age.

One week after this explicit critique of the Uncle Tom model, however, *The Freeman* announced a new series of weekly columns by "Uncle Tom" that presented a more forgiving perspective on the old man. Reconstructing Uncle Tom as an uneducated older man with his own folksy wisdom, the columns exemplify nineteenth-century conceptions of the uneducated, unthreatening Old Negro. *The Freeman* adopts a gently mocking tone in introducing the series, "written in 'Uncle Tom's' quaint vernacular, on the social, political and religious foibles of the race generally. 'Uncle Tom' is one of the race's most brilliant thinkers and writers and his effusions will well repay perusal. Watch for them."[29] The three-part series dramatizes the tensions between the old and the new, as Uncle Tom, a late-nineteenth-century Old Negro, confronts the effects of urban migration. In the inaugural column, Uncle Tom introduces himself as an "old man, born afore the war" on "a big slave plantation, in ole Virginy," who now lives in rural Virginia with his daughter, Betsey Jane, and his dog, named George Washington Andrew Jackson with uncritical patriotism.[30] Although Uncle Tom is uneducated—"not learned in the books like some of the young chaps what write for big city papers"—he still wants to share with *The Freeman*'s readers "how things in these newfangled days look to an old man who ain't got long to stay here." Perhaps his few remaining days make his perspective welcome. The topic of Uncle Tom's first column is his name: even though the war is over, and he is "as much gentleman as any white man," white people still call him "Uncle Tom" since they don't want to call him "Mister." "I often wonder," he reflects, "if the white angels calls [*sic*] the black ones uncles and aunts. Well, I don't want none of that foolishness with me in heaven; for when I get there I want to be treated like any other gentleman is." Uncle Tom resents these racist practices of address and notes the similarities between slavery and the postbellum social order, but he's not particularly interested in fighting for it now; heaven, he hopes, will soon settle the score.

The next two columns light-heartedly describe a clash between the old Negro's rural South and the new Negro's urban North, a theme that clearly reflects the emerging intraracial tensions of the Great Migration. Recently, Uncle Tom writes, a local girl named Mahala Jane returned to Virginia after spending two years in New York City. Mahala Jane, now "full of them city ars," comes to Uncle Tom's home to visit his young daughter and insists on calling Betsey Jane "Jennettee" because in the city the name Jane is too "old fashioned."[31] The movement from rural South to urban North entails a new kind of language, one visible in the differing dialects given to the column's characters. When Betsey Jane tells Mahala Jane that she is engaged to be married next Thanksgiving, the city girl again urges her country friend to modernize her old-fashioned ways, suggesting that she find a gentleman in addition to her fiancé, one who will take her to the theater, give her money, and buy her nice things. Winking, Mahala Jane says, "Caunt you understand?" and then whispers something in the girl's ear. Here, as in Paul Laurence Dunbar's novel *The Sport of the Gods* (1902), the typical elite attribution of virtue to the self-improving Northerners and of degradation to the uncivilized and poor Southerners is inverted: the city girl is promiscuous, while the country girl is chaste. This chastity is not passive; the country folk are not shy about standing up to Mahala Jane and her New York ways. In the third and final column, headlined "Uncle Tom Mad, Very Mad!," both Betsey Jane and Uncle Tom give Mahala Jane a piece of their minds about what is obviously a suggestion of adultery, if not outright prostitution. Betsey Jane insists that her good character would never allow her to be anything but sexually pure for her husband and tells Mahala Jane that she never wants to speak to her again. "When you get back to New York, you just stay there," she says. Meanwhile, Tom, "mad that such good-for-nothing no count low-down trash was trying to ruin my gal right in my house," insults Mahala Jane viciously and then gives her a hard knock on the head with a piece from a split-bottom chair he's been repairing. The city girl runs away, with George Washington Andrew Jackson chasing her all the way to the fence. "If ever old Tom ketch you here agin he'll make you jump highern that," Tom calls as she disappears from sight.[32] This conclusion leaves the rural Southern values of

Uncle Tom and his daughter intact, Mahala Jane's immorality and material-
ism successfully relegated to the cities of the North. Old and old-fashioned
Uncle Tom is the story's hero, even willing to use a little violence to defend
his daughter's virtue. Indeed, such a stance of resistance was not yet incom-
mensurate with the notion of Uncle Tom. In 1895, *The Freeman* compared a
black man who had stood up for his family against the insults of a group of
white men—and been shot dead for it—to Uncle Tom.[33] Like Stowe's hero,
the man had been murdered for courageously protecting others.

The New "New Negroes"

As long as Uncle Tom was "a historical factor of a time and period long since
swallowed up by the sturdy advance of civilization and new customs," as a
1903 account in *The Freeman* put it, he sparked limited antagonism.[34] This
would change, however, when instead of quietly passing away the Old Negro
developed power both within the race and with whites, and then used it to
support a racial order dangerously close to antebellum slavery. The new century saw the emergence of a growing intraracial critique of race leaders who
had been unable to halt the rapid deterioration of black civil rights in the
post-Reconstruction years, what Rayford Logan famously called the "nadir"
of African American experience.[35] With the 1877 Compromise, which gave
Republican Rutherford B. Hayes the Presidency in return for the withdrawal
of federal troops from the South, Reconstruction ended, opening the door to
a new era of black unfreedom. The gains of the Reconstruction era quickly
gave way to a determination among white supremacists in the South to create a caste system as close as possible to the social order of slavery, a process
to which the North all too willingly consented.[36] In 1883, the Supreme Court
declared the 1875 Civil Rights Act unconstitutional, thereby limiting the
rights that the nation had so recently extended to blacks. In an effort to
prevent blacks from voting, the South instituted poll taxes, literacy requirements, "understanding" clauses, and "grandfather" clauses. From 1887 to 1891,
white Southerners passed a series of Jim Crow laws, giving an official stamp
of approval to discriminatory practices already in place in schools and public
transportation. Meanwhile, the Ku Klux Klan rose in power, and along with
it the extralegal violence of lynching, which increasingly targeted Southern

blacks. The U.S. Supreme Court's 1896 *Plessy v. Ferguson* decision introduced the impossible category of "separate but equal" to American jurisprudence, thus condoning the South's shift from de facto to de jure segregation and propelling the undoing of black civil rights. In the North, black Americans maintained political rights, at least on paper, but rules and customs increasingly mandated segregation in education, housing, and employment.

In this environment, the path to advancement was not immediately clear. At the turn of the twentieth century, black leaders, most prominently Booker T. Washington, generally continued to promote a doctrine of self-help, asserting that hard work and cultivation were the best means of advancement. Yet tensions between this worsening racial situation and the rising aspirations of young black Americans produced a mounting opposition to the dominant leadership. Although Washington and his supporters had described themselves as New Negroes, early in the new century the rhetoric of a younger generation of leaders turned the Washingtonian New Negroes into Old Negroes whose Southern slave mentality was an active threat to the race's progress. A *new* New Negro movement emerged, charging the older generation with ineffective and even counterproductive leadership. Uncle Tom, the perpetual Old Negro, transformed from an unthreatening old slave to an old-fashioned leader who reproduced the dynamics of slavery. The New Negro now defined himself not by acquiring civilization but by self-assertion, and the importance of education was less as a marker of cultivation than as an experience that encouraged assertive resistance.

At the heart of this new breed of attacks on the older generation was a charge of insufficient manliness. This reflected the emergence of a new black masculine ideal which, following a turn-of-the-century "crisis of masculinity," replaced the standards of civilization and Christian virtue with self-assertion.[37] In the twentieth century, American men increasingly invested themselves in what Theodore Roosevelt called "the doctrine of the strenuous life," in which brawling and physical play were no longer boyhood activities to be left behind as one developed the self-control of manhood, but rather badges of masculinity. To help boys become men and to keep men in touch with their newly appreciated "animal instincts," male leisure institutions such as the Boy Scouts of America, men's clubs, and lodges flourished. Boxing became a national obsession. The new masculine ideal

of self-assertion extended to religious matters as well: a flourishing "muscular Christianity" transformed the nineteenth century's self-sacrificing faith
into a more physically active and aggressive religion.[38] At the time, these
transformations even affected images of Jesus: whereas nineteenth-century
images of Christ usually represented him with long hair, flowing robes, and
a welcoming gaze, the twentieth-century Christ tended to be muscular and
stern-jawed, virile rather than lamb-like.[39]

This shift in white masculine ideals extended to the black community as
well, ultimately leaving little patience for humble Christians like Uncle Tom.
With the turn of the century, the masculine traits praised by nineteenth-
century leaders such as Frederick Douglass and Booker T. Washington
became the basis for a new generation's critique of the old leadership. In
Douglass' famous "Self-Made Men" speech, first composed and delivered in
1859 and delivered more than fifty times throughout the rest of his life, he
championed hard work and self-sacrifice as both the material and the ideal
of manhood.[40] Similarly, Washington, the acknowledged leader of the race
for the fifteen years after his 1895 Atlanta Exposition address, repeatedly
affirmed the Victorian masculine values of autonomy, self-discipline, and self-
sacrifice.[41] Moreover, Washington believed that cooperation between blacks
and whites was necessary for the race's progress. In his Atlanta Exposition
address, he advised, "Cast down your bucket where you are," further specifying, "[C]ast it down in making friends in every *manly* way of the people
of all races by whom we are surrounded" (my emphasis).[42] This advice—to
develop associations with whites in a "manly" way—appears again and again
in Washington's speeches, reflecting his conviction that blacks could form
honorable relationships with whites. He was resolutely opposed to political
agitation, which he thought would achieve nothing but continued racial friction. Rather, he urged members of the race to devote themselves "to the more
fundamental principles of citizenship, education, industry and prosperity."[43]

But with the turn of the century, a more assertive understanding of manliness increasingly dominated black political rhetoric, urging opposition to
white supremacists rather than the formation of relationships with them.
Washington was himself aware of this development. "Unconsciously we seem
to have gotten the idea into our blood and bones," he wrote to his close friend,
Timothy Thomas Fortune, in 1899, "that we are only acting in a manly way

when we oppose Southern white men."[44] Indeed, when W. E. B. Du Bois rose to prominence as Washington's chief critic, he did so by championing an aggressive and oppositional masculinity that, he insisted in a chapter of his *Souls of Black Folk* (1903), Washington lacked. "Of Mr. Booker T. Washington and Others" is prefaced by two snippets from Byron that signal the essay's twinned investments in manliness and self-assertion. The first line, from Byron's "Canto the Second," equates slavery with emasculation: "From birth til death enslaved; in word, in deed, unmanned!" The second Byron quotation, from the narrative poem "Childe Harold's Pilgrimage," asserts that slaves can free themselves only through their own force: "Hereditary bondsmen! Know ye not / Who would be free themselves must strike the blow?" Throughout the essay, Du Bois repeatedly impugns Washington's masculinity, charging him with being too submissive to whites, too lacking in manliness, to "strike the blow" that is necessary for the full citizenship of the race. Washington's program, Du Bois charges, represents "the old attitude of adjustment and submission" in Negro thought, and as such, it would "sap the manhood" of any race.[45] For Du Bois, "true manhood" was more often than not found in the North. "In the North," he writes, "the feeling has several times forced itself into words, that Mr. Washington's counsels of submission overlooked certain elements of true manhood."[46] Practically, "true manhood" required full political participation, for, as he wrote, "voting is necessary to modern manhood."[47] Du Bois concluded his essay by charging Washington's critics—"those black men, if they are really men"—with the duty of speaking out and opposing him by all civilized means.[48] It was time for a new generation of "real men" to step up, push self-assertion to the limits of civility, and take the place of an insufficiently masculine leader.

Du Bois' more antagonistic conception of manliness exemplified black political thought in the first decades of the new century. While nineteenth-century leaders largely embraced Christ's self-sacrifice and humility even when they did not want to emulate it, the subsequent generation explicitly critiqued this model. In a 1902 private letter to Booker T. Washington, the black journalist and pastor William H. Ferris suggested that the Tuskegeean should develop a champion boxer's aggression instead of the patience and love of Christ. "Now Prof. Washington," Ferris wrote, "there are many colored people and a number of white people who think that you kiss the hand that smites your race too much. There is a time when patience ceases to be a virtue and when love for your enemies becomes a slave's love rather than a man's love. I wish you had less of the Christ and more of the John L. Sullivan."[49] Sullivan, a prominent white boxer who consistently refused to meet a black man in the ring, was perhaps an odd exemplar for Ferris. Equally surprising was the pastor's criticism of Christ and his teachings. But Ferris' metaphor underscores the American cultural transition from a notion of manliness that idealized Christ's loving self-sacrifice to one that described such behavior as "a slave's love rather than a man's love." Christ's example was fine for slavery times, and it certainly didn't need to be cast away entirely, but the new century demanded less of Christ's love and submission, and more of the boxer's punch.

With this paradigm shift, the Christ-like Uncle Tom was incorporated into critiques of the old leadership. Washington, Ferris would write in 1913, was "an Uncle Tom in real life," one who didn't understand that in the present day Christ's advice to turn the other cheek was "to be figuratively and not literally taken."[50] (Actually, Ferris objected to turning the other cheek both figuratively *and* literally.) The comparison between Washington and Uncle Tom had already been made in the black press. In a 1905 critique of Washington as "the apostle of servility and submission," the St. Louis (Missouri) *Advance* suggested that Haitian revolutionary Toussaint L'Ouverture, with his bold resistance, provided a far better model for the race. *The Advance* proposed a new interpretation of Christianity that equated resistance to tyrants with obedience to God. Counterposing "slave" and "man," it contended that "[t]he faithful slave is no example for men." "We pity 'Uncle Tom,'" *The Advance* continued, "we neither emulate nor admire him.... [T]rue Negroes are proud of Toussaint L'Ouverture, not of some semi-idiot who believes that, in order to be Christian, he must be servile."[51] The implication of such language was that servility and unwillingness to resist was not simply a mistaken approach but a position that made one somehow less authentically black.

The consequences of this view for a figure like Uncle Tom are clear in a 1906 political cartoon critiquing Thomas Dixon, published in the black newspaper *The Topeka Plaindealer*. As we have seen, Dixon's novels and plays, intended and received as a counterblast to *Uncle Tom's Cabin*, celebrated the Ku Klux Klan as the South's savior against the depraved plots of black criminals. Their popularity was emblematic of the deteriorating racial situation, of the success of robust cultural and political efforts to undo the work that *Uncle Tom's Cabin* had accomplished some fifty years earlier. The visually cluttered drawing, which shows Dixon, members of the Klan, and Uncle Tom gathered before St. Peter at the gates of heaven, presents Uncle Tom's sympathetic Christianity as inadequate in an age of vicious propaganda and violence. As an extended caption explains of the image, although the KKK confesses Dixon's sins, Dixon himself insists on trying to enter heaven because he believes that his views are righteous. Uncle Tom's compassionate response advocates a retreat from eternal justice. "As Dixon seeks to supplant the already accomplished mission of Uncle Tom's Cabin with his tommyrot," the caption continues, "Uncle Tom sheds tears for him and begs 'Mr. Peter' to be lenient. But St. Peter upon finding that Dixon's record is too badly stained to justify any exercise of leniency, points out the road to him that saints do not travel."[52] St. Peter, who is ultimately responsible for weighing the balance of man's virtues and sins, ignores Tom's pleas and sends Dixon straight to hell. Even this heavenly figure knows that Uncle Tom's Christianity is inadequate in the face of Thomas Dixon and the KKK.

Turning Traitor

In the 1910s, after several decades of flux, Uncle Tom became widely understood in black political rhetoric as an old-fashioned man whose submissive mentality seriously jeopardized racial progress. Where earlier New Negroes had incorporated the Old Negro as an originating figure in their narratives of racial advancement, one bound to fade away in the march of progress, the *new* New Negroes saw the Old Negro as one of the greatest problems facing the race, one that needed to be eradicated. Uncle Tom could stand for a variety of qualities: an attitude (acceptance and even encouragement of the spread of Southern racial practices such as segregation to the North), an image (perpetuation of a submissive version of modern black manhood), a strategy (submission to racial injustice rather than vigorous contestation), and a performance (an act knowingly affected in order to get ahead). Emerging critiques of Uncle Tom and the Old Negro during the 1910s revealed the frustrations of a younger generation educated for futures that turned out to be impossible for them. Even as the race became more widely educated, its rights were withdrawn. But what was the most effective means of racial advancement? Was it best to pursue education and cultivation and trust that whites would be forced to recognize this progress? What if whites objected to the race's advancements with mob violence? Was political protest necessary? If so, what kind, and how much?

As late as 1909, there were black leaders who endorsed the Uncle Tom model. The prominent A.M.E. pastor J. M. Henderson, for example, argued that protest was unnecessary and that race would stop being an issue only once black people stopped treating it as such. In an opinion piece that would read like satire if only it did not square so neatly with the conservative tone of his other writing, Henderson proposed to the Indianapolis *Freeman*, "The educated Negro has got to sit down at the feet of Uncle Tom and learn the good old lesson of knowing how to be whatever you are and going on with a jolly laugh and an unblinking eye."[53] Older folks had grown up knowing how to navigate interactions with whites, even if it meant masking their real feelings, and the younger generation needed to realize that the same racial limitations applied to them regardless of their education. Henderson's "good old lesson" of careful appeasement was of the sort Richard Wright would later describe as his "Jim Crow education": an informal system of instruction in Southern racial dynamics that occurred alongside more formal academic and vocational education. As one principal of a black Texas college reported in 1915, educators needed to teach their students not only college subjects but also how to survive in the South. These lessons would best come from the model of the older generation: "Uncle Tom and Aunt Nancy, Uncle Jim and Aunt Susan who the old pioneers had the highest regard for, are all passing from the stage of the living and the young Negro is coming on the scene. He has to have that teaching that will enable him to live in perfect harmony with his white brother."[54] Such teaching, as vital to black progress and indeed survival as any academic subject, asked the "young Negro" to model himself after the old uncles and aunts, in effect recreating antebellum race relations. While this situation was certainly not ideal, the alternative was all too likely to result in violence against black people.

Many members of the younger generation, however, refused to mimic the behaviors of the slavery era, especially in the North. To them, the recommendations of men like J. M. Henderson were hogwash and amounted to something like perpetual enslavement. They argued that the older generation, with its inability to break free of antebellum constrictions, was itself a great danger to the race. In 1910, *The Chicago Defender*, the most politically radical black periodical in the city as well as the most widely and extensively distributed black weekly across the nation, offered a disgusted report on a Fourth of July celebration in which a black group had agreed to march at the rear of a parade. The newspaper framed its critique of this segregated parade as a contest between a "young progressive class" of educated Negroes and an uneducated "Uncle Tom class," beloved by the South. Those who assented to march in "tenth place" were not, *The Defender* reported,

> those who represent that young progressive class, that class that represent our colleges, that class that represent our business and professional side; but they are the class that the South is preparing to raise a monument to, the "Good Nigger," the Uncle Tom class, if you please, who by their lack of education they cannot ride beyond the scope of an errand boy to answer the bells or raps of a man and who would die for him because of the fact that they have no hopes, and if they had, their lack of training would prevent them from hoping. . . . [T]hose of the race who will be hauled on the float asleep on a bale of cotton will not be our representatives, and for the sake of the Fourth of July and our unborn generations, we the educated classes, protest.[55]

Drawing insistent distinctions of age, education, and region, *The Defender* condemned the unseeing Old Negro for the "lack of education" and "lack of training" that prevented him from imagining a life beyond servitude. The Old Negro was content to be "hauled on the float asleep on a bale of cotton," his eyes shut in blissful, cotton-field sleep. His contentment with the status quo was the reason why the older generation was favored by the white South but resented by the younger generation. Yet in the wide-open eyes of the educated New Negro, protesting segregation was vital.

Representing the Race

The real danger posed by the Old Negro was not so much in his old-fashioned attitude as it was in his status as a representative of the race. If instead of passing away the Old Negro was becoming immortalized in monuments and marching in (the rear of) Fourth of July parades, he posed a threat to the race's progress. Of course, whether or not the "young progressive class" assented, Jim Crow was influencing the North, a circumstance sharpened by the northward movement of African Americans during the Great Migration. As Southerners moved to Northern cities in increasing numbers, regional and class divisions within the race became more pronounced. Northward migration began around 1890, with the first major wave beginning in 1910 and a drastic increase during World War I. Scholars of the Great Migration have documented Northern concerns about the "respectability" of these migrants, showing how various local groups educated arriving migrants in the conventions of proper behavior.[56] Among these were the "dos and don'ts" lists published in black newspapers to guide new arrivals in the rules of public comportment.

Those already living in Northern cities were interested in the "respectability" of the migrants because they were concerned that the newcomers were somehow bringing Jim Crow with them, thereby encouraging race relations in the North to mimic those in the South. Indeed, there's no question that the migration of Southern blacks to Northern cities accelerated racial segregation, a process powerfully demonstrated in the case of Chicago. In the late nineteenth century, black people lived only in certain sections of the city, but they were interspersed among white residents. As the black population grew, however, white Chicagoans organized to prevent black people from moving into their neighborhoods, at times using terroristic violence. As a result, the city's racial geography became drastically more concentrated.

As black Chicagoans found themselves losing some of the limited freedoms they had once enjoyed, some wanted Uncle Tom and his old Southern ways to turn right back around. Beginning in 1910, Uncle Tom became a recurrent figure in condemnations of Southern migrants published in *The Defender*. Although the newspaper's editor, Robert Abbott, later spearheaded a national campaign for northward migration and employed railroad porters to distribute the newspaper along Southern train routes, initially the publication expressed reservations about whether these migrants would diminish the advantages Chicago residents enjoyed. For example, when a migrant from Georgia tried to assemble a petition for a segregated school in Chicago, *The Defender* had harsh words for "southern white folks' lovers" bringing Jim Crow to the North: "If such negroes of Georgia are satisfied with Jim Crow schools and theaters and being black wenches for ignorant white crackers and rich ones as well, let them keep it South," declared the paper. Calling on "all the better families of the city to kill the Southern viper and save Chicago, the only city in America where the Negro is treated as a man and where his children may associate with other races freely and be at ease while so doing," *The Defender* urged the petitioner to leave Chicago and "beat it back to her dear old southern home, where all the Uncle Toms and Topsys should be."[57] Referring to "Uncle Toms and Topsys" as a generic term for the antebellum type, *The Defender* angrily characterized the migrants as complicit in segregation and servitude, with questionable morals to boot. The paper suggested that such conditions were fine for those below the Mason-Dixon Line. Northern elites, on the other hand, wanted to be treated "as a man" and left free to enjoy racial integration. The problem with Uncle Tom was not, then, that he existed but that he was coming to the North and bringing his submissive Southern sensibility with him. Northerners could no longer rest easy from "the southern viper" in the comparative racial integration of Chicago.

During the 1910s, the figure of Uncle Tom was invoked in critiques of railroad porters more than in any other context outside of *Uncle Tom's Cabin* itself. Working as a railroad porter was at the time one of the best jobs available to black men, putting such individuals in a privileged class within the race. Railroads were also the most visible link between the North and South. In a 1911 article for *The Defender*, one Northerner, John R. Winston, viciously criticized the Southern "monkey porters and Uncle Toms, and end men, who are making it hard for men who stand on their merits in securing a position."[58] The images perpetuated by Southern porters were dangerous to those who wanted to be employed for their talents rather than for fulfilling the old minstrel stereotypes. But Winston had no interest in enlightening these uncultivated Southerners on how they might access their merits. Rather, his solution to the problem of "Too much South," as he called it, was indistinguishable from the language of white supremacists: "Brand them and send them back to the uncut timber and sage bushes and let them juggle cocoanuts [*sic*] with their brothers." In rejecting Southern blacks as uncivilized, monkey-like barbarians, Winston's nasty critique underscored the perceived threat of Southern encroachment.

Some porters were also concerned that the behavior of Southern porters would encourage Northern men to put on a similar act. Indeed, the notion

that one could "play" Uncle Tom was fundamental to the figure's transformation into a traitor to the race. Southerners of what *The Defender* called "the
Uncle Tom class" might be foolish and dangerous to the race, but they probably didn't know any better. Those who *chose* to adopt such a humble image,
however, were ultimately a more pernicious threat. "All porters who are playing Uncle Tom for passengers on the train should cut it out," asserted *The
Defender* in 1912. "Work on your merits and manhood. You will remain in the
service much longer."[59] *The Defender* again invoked Uncle Tom when a porter
named James Walter Lange was dismissed for defending himself against a
"poor white 'drunk'" on his train. "Had Mr. Lange played 'Uncle Tom' he could
of [*sic*] had a chance to remain in the service under those southern 'snake dig-
gers.'"[60] Was the trade-off worthwhile? Willingness to defend oneself could
lose a man his job, but unwillingness to do so could rob him of his manhood.

At the start of World War I, derogatory references to Uncle Tom in *The
Defender* shifted away from a focus on the figure's Southern status. There
were plenty of war industry jobs in Chicago to go around, and a vibrant
community of migrants was developing, making *The Defender*'s Abbott a rich
man. Now Uncle Tom became closely tied to an old-time submissiveness
that allowed and even encouraged continuation of slavery-era policies. During the war, *The Chicago Defender* published numerous invocations of Uncle
Tom targeted at those who supported segregation. In 1916, the paper used
the term to criticize a Dallas educator who had issued a statement in favor
of segregated schools. "Like Uncle Tom of 'Cabin' Fame This Man Is Ready
to Submit to Anything a White Man Tells Him—Men of This Stripe Not
Even Fitted to Train Skunks Much Less Children." This parallel between
segregation and the "Uncle Tom's Cabin days" of slavery made rejections of
Uncle Tom all the more urgent. Later that year, *The Defender* protested the
exclusion of a black women's Republican group in Chicago from the city's
loop of national headquarters. "The 'Uncle Tom's Cabin' days are passed," the
paper told its readers, and urged the women to "demand what other women
demand, and not a separate place."[61]

Just as World War I brought a new hopefulness to the black community, it
brought a new energy to rejections of Uncle Tom. At the start of the war, there
was a widespread conviction among the race that black men could prove that
they deserved full citizenship rights through their performance on the battle-

field. As an Ohio minister, Reverend C. S. Williams, reflected in a 1922 speech, "When [the Negro] went to the War under the slogan of making the world safe for democracy, he expected, when he returned, to find no more segregation and discrimination."[62] In a 1915 open letter to Secretary of War Lindley M. Garrison, the black Spanish War veteran R. P. Roots adopted the rhetoric of the New Negro and Uncle Tom to protest unfair treatment of black soldiers, particularly their restriction to service positions. Roots demanded that the military respect the black serviceman as a social equal and give him the opportunity to be promoted based on his merits. "He can fight and will," Roots insisted, "but will fight better with an incentive than without one. He is a citizen regardless of all laws to the contrary; also he is the NEW Negro, and NOT of the 'Uncle Tom' class, the passing of whom so many white citizens regret."[63] Roots' letter underscored the burden of the old "Uncle Tom class" to the younger generation. While many whites, nervous about this rising class of educated blacks, increasingly celebrated the antebellum slave, New Negroes felt hampered by the old "Uncle Tom" model. Despite this frustration with the segregated military, many black Americans still held hope that military service would bring racial progress. W. E. B. Du Bois, for one, had such faith that black military valor would ultimately promote better treatment of the race that, in his famous 1918 "Close Ranks" editorial for *The Crisis*, he broke with his anti-segregation policy to support racially segregated officer's training camps.[64] Du Bois saw this concession as a means of getting black servicemen out of supporting roles and into combat. But as the angry responses from the black community suggested, Du Bois' optimism was already out of place.

Indeed, the nation showed little interest in black rights during the war. Those who attended training camps in the South discovered racial segregation on military bases and violent attacks beyond; it was dangerous for a black soldier simply to walk off military property in uniform. Then, after being relegated to service positions during the war, returning soldiers found that the nation was no more willing to accept them as full citizens than it had been before their service. If anything, Southern racial policies and attitudes were crossing the Mason-Dixon Line: residential segregation was on the rise in the North, as was mob violence against blacks. In postwar race relations, as C. Vann Woodward observed, "the Southern way" was now "the American way."[65] Of course, this did not sit well with those who had just bravely served their nation. At a victory parade for returning soldiers in St. Joseph, Missouri, parade organizers wanted black soldiers to march at the end of the parade. But they refused, and the black newspaper *The Wichita Protest* applauded the "manhood and grit" of those who had told the white folks "that there was a new Negro on the stage of action who would at all times expect the treatment due a real man and that he would govern himself accordingly."[66] The new Negro, then, was "a real man," and this meant that he would demand more than those who had come before him.

After World War I, the heightened expectations of the younger generation collided with the worsening position of the race, producing a newly forceful mode of protest that relied on both political and physical self-assertion. Politically, the postwar break of the New Negro from the Old involved a sharp turn against a Republican party that had sold out the race for so many years and against an old leadership that continued to maintain allegiance to the party despite its many betrayals. While the Old Negro retained faith in the Republican Party and sought racial progress by "begging or asking," the New Negro, according to the black activist Hubert H. Harrison, was "demanding elective representation."[67] Gesturing to Du Bois, Harrison described such demands as the result of the recent development of "a new manhood" in "the souls of black folk."[68] Patience with old-fashioned submissiveness was wearing thin. "The day has passed," asserted the Chicago *Broad Ax* in 1918, "when black men will take orders absolutely from white men, especially when they have the power to do otherwise. The day has passed when black men are so indifferent to their welfare that they will permit a white man to do a thing or to select a man to represent them and tell all of the colored citizens that they must take him whether they want him or not."[69] This repeated insistence that "the day has passed," however, betrayed anxiety about whether or not such a time or such men really had disappeared from the contemporary scene. Indeed, it was the persistent power of the Old Negro that made him most troubling. "It is the young colored Americans who are defending the rights and liberties of their people," editorialized *The Washington Bee* in 1919, "and the old school politician is the dangerous element in society."[70]

The postwar critique of the Old Negro involved two complaints: first, that the Old Negro was too submissive to the dictates of whites, and second, that he didn't care enough about himself to look out for his own interests. Accordingly, Uncle Tom, an Old Negro with less regard for his earthly body than his heavenly soul, became associated with this kind of submission. An "Uncle Tom," according to the 1918 *Broad Ax* account, submitted to whites even when he had the power to do otherwise because he had too little regard for his own welfare. By doing so, however, he harmed others. "Uncle Tom" politicians betrayed the race from within by assenting to racial segregation, whether by taking a Jim Crow job, accepting Jim Crow schools, or advocating segregation in other contexts. In St. Joseph, Missouri, for example, a local black man appointed to handle the claims of black World War I veterans was charged by *The Chicago Whip* as an "'Uncle Tom' politician" for accepting a Jim Crow job: "As long as we take these political handouts, as long as our 'leaders' are too hungry to refuse them, of course they will be tendered our race."[71] Such trade-offs brought limited personal advancement to the individual at a grave expense to the race.

"Dying, but Fighting Back"

During the last six months of 1919, some twenty-five race riots erupted in cities across the nation. Unlike the earlier generations, who found masculine values in the mind and the soul, this new generation of New Negroes prioritized the body as the primary location of masculinity. They described violence not only as the most effective means of fighting for equality but also as a masculine virtue in and of itself. Even some pastors joined in this rhetoric, rejecting Christ's self-sacrificing example in favor of physical resistance.[72] Speaking against a Jim Crow school, Ohio Reverend C. S. Williams told a crowd that, although he was a minister, he would rather "have hell on an equality basis than heaven on servility and jim crowism [*sic*]."[73] Unlike Uncle Tom, he declared, he had no patience for heaven's rewards: "The day of the belly-crawling, hat-in-hand, lick-spittle and Uncle Tom type of leadership is past," he announced. "[T]he leader of the future must not only have brains and heart, but also backbone." For this generation, death was preferable to the stasis that they ascribed to past leaders; at least it allowed one some measure of manliness and self-respect. In contrast with "the old reactionary Uncle Tom doctrine—a half loaf is better than no loaf at all," wrote a columnist for *The Chicago Whip* in 1921, "there are some black men, some

real men left, thank God, who want liberty, unqualified liberty, or death."[74] A
"real man," the newspaper implied, would embrace Patrick Henry's rousing
call: "Give me liberty or give me death!" Indeed, black newspapers of the era
almost uniformly favored armed defense, urging black Americans to fight
lynch mobs even if this likely meant death.[75]

Like earlier New Negroes, those who came of age in the months of mob
violence known as the Red Summer of 1919 constructed an oppositional Old
Negro figure. The Kansas City *Call* observed that the summer of violence had
introduced white mobs to a "new type of Negro" whose willingness to die in
self-defense set him apart from the kowtowing "old time Negro": "The NEW
NEGRO, unlike the old time Negro, 'does not fear the face of clay.' . . . The
time for cringeing [*sic*] is over. If we are driven to defend our lives, our homes,
our rights either by responsible or irresponsible mobs, let us do it MAN
FASHION . . . defending our lives, our homes, our rights from the attacks of
white men."[76] Contrasting the "cringing" posture of the Old Negro with the
steely stance of the New, this critique asserted that physical defense of lives,
homes, and rights from white mobs took precedence over heavenly salvation.
This bodily contrast between the Old and New Negroes also appears in "Be
a Man!," a poem by Carita Owens Collins published in Marcus Garvey's
Negro World in 1919. Like "If We Must Die," Claude McKay's defining poem
of the Red Summer, Collins' poem couples violence and self-respect. But it
departs from McKay's focus on a united racial "we" by positioning the violent
and self-respecting New Negro against an older generation and its old-time
religion. The time is past, the poem asserts, "[w]hen black men, laggard sons
of Ham, / Shall tamely bow and weakly cringe, / In servile manner, full of
shame."[77] The cringing physical stance of these Old Negro "sons of Ham,"
who accept the primary Biblical justification for racial difference, matches a
weak character. By contrast, the New Negro takes an unyielding position of
self-respect and brave self-assertion. He must, the poem insists, "Demand
what is right, / Not a weak suppliant demand; / But an eye for an eye, and a
soul for a soul, / Strike back, black man, strike!" Despite the poem's firm and
ecstatic energy, Collins complicates McKay's celebration of resistance; "Be
a Man!" acknowledges that the rejection of Christ's turn-the-other-cheek
submission involves the sacrifice of souls as well as bodies: not just the Old
Testament's "eye for an eye" but also "a soul for a soul." For Stowe's Uncle

Tom, and for the older generation, the soul is more important than anything; for Collins, manly self-respect trumps the loss of one's soul.

Certainly, the anger of the Red Summer was not directed solely at the older generation. Yet the New Negro of this time inflicted a special rage on the Old Negro as a figure of complicity best abandoned in the grave. "The Old Negro and his futile methods must go," editorialized the New York *Crusader* after a long hot summer of race riots, blaming the old leadership for bringing no improvement to the American racial situation. "His abject crawling and pleading have availed the Cause nothing. He has sold his life and his people for vapid promises tinged with traitor gold. His race is done. Let him go. The New Negro now takes the helm. It is now OUR future at stake. Not his. His future is in the grave."[78] This sense that the race—or at least certain portions of it—was itself responsible for the dreadful racial situation served a dual role: as an outlet for rage and as a relief from feelings of victimhood at the hands of whites. Perhaps there was some fraught comfort in understanding injustice as a product of the methods of both whites and blacks, and therefore something that could be ameliorated with a new set of leaders.

The Old Negro's place, according to *The Crusader*, was "in the grave." The same went for Uncle Tom, whose death would be alternatively advocated and celebrated in black politics for several decades, especially by followers of the black nationalist Marcus Garvey and the labor leader A. Philip Randolph. At the parade that opened the first convention of Garvey's Universal Negro Improvement Association, protest signs proclaimed, "Uncle Tom's dead and buried." And in an address to the convention, Reverend George Alexander McGuire declared that "the Uncle Tom nigger has got to go and his place must be taken by the new leader of the Negro race . . . not a black man with a white heart, but a black man with a black heart."[79] The Uncle Tom figure was particularly useful to Garveyite black nationalists because invoking him helped them differentiate their kind of racial separatism, which was based on choice and ideas of black superiority, from segregation imposed by white supremacists.

But no matter how many people would try to kill Uncle Tom in the next century, he would not die. The figure's endurance had something to do with the slippage between *being* and *playing* an Uncle Tom, and with the radical potential of sneaking into the enemy's territory and hiding in plain sight. An imaginary dialogue published in Randolph's *Messenger* in 1927, "Dialogue of the Old and New," clearly riffs on the rhetoric of the New and Old Negro, with a "New Porter" trying to convince an "Uncle Tom Porter" to join Randolph's union, the Brotherhood of Sleeping Car Porters. (This was the first union of the Pullman Company, a major employer of African Americans.) A holdover from old times rather than a conniving race traitor, the Uncle Tom Porter is the dialogue's foil for explaining the values and strategies embraced by a younger generation trying to organize into unions to advocate for rights while struggling against the legacies of slavery. When the older man questions the effectiveness of unionizing and worries that black porters may be replaced by immigrants if they try to unionize, the New Porter dismisses his concerns as "nothing but the slave psychology in you, Pop. You don't think a black man can do anything a white man can do."[80] Such fear, the New Porter continues, is "just like those ghost stories about old slaves scared to death at a bed-sheet over the head of their masters." Scoffing at a caricature of frightened old slaves, the New Porter begins to reveal the potential weakness in his perspective. Given that the Ku Klux Klan and its white hoods reached peak popularity during the 1920s, the scenario invoked by the New Porter is curiously ignorant of the real danger of white men with sheets over their heads. Like many New Negroes before him, the New Porter defines himself against an Old Negro still mired in the lingering effects of slavery and not manly enough for present times: "Get that rabbit out of you, old man," says the New Porter, "and be a real man. . . . This is the 20th Century. Understand that 'a man's a man.'"

But the conversation ends with a twist: at the end of the dialogue, the Uncle Tom Porter reveals that he has actually been a member of the Brotherhood all along. In words that anticipate the deathbed confession of the grandfather in Ralph Ellison's *Invisible Man*, he admits, "I'm bluffing these white folks to death. They think I'm the worst enemy of the Union in the service."[81] Although his "Uncle Tom" mask has fooled even the New Porter, he's been working against the railroad bosses all along. Randolph's Uncle Tom in disguise suggests the radical possibilities of a man so inoffensive to whites that he doesn't arouse suspicion. In the remainder of the century, a question about this man's power would endure: Could such a man achieve progress for the race, and would that progress be worth the sacrifice required?

CHAPTER 6

WRITING OFF UNCLE TOM

PERHAPS NO ONE used the "Uncle Tom" slur more frequently than did the black nationalist Marcus Garvey, who often railed against those who, he asserted, "allow[ed] themselves to be used [by whites] even as Uncle Tom and his bunch were used for hundreds of years."[1] When a group of black men and women warned the U.S. attorney general about Garvey's threatening tactics against rivals, he published a pamphlet titled "Eight 'Uncle Tom' Negroes" (1923).[2] Yet while he was serving time in prison for mail fraud in 1925, Garvey's wife published a volume of his writings and advertised it as "A Second Uncle Tom's Cabin with the appeal of Bunyan's Pilgrim Progress."[3] Revising Stowe's call in *Uncle Tom's Cabin* for Americans to "see to it that they feel right," the advertisement heralded "A Book that will set you Thinking Right," positing intellect, rather than emotion, as the most effective means of transforming American politics. Garvey was hardly the first writer, black or white, to hope that his book would achieve the popularity and influence of Stowe's famous novel, but he was probably the first to use the Uncle Tom epithet so liberally while doing so.

By the 1920s, the political threat of the "Uncle Tom Negro" was clear to many black Americans. Yet the status of Uncle Tom in literature and popular culture was far less clear-cut. While James Weldon Johnson, as we have seen, found political, spiritual, and aesthetic value in the story of Uncle

Tom, most black critics of his era saw nothing to gain from nineteenth-century literary aesthetics and topics. In the 1910s and 1920s, black critics called for American literature to forsake the old types and represent the Negro of the new day using the techniques of realism. Writing for *The Dial* in 1916, Benjamin Brawley reminded readers that "[t]he day of Uncle Remus as well as of Uncle Tom is over," dismissing the postbellum and antebellum Old Negroes in one fell swoop.[4] A decade later, Alain Locke's triumphant introduction to his era-defining collection, *The New Negro* (1925), echoed Brawley by announcing that "[t]he days of 'aunties,' 'uncles' and 'mammies' is ... gone. Uncle Tom and Sambo have passed on."[5] These optimistic declarations of the passing of Uncle Tom and the Old Negro celebrated a liberation that was both historical and aesthetic: not only were the days of slavery over but so, too, were the sentimental methods of characterization typically used in representing it. With the Old Negro safely ensconced in the literary past, the New Negro writer would replace the old-fashioned sentimentalism and outworn characters of the past with a modern realist aesthetic and proud racial expression.

How could Locke, the Howard University professor who would become the "dean" of the Harlem Renaissance, so breezily dismiss Uncle Tom at the same time that many of his peers harshly derided "Uncle Tom Negroes" for impeding the race's progress? As we have seen, anger at "Uncle Tom Negroes" in politics required a widening pool of race leaders and the emergence of a younger generation who, frustrated with social and political stagnation, blamed those who came before them. In literary culture, a forceful critique of the Uncle Tom character developed in much the same way, first cropping up in the tensions between older and younger Harlem Renaissance writers with competing visions for black literature. However, vigorous censure of the Uncle Tom character did not develop until the late 1930s and early 1940s, when black Americans, armed with social scientific research showing the influence of popular culture, protested the continued proliferation of the Uncle Tom type in American culture, and especially in American film. Uncle Tom images of subservience and inferiority in popular culture were now just as pernicious as Uncle Tom behavior and thinking in real life.

Characterizing Uncle Tom

With the triumphant debut of the New Negro, Alain Locke and other critics of his era believed that sentimental fiction's Uncle Tom type was certain to retreat. Indeed, for the jubilant, forward-looking writers and thinkers of the 1920s, it was as if the "tortured past could be erased with rhetorical flourish and fiat, with the mere proclamation of 'the new.'"[6] In Locke's introduction to *The New Negro*, he casually dismissed this figure both aesthetically and historically. While Locke's New Negro is vibrantly alive, exerting agency and power through his creative and critical efforts, his Old Negro is a set of abstractions: "more a myth than a man," "more of a formula than a human being," and "a stock figure perpetuated as an historical fiction."[7] The essay does not tell readers what this figure looked like, where and when he came from, how he behaved, or what he believed. It even displays skepticism about whether he ever existed. Locke's account of the transition from old to new invoked several metaphors of slipping off an outer shell of old thinking— "slip[ping] from under," "shaking off," "shedding the old chrysalis"—and thereby revealing an inner sensibility that was previously "suppressed."[8] Envisioning a New Negro literature defined by contemporary racial expression, he suggested that one could throw off the vestiges of the Old Negro as easily as one could remove an ill-fitting jacket.

At the same time that Locke and other critics heralded the future of "Negro literature," a category that until at least the 1930s included literature both by and about black Americans, they also assessed American literary history.[9] And they concluded that, as William Stanley Braithwaite observed, the Negro had for generations "been accorded as little artistic justice as social justice."[10] Deriding sentimentalism and melodrama as the regressive literary tools of white Southern conservatives, black critics championed realism as an inherently progressive literary mode. Although Locke believed that for the most part "literature has merely registered rather than moulded public sentiment" about the Negro, he was confident that realism would significantly expand the social power of literary characters, transforming them from evidence of social views to shapers of racial attitudes.[11] In his introduction to *The New Negro*, Locke described sentimentality as a "social distemper"

whose cure was realism; satire and irony were "good medicines for the common mind" and "necessary antidotes against social poison."[12] This faith in the
power of realism extended into the 1930s, with Locke theorizing realism as
a "saving grace" against Old Negro stereotypes and Sterling Brown describing social realism as a "sharper weapon" than melodrama for molding public
opinion, a mode that gave "the greatest justice to Negro life and character."[13]

Given the path-breaking prominence of *Uncle Tom's Cabin* in American literary and political history, it was no surprise that New Negroes used
the figure of Uncle Tom to symbolize the sentimental Old Negro literature
against which they defined themselves. But how could any champion of realism explain the extraordinary influence of a novel like *Uncle Tom's Cabin*, a
work H. L. Mencken derided as the apotheosis of mid-nineteenth-century
sentimental romanticism?[14] And how could one easily dismiss Uncle Tom, a
character who Braithwaite acknowledged was "unequalled in its hold upon
the popular imagination to this day"?[15] Ultimately, critics had to accept a
paradox in which it was true both that realism was more politically powerful
than sentimental romanticism and that the most influential novel in the nation's history was, as they saw it, sentimental romanticism of the worst kind.
Both Braithwaite and Locke censured Stowe's novel for its melodrama and
stereotypes but ascribed its historical effectiveness to precisely these aesthetic
offenses. For Braithwaite, the problem with Stowe's Uncle Tom was the form
rather than the content of his character. Describing *Uncle Tom's Cabin* as
"sentimentalized sympathy for a down-trodden race," he suggested that "the
moral gain and historical effect of Uncle Tom have been an artistic loss and
setback. The treatment of Negro life and character, overlaid with these forceful stereotypes, could not develop into artistically satisfactory portraiture."[16]
Locke soon echoed Braithwaite's assertion by observing in his 1926 essay
"American Literary Tradition and the Negro" that Stowe's novel, with its
"melodramatic stereotypes," showed that "[t]he artistic costs of all revolutions
and moral reforms is high."[17]

Caught in this tension between realist aesthetics and the revolutionary power of Stowe's novel, Locke and other Harlem Renaissance critics
advanced a critique of the Uncle Tom character that was largely aesthetic.
Locke suggested that the white South had "borrowed [Stowe's Uncle Tom]
back as counter-propaganda" in order to "glorify the lost tradition and balm

[its] inferiority complex after the defeat."[18] In Locke's view, realism gave power to the white South's "refurbished" Uncle Tom character.[19] He suggested that the postbellum "old Negro" character had ultimately usurped Stowe's character in Northern public opinion because fiction writers such as Thomas Nelson Page and George Washington Cable had used the literary tools of realism to "paint . . . more convincingly human and real" characters.[20] Page and Cable had used the right mode (realism) for the wrong subject (the devoted servant). Locke wanted these literary methods to be turned toward representing the New Negro.

New Negro critics who found proof in the literature of the Harlem Renaissance of a new aesthetic and an emancipatory mentality were confident that the days of Uncle Tom were over. But to writers who operated outside of Locke's camp and still felt that their expression was shackled, the character seemed more relevant. Modernist writers and critics including Wallace Thurman and George Schuyler positioned their work not against previous portrayals of the race, as Locke did, but rather opposite the race's ongoing demand for "respectable" literature, in which black characters "must always appear in public butter side up."[21] Thurman chose to open the first (and only) issue of *Fire!!* by thumbing his nose at readers who demanded such respectability, publishing a sketch in which the narrator casually recalls his unwitting role in turning a promiscuous young woman into a prostitute.[22] Only at the very end of the issue did Thurman directly address the question of how the Negro should be represented in literature—and he argued that the question itself was a ridiculous one. Authors should concern themselves with whatever catches their interest, he maintained. Limiting literary characters to the race's "well bred, well behaved church-going majorities" meant pigeon-holing the race anew, creating characters that were "as ridiculous and false to type as the older school of pseudo-humorous, sentimental writers made their Uncle Toms, the[ir] Topsys, and their Mammies, or as the Octavus Roy Cohen school now make their more modern 'cullud' folk."[23] Such limits would get no closer to the serious and realistic portrayals that both Thurman and Locke advocated.

In using a comparison with Uncle Tom and his ilk to criticize other black writers, Thurman began a tradition of invoking Uncle Tom for intraracial literary critique, one that would fade during the Depression era, when the

Harlem Renaissance was no longer in vogue, and resume in the late 1930s. Just as the figure of Uncle Tom allowed black political leaders to denounce their contemporaries, alluding to Stowe's novel and its characters enabled writers to charge their literary rivals with being exactly the "Old Negroes" against whom those rivals had positioned themselves. Often, this critique worked through an accusation of old-fashioned sentimentalism. In a 1927 *New Republic* essay, "Negro Artists and the Negro," Thurman extended the critique he had initiated in *Fire!!* by equating the "respectable" literature often demanded by black readers and "sentimental whites" with the sentimental fiction of the past.[24] Connecting submissiveness, the feminine mode of sentimentalism, and *Uncle Tom's Cabin*, Thurman's critique of Walter White's *Fire in the Flint* (1924) as "a direct descendant of *Uncle Tom's Cabin*" anticipates James Baldwin's takedown of Richard Wright in "Everybody's Protest Novel" (1949).[25] According to Thurman, White's novel, with its suffering black martyrs and evil Southern whites, is a typical romantic propaganda, "follow[ing] the conventional theme in the conventional manner."[26] Using *Uncle Tom's Cabin* as a tool of intraracial critique, Thurman differentiated himself from the writers and works to which he objected by suggesting that they not only used the same literary conventions as white-authored texts but also produced the same responses in readers: head-shaking protest for sympathetic whites, outrage for blacks. These works, Thurman concluded, produced little more than feelings. Like the Uncle Tom leaders who counseled moderation, writers of the 1920s did not produce the transformative change they claimed.

The figure of Uncle Tom also proved useful for questioning the New Negro's account of American history. In "The New Negro Hokum" (1928), Gustavus Adolphus Stewart disparaged the political and artistic manifestations of the New Negro movement as nothing more than publicity stunts. Building on the skepticism of George Schuyler's "The Negro-Art Hokum" (1926), Stewart's essay challenges the typical 1920s account of a racial transformation from the old Uncle Tom type to the New Negro, in which before the Great Migration and World War I "only 'old' Negroes peopled the land, 'old' Negroes being the wooly headed Uncle Toms, bland and obsequious, spineless and grinning, tale bearing and treacherous, accepting obloquy with one hand and old clothes with the other from their adored white patrons."[27] This image, a conflation of the Old Negro and a traitorous Uncle Tom, allowed the purported New Negroes to claim for themselves resisting attitudes and behavior that in fact had always been in evidence in the black community. In lieu of this popular account of sudden racial transformation, Stewart insisted that much of the race's past and present progress in politics, education, and popular culture relied on precisely the "old" Negro that the New Negroes were so quick to dismiss. What none of these critics realized, however, is that the Old Negro would resurge on the silver screen with greater cultural power than ever.

"'Uncle Tom' in Natural Colors"

At the same time that New Negroes were casually writing off the days of Uncle Tom in literature, Universal Studios produced and released the ninth film adaptation of Stowe's novel in less than twenty-five years.[28] *Uncle Tom's Cabin* was a popular vehicle for American filmmakers during the silent film era, beginning in 1903 when Edwin S. Porter made a one-reel adaptation at Thomas Edison's studio that preceded even *The Great Train Robbery*. Before sound, any information not communicated in an image could be added only through interpolated title cards (e.g., "Eliza Pleads with Uncle Tom to Run Away," the first intertitle in the 1903 film) or a live host hired to narrate the story. In silent film, storytelling became easier for the filmmaker if an audience was already familiar with the characters and plot.[29] This was certainly the case with *Uncle Tom's Cabin*.

Although the "Uncle Tom Negro" slur was already entrenched in black political rhetoric when Universal announced its production of *Uncle Tom's Cabin*, the black community responded enthusiastically. Why didn't they protest this big-budget resurrection of the "days of Uncle Tom"? Initial support for the film came from Universal's heavily publicized decision to cast a black actor in the role of Uncle Tom, a choice that made it the first major studio to showcase a black actor in a feature film. Judging by the headlines in the industry magazine *Variety*—"'Uncle Tom' in Natural Colors," "'Uncle Tom' for U[niversal] with Colored Actor"—the casting was the biggest news about the production.[30] In the 1920s, black feature characters were rare in Hollywood film, and when such roles did appear, studios usually cast white actors in blackface. Black actors hoping for roles within the studio system usually found themselves limited to "creat[ing] atmosphere" as extras in jungle-themed films.[31] Given this scarcity of opportunity, the black press vigorously promoted the careers of black film actors and puffed up even minor appearances.[32] And so, when Universal selected the relative unknown James B. Lowe for the role of Uncle Tom, *The Afro-American* responded with characteristic enthusiasm, cheering that the role "places Lowe in the foremost rank of motion picture stars and establishes a record for rapid achievement unapproached by any actor."[33] Although "playing Uncle Tom" in political and social life was a behavior for censure in the 1910s and 1920s, playing the *role* of Uncle Tom in film or theater was an achievement. After all, Uncle Tom was still the rare serious feature role for a black actor. For this reason, when *The Pittsburgh Courier* looked back at the life of the champion boxer Peter Jackson in 1927, among the highlighted accomplishments was his performance in the role of Uncle Tom in an 1893 production (see figure 6.1)[34]

Universal's *Uncle Tom's Cabin* was also a particularly exciting development for the race because in addition to the role of Uncle Tom and possibly that of Topsy as well, the film's director, Harry Pollard, planned to hire black extras.[35] *The Plain Dealer* approvingly reported that Mildred Boyd, the recent winner of a "Bathing Beauty" contest, was selected "to dance and play one of the important slave girls of the St. Clair household."[36] To be sure, the role of a dancing slave girl might not have been one that Mildred Boyd would have designed for her cinematic debut if left to her own devices, any more than Stepin Fetchit necessarily dreamed of playing a series of comic buffoons. Yet as long as the jobs for black actors were so few and far between, it seemed more important to cheer achievements than to critique the particularities of film roles. Even when their films implicitly reinforced a racial hierarchy, black stars who found commercial success in stereotypical roles often inspired pride in the black community.[37] Such roles were part of the uneven process of integrating Hollywood, a process that remains far from complete today.

The disparity between the achievement of playing the character of Uncle Tom and the opprobrium of being an "Uncle Tom Negro" was not lost on the film's commentators. Once production wrapped, *The Afro-American's* Rodney Ayers triumphantly heralded Lowe's performance as a "credit to the Negro

Figure 6.1. Peter Jackson as Uncle Tom in Chas. E. Davies' *Uncle Tom's Cabin*, ca. 1893. George C. Howard *Uncle Tom's Cabin* Collection, Harry Ransom Center, University of Texas at Austin.

race" and suggested that his Uncle Tom was in line with Stowe's character and not the contemporary meaning of the term. Lowe's interpretation of Uncle Tom, Ayers wrote, was "a Black Christ on earth, suffering not because he was a coward but because he feared no man or any physical suffering he could inflict. As played by Mr. Lowe, Tom's one ambition is to help his fellow slave and master, and he makes 'Tom' a feelingly sympathetic person." Ayers' description of the nobility of Tom's suffering admitted a meaningful difference between the consequences of the character on the screen and of the Uncle Tom type of leadership in everyday life, where sympathy was no longer adequate. Nevertheless, he was optimistic that the public release of the film would give "a new meaning" to "the phrase 'Uncle Tom Negro.'"[38] The following week, the paper featured a large photograph of Lowe, headlined "Portrays Uncle Tom."

To be sure, Ayers' prediction that Lowe would drain the phrase "Uncle Tom Negro" of its negative implications was, like much of the black press' film criticism during the era, naively optimistic. But in 1927 the production of Universal's new *Uncle Tom's Cabin* upset conservative white Southerners far more than it did anyone else. Southern antagonism to Universal's film began during production on location in the South, as director Harry Pollard and the cast and crew spent several weeks on a Mississippi riverboat traveling from Memphis to Natchez.[39] They soon met challenges from white conservatives, who tried to prevent the production from proceeding because they worried that the film would too closely follow Stowe's allegedly "distorted" portrayal of slavery.[40] In the fall of 1926, the General Nathan Bedford Forrest Chapter of the United Daughters of the Confederacy, named after the confederate general who served as the Ku Klux Klan's first Grand Wizard, unanimously protested the filming of scenes in Memphis and along the Mississippi River.[41] Writing to *Los Angeles Times* columnist Grace Kingsley, Universal publicity representative Sam Jacobsen reported that "Memphis seemed to be doing all in its power to put the banshee on us."[42] To some extent, that was to be expected. Beyond the inherently controversial status of *Uncle Tom's Cabin*, a work that Southerners had been vigorously protesting for seventy-five years, the choice to cast a black actor in the role of Uncle Tom was a risky one for any studio hoping to market its films in the South. Under Jim Crow, whites rejected integration on movie screens just as much as in movie theaters. As Universal acknowledged, "the use of colored players in these roles may not be received with sympathy or enthusiasm in certain sections of the country."[43]

Even so, protests of the Universal film differed from previous action against stage and screen adaptations because some protesters were open to amending the film rather than summarily banning it. When Pollard's team began to set up filming in Natchez, Mississippi, the white Association of Commerce wrote to Universal that they would object to the film if it followed Stowe's novel fully. However, if production would "remove all objectionable features from the film, such as brutality towards the Negro, Natchez would welcome the cameraman with open arms."[44] *Uncle Tom's Cabin* could be tolerated as long as it was modified to fit the romantic vision of the antebellum South that had come to dominate American culture. Long-held white fears that acknowledging the cruelty of slavery would somehow harm white interests in the region made this revisionist narrative of slavery seem necessary.

Universal took Southern antagonism to *Uncle Tom's Cabin* seriously because it, like other big studios, believed that Southern movie ticket sales made the difference between a profitable film and a financial failure.[45] Whether or not this assumption was correct, it encouraged studios to make special efforts to avoid offending the South—or at least the white South. Each major studio regularly consulted "Southern white counselors" charged with evaluating the salability of proposed film treatments in the Southern market.[46] Under Hollywood's unofficial "industry policy," studios submitted prospective film treatments to the motion picture industry's Production Code Administration not only for guidance about the Code's moral and religious rules but also to vet scripts for potential problems with the representation of racial, ethnic, regional, and professional groups.[47] Because studios did not want to offend white Southerners, this industry policy had a profound impact on the political messages of films, the casting of black actors, and the range of roles envisioned for them. While groups from journalists to Italians had their own Hollywood liaisons beginning in the 1920s, there was no such formal advocacy group for black Americans until the 1940s.

In the case of Universal's *Uncle Tom's Cabin*, Pollard had assured protesting white Atlantans that his Virginia and Kentucky heritage meant that the "grand old south will lose no glamour or prestige at my hands."[48] Nevertheless, Universal's in-house Southern consultant, Lamar Trotti, predicted that many white Southerners would respond poorly to the film. So when an early cut was ready, the studio set up focus groups of white Southerners to help guide the editing process.[49] An opening sequence set in 1840, in which a young Cassy is purchased by Legree at the New Orleans slave market and her infant daughter Eliza is torn from her arms and sold to Mr. and Mrs. Shelby, prompted enough opposition that Universal cut this scene and replaced it with one that put the North and the South in the same moral position.[50] Now the film began with an image of Robert E. Lee looking dignified in his Confederate uniform. The image was soon transposed with text indicating that neither the North nor the South supported slavery: "There are few, I believe, in this enlightened age who will not acknowledge that slavery as an institution is a moral and political evil. —Robert E. Lee, Dec. 27, 1856." Following this unifying claim, the film's first scenes depict a joyous plantation celebration of the wedding of Eliza and George Harris. (Blacks and whites celebrate separately.) An intertitle identifying the plantation owners as Mr. and Mrs. Shelby, "whose gentle rule of the slaves was typical of the South," implies that slavery was a pleasant institution for all.[51]

Despite this change, Universal's *Uncle Tom's Cabin* did not satisfy conservative whites on either side of the Mason-Dixon Line. The cuts still left intact a crucial element of offense to the white South: the film's integration of the Civil War. Previous adaptations, such as those from 1903 and 1914, gesture toward the Civil War with concluding montages of images related to the war. Pollard's *Uncle Tom's Cabin*, however, weaves the war into the plot. In doing so, it makes what was at the time a controversial suggestion: that Emancipation was central to the war. When Uncle Tom is sold to Simon Legree, Pollard's cinematography cuts between scenes of Legree's rising violence and depravity toward Tom, Eliza, and Cassy and of Sherman's troops moving through Georgia. As this "stream of blue" comes to save the day, white bystanders are terrified and black Southerners are jubilant. To be sure, this exciting, tension-filled cinematic device was likely added in order to show off what film could do that the theater could not. But in switching back and forth, the film links the defeat of its villain with the victory of the Union army, making the Confederates into bad guys by default. This was not a story that could survive the South.

Slavery on the Silver Screen

After *Uncle Tom's Cabin* premiered in New York City in November of 1927, *The Pittsburgh Courier*'s Floyd Calvin wrote a review suggesting that those who hated D. W. Griffith's *Birth of a Nation* should "flock" to see Universal's *Uncle Tom's Cabin* because the film's producer, Carl Laemmle, "seems to have tried to take just the opposite view of the Negro that Griffith took. Where Griffith's film inspired the rankest kind of race hate, the Laemmle film pictures the Negro being taken advantage of by a stronger race that is cowardly in its strength."[52] Indeed, with the devoutly Christian Tom at its center, Universal's adaptation inverted *Birth of a Nation*'s mythology of black assaults on white victims.[53] For Harriette Underhill of the *New York Herald Tribune*, the vivid portrayal of Uncle Tom's violent death at the hands of Legree crystallized slavery's cruelty in a way that simply knowing the facts did not.[54] Yet portraying slavery on the silver screen was an inherently risky business. Most everyone in the race could agree that Griffith's tale of racial strife during the Reconstruction era was a dangerous attack on black character, one that encouraged ongoing racial prejudice and violence. But *Uncle Tom's Cabin* was a trickier case, because it portrayed a history that was both inspiring and humiliating. Some argued that the nation, and particularly the South, needed to come to terms with its unjust history; sweeping the inhumanity of American slavery under the rug would only encourage continuing injustices. Mary Church Terrell, for example, continued her lifelong support of *Uncle Tom's Cabin* by praising Pollard's film for representing slavery "as it actually was" and offering a valuable "lesson in the history of the United States which everybody—North, South, East and West—should learn."[55] Moreover, Terrell argued that young people's exposure to the history portrayed in the film could be effective in contemporary efforts against lynching and other racial injustices.

Others, however, saw disadvantages to vividly reconstructing this history. *Uncle Tom's Cabin*, and especially the scenes of Legree's violence against Uncle Tom, asked black audiences to watch the horrors of slavery writ large on the big screen. It forced them to confront an inherent tension between a desire for the nation to face the true injustices of slavery and a fear that such portrayals would negatively impact perceptions of the race. Under slavery, the survival of the race relied on the millions who found a way to preserve a sense of agency and meaning despite the many horrific injustices of an enslaved life.[56] Many endured because of deep Christian faith that subordinated earthly justice to eternal grace. While this faithful endurance was not a model that most twentieth-century people wanted to emulate, neither was it one that could be denigrated without disrespecting the sacrifices made by one's ancestors.

Floyd Calvin's *Pittsburgh Courier* review of the film balanced praise for Lowe's performance with concern about the effects of seeing a black man abused on film. According to Calvin, the film had "many lessons to teach the thoughtful person."[57] Seeing the forbearance of the slave characters as they headed down the river and the "eternal hope" in Tom's eyes in the film's final scenes inspired Calvin to help the Negro people. Nevertheless, he thought that the film was "humiliating for the colored spectator" because seeing one's race mistreated on film provoked shame, no matter whether one was black or white.[58] Such feelings could not help but influence responses to the Uncle Tom character.[59] Indeed, in 1925 William Pickens had suggested that the representation of slavery on the stage had something to do with the transformation of Stowe's "real 'Uncle Tom'" character into the derogatory "'Uncle Tom' Negro."[60] Pickens noted that the character, who was whipped to death because he refused to do any violence to "an unfortunate woman of his group," was "quite the opposite" of "the lick-spittle, belly-crawling Negroes [often called] "'Uncle Tom' Negroes": "There is no greater and cleaner hero than he who gives his life in defense of the weak and anticipates no glory in so doing. That was the real 'Uncle Tom.'"[61] Despite the character's spiritual nobility, however, Pickens believed that the very fact that Uncle Tom was whipped over and over again—"driven across the stage in a thousand cheap dramatizations, and beaten by the whip of 'Legree' and his cowardly slave minions"—compelled a psychological urge in the black viewer to reject him. In "a curious bit of psychology," he reflected, Uncle Tom's forced subjection to cruelty made black audiences regard him with scorn. It was as if, in being the repeated victim of racial violence, the character became complicit with it.

This ambivalence about representing the violence of slavery applied to James B. Lowe's experience filming the role of Uncle Tom in the South, where locals ultimately provided services to the cast and crew and even took small roles in the film. As Lowe recollected to *The Chicago Defender*, filming on the Mississippi River brought him "opportunities to come in contact with the best and worst of the white race" as well as connection to "his own race in its darkest stage"—a comment that elided the difference between the enslaved and their free descendants.[62] Working alongside white Southerners to film a story that "condemns the South more than any single publication before or since slavery" and using white men and women who had lived in and defended Dixie for generations was an odd experience.[63] It seemed possible that the participating whites wanted to make up for former error by "helping to broadcast the true facts." The more likely scenario, though, was that Southern whites joined the production "in order to live again, if for a few days only, the period they loved so well—maybe they wanted to lash slaves again, and to hear the wails, and weepings again. Maybe they wanted to imagine that their old life had returned." These two possibilities point to the ambiguous implications of any cultural production that tried to be true to the horrors of slavery. Representing the violence of slavery in graphic detail could set the record straight at a time when a revisionist memory was invoked to justify continued racial oppression. But it could also become a way for disempowered whites to relive the sadistic pleasure of that violence.

When Calvin observed that Universal's *Uncle Tom's Cabin* showed the Negro "to splendid advantage, if a slave can be shown to advantage," the conditional statement reflected his concern that there might be no advantageous way to represent slaves. Even as he praised James Lowe's "superb" acting in the Uncle Tom role as the film's "great attraction," he was ambivalent about the character as a figure in the contemporary moment: "His humility makes you want to give him a swift kick at times," he wrote, "but when you reflect he is portraying a former condition you forget it."[64] This was the difference between the Old Negro character in the past and in the present. The humble posture was aggravating from a twentieth-century perspective but it made sense to Calvin in the context of slavery, when religious faith brought many through their darkest hours. Out of this ambivalence about the film's combination of inspiration and humiliation, what finally made the experience for Calvin was the knowledge that James B. Lowe was making five hundred dollars a week for his acting. Even if a character was not ideal, the fact that a black actor was earning a hefty paycheck in one of the most expensive films ever made was a victory for the race.

Despite this ambivalence about depicting slavery on the silver screen, some black Americans took a more protective view of Universal's *Uncle Tom's Cabin* as the film continued to encounter significant opposition from white conservatives in the South despite additional cuts. Universal released *Uncle Tom's Cabin* into a culture that was reluctant to depict the violence of slavery for many reasons, some of them in opposition with each other. For some Southerners, it was still vitally important that Americans believe that Stowe's novel greatly exaggerated the cruelty of slavery. They maintained that the scenes in which Legree beats Uncle Tom were historically inaccurate, making the film a libel on the South and its history. In a letter to the editor of *The Chicago Tribune*, a Kentuckian named Emmet V. Mittlebeeler encouraged readers to "forget *Uncle Tom's Cabin*" because it "cost the lives of the best and bravest men in the country" and "set back the north by ten years and the south by fifty."[65] These scenes of violence were also problematic for some whites North of the Mason-Dixon Line, who objected that the violence was not "in good taste" and wondered why it was necessary to bring up the old wounds.[66] When the film premiered at the Central Theatre in New York in November 1927, the director of the New York Board of Censors, James Wingate, wrote to producer Carl Laemmle calling for cuts to the film's unusually graphic violence, especially in the scenes between Legree and Tom. Wingate's communication with Laemmle, part of a local and state censorship system in place during the studio era, indicates the extent to which the memory of slavery was already sanitized in the North. According to Wingate, the first six reels of the film were wonderful, but the last seven, which take place primarily on Legree's plantation, were excessive. Indeed, a reviewer for *Billboard* magazine found that the depiction of Legree and his two helpmates whipping Tom to death was "so realistic, in fact, that this sequence took on an aspect of pathos and horror never before equaled" in film.[67] Wingate reported that after the screening audience members expressed horror at seeing the mistreatment of slaves: "It was so horrible I couldn't look at it," one said, while another confessed, "I kept saying to myself it wasn't so."[68] Audience members had also commented that the film was unnecessarily harsh in its depiction of the South. Comments such as "Why open the old sores?" and "Why give offense to Southern people?" indicated discomfort not simply with the film's violence but also with its presentation of history.[69]

In addition to calling for the film to show more of "the delightful character of the Southern people," Wingate demanded the reduction of Legree's cruelty toward Tom: "Eliminate scene of Legree kicking Tom after knocking him down"; "Eliminate views of Legree's face with blood streaming down it."[70] While it was too late for Universal to film entirely new scenes, it appears that the studio consented to Wingate's suggested cuts, as studios often did when censors objected to violence.[71] Despite these cuts and others added in anticipation of Southern objections, however, Pollard's film met resistance in the South. After Kentucky's Uncle Tom's Cabin Law prevented the studio from releasing the film in that state, the first Southern showing took place on April 26, 1928, Confederate Memorial Day, at a Universal-owned theater in St. Augustine, Florida. Edited to leave out all scenes of Sherman's March, the picture played without incident.[72] The case was different, however, in Atlanta, a city that had a longstanding tradition of banning dramatic adaptations of *Uncle Tom's Cabin*. One Atlanta resident, Sam W. Small, claimed that he knew from "abundant testimonies at first hand that most of those in the north who read the book or see a 'Tom show,' as they are called, get an ineffaceable conviction that southern people are heartless, brutal and un-Christian."[73] In August, a preview of the film drew an audience of 1,100 people—the number suggests that curiosity overcame principle—but also demands that the mayor ban it because the "sensibilities" of local white citizens were "outraged."[74] After a meeting between Atlanta's mayor, a Universal representative, and members of the local motion picture review board, the mayor ordered all scheduled showings of the film to be canceled and vowed to prevent its booking in the future, explaining that he was doing so "for fear racial prejudice might be stirred up."[75] Universal's film now met the same fate as the widely banned footage of the black boxer Jack Johnson's 1910 win over the white Jim Jeffries, which many white Americans worried would upset the racial hierarchy. Indeed, as a cover of *Puck* magazine warned before the fight, a Johnson victory could make Uncle Tom knock down Simon Legree (see figure 6.2).

This opposition came as no surprise to the black community. A writer for *The Pittsburgh Courier* recalled that when the film came out, "it was the expressed opinion of almost every Negro who saw it that few, if any, Southern communities would permit the film to be shown in their local

theaters."[76] After all, even though Pollard "pretty thoroughly sugar-coated" the story, "it was impossible to film it without showing the horrors of chattel slavery and the victorious Union Army putting an end to it. . . . Nothing can be shown in the South, especially in such a Confederate state as Georgia, that will cast any reflection on Southern chivalry and honor of the white variety."[77] Those who wanted to ban *Uncle Tom's Cabin* were fervently attached to a totalizing conception of "Southern chivalry and honor" that could no more acknowledge slavery's violence than it could positively envision a society in which blacks and whites had equal rights. Even if Universal's adaptation added a rosy tint to Stowe's anti-slavery story, the film regained some of its progressive symbolism to black Americans by the very fact that ex-Confederates hated it. When Birmingham, Alabama, banned the film, *The Defender* and *The Afro-American* pointed out that, in a state with "hundreds of Ku Klux Klan lynchings and whippings to its credit," the real concern about the film came from the "ruling class of business men and white planters [who] fear that it would encourage rebellions on the part of the innumerable workers alleged to be held in peonage and serfdom in this state."[78] The anti-slavery politics of *Uncle Tom's Cabin* remained dangerously revolutionary in Jim Crow Alabama.

Black responses to these protests differed from earlier defenses of *Uncle Tom's Cabin* on stage and screen because they were less about the inherent value of *Uncle Tom's Cabin* than about the implications of Southern resistance to a story that they did not think should still be considered radical. To *The Chicago Defender*, the fact that Georgia banned *Uncle Tom's Cabin* while still allowing D. W. Griffith's *Birth of a Nation* to play was "a fine illustration of why the 13th, 14th and 15th amendments are not enforced, and why we can expect no justice in the South."[79] A region that was so adamantly opposed to admitting the truth about slavery had little chance of abolishing contemporary injustices such as peonage and the convict lease system. Even white Northern newspapers understood that these white Southern protests indicated a broader social and cultural problem. Reporting on the Atlanta protests, *The Boston Daily Globe* reflected that this "attitude toward Uncle Tom indicates that the South resists change more steadfastly than most people realize."[80]

However, the film became less appealing to black audiences when Southern objections moved Universal to make further cuts to the film; these included deleting more of the film's "'cruelty' footage" of Legree beating Tom, adding a prologue title card explaining that such cruelties "were not the usual thing in the South of pre-war days," replacing "Civil War" with "War between the States," and making Simon Legree a Yankee, an edit that was in accordance with the novel but bucked the stage tradition of giving him a Southern accent.[81] When the film headed to Dallas, initial protests by local members of the United Sons and Daughters of the Confederacy were withdrawn after a delegation saw a private showing of the amended film. Exhibitors in Montgomery, Alabama, and Nashville, Tennessee, advertised the film as a departure from "anything you have heard—thought—or seen—of any form of production of *Uncle Tom's Cabin*" and claimed it for the mythology of "the glorious days of the Old South."[82] The amendments were thorough enough that some black Americans concluded that the film was "a cheap travesty on the original."[83] Even so, amendments to the film did not uniformly smooth its entrance into all parts of the South. In the fall of 1928, the Augusta chapter of the UDC passed a resolution against *Uncle Tom's Cabin* and requested that authorities forbid it from showing in local theaters.[84] In the following months, other women's groups in Florida and Georgia also successfully prevented the film from showing.[85]

Southern efforts to ban the film provoked a debate in the black press about the potential consequences of portraying slavery in popular culture. William N. Jones argued in *The Afro-American* that if the race wanted the South to cease its racial antipathy, then it also needed to relegate to the past "anything which would preserve hatreds in ourselves"; the memory of slavery, even as shown in the amended *Uncle Tom's Cabin*, was one such thing.[86] *The Defender*'s J. Ernest Webb, who had observed packed houses for the film in Indianapolis' Indiana theater, was pleased with the film as a human interest story but not with its subject matter, which he was sure could not help but awaken "sleeping race hatred, as no real Race man can view the right reels of 'Uncle Tom's Cabin' and still feel like loving his white neighbor."[87]

Some also worried that portraying slavery, truthfully or not, would impede the race's progress in the contemporary moment. After *The Chicago Defender* criticized the successful banning of *Uncle Tom's Cabin* in Atlanta, a New Yorker named Thomas Cauldwell wrote a letter to the editor arguing that the ban was in fact a good thing. After all, reminding white people of the race's former servitude might naturalize the old order. "The most detrimental and obstructive piece of legislation," Cauldwell wrote, "is no more harmful to our group than those moving pictures that remind the American people of the former condition of servitude of a people now struggling to be recognized as full American citizens."[88] But such a perspective overlooked the fact that the South was still perpetuating slavery under another name through peonage and the convict lease system. Responding to Cauldwell's letter, O'Dell Hatchett urged *The Defender*'s readers to recognize the importance of facing both the good and the bad in the nation's past. "Every nation makes its own history," he reasoned. "America made hers; if she made a mess of it, then let the world know it."[89] To Hatchett, *Uncle Tom's Cabin* reflected poorly only on whites.

The question of whether or not to portray the cruelty of slavery was particularly complex when it came to mixed-race audiences. As James Weldon Johnson reflected in his 1928 essay "The Dilemma of the Negro Author," black audiences had markedly different criteria for what could be shown to white and black audiences.[90] A white gaze could transform a comic performance into a dangerous one. Likewise, showing the brutality of slavery to a black audience was less concerning than doing the same before whites. For that reason, productions of *Uncle Tom's Cabin* put on by black theater groups garnered praise, not protest. For example, in the spring of 1929, a Pittsburgh theater group called the Emco Art Players put on a production of *Uncle Tom's Cabin* in several area churches. In a review, *The Pittsburgh Courier* praised the heart-felt spirituals performed in the opening scene, suggesting that only the descendants of slaves could render these songs so movingly. The standout actor in the production was the melodious Clarence Blakey as Uncle Tom, who "radiated the spirit of the sincere Christian who is striving to save his fellowmen."[91] Perhaps one felt freer to be moved by Uncle Tom's Christian devotion when it was not depicted in front of whites.

Ultimately, concerns about the effects of representing slavery prompted the first organized protest of *Uncle Tom's Cabin* by black Americans. During the summer of 1929, residents of Gary, Indiana, protested the presentation of the Universal *Uncle Tom's Cabin* at the Roosevelt Theatre, a "mixed house" owned and operated by whites. Those protesting did not mention the film's

racially stereotyped characters. Indeed, the particular character traits of
Uncle Tom and the other black characters did not come up. According to
The Afro-American, what moved them to protest were the same scenes that
had most angered whites throughout decades of Southern protests against
the stage and film adaptations: "the scenes depicting slavery in the South
in its most brutal form, and the selling of slaves from the auction block."[92]
While conservative whites took issue with the accuracy of these scenes, some
blacks posited that the represented mistreatment might become normalized.
Nevertheless, a black protest against *Uncle Tom's Cabin* was unusual enough
that when the story reached *The Chicago Defender* a few weeks later, the facts
changed: now the protesters were said to be white.[93] After all, *The Defender*
had criticized the cancellation of a student performance of *Uncle Tom's Cabin*
in the Philippines just a few months before.[94] It was hard to imagine that the
same work could be protested from such opposing perspectives.

Servants, Maids, and Slaves

If Universal's *Uncle Tom's Cabin* opened the door to feature roles for black
actors, it was the advent of sound that truly expanded opportunities for the
race in Hollywood. "Up to the introduction of the 'talkies,'" wrote Harlem
social commentator Geraldyn Dismond in a 1929 article for *Close-Up*, "*Uncle
Tom's Cabin* was the outstanding achievement of the Negro in the movie
world."[95] Indeed, according to a 1929 report from the Motion Picture Research Council's National Committee on Social Values, black performers
appeared in American film "only to create a laugh on the screen, excepting
for *Uncle Tom's Cabin*."[96] As American cinema adjusted to the opportunities and challenges of pairing moving images with sound—those who were
extraordinary in silent films sometimes fell flat when they spoke—some in
Hollywood concluded that the "rich resonance" of black voices recorded
more authentically than white ones.[97] In 1929, both Fox and MGM released
films with all-black casts, *Hearts in Dixie* and *Hallelujah!*, respectively.[98] According to film critic Robert Benchley, *Hearts in Dixie* made the first real
case for the future of talkies. "In the Negro," he wrote in *Opportunity* magazine, "the sound picture has found its ideal protagonist."[99] In the sound era,
studios became less likely to use white actors in blackface to play black char-

acters and more likely to cast "real blacks with black voices," giving expanded screen time to black actors.[100]

1929 was also, of course, the year of the stock market crash that brought on the Great Depression. As the economy soured and left millions unemployed, American film's new interest in black characters met a cultural climate in which the movie theater took an increasingly important role. To meet the needs of struggling Americans during the Depression, Hollywood embraced an escapist sensibility. Black servant and slave characters quickly became essential to this trend.[101] The plantation melodrama, which depicted the plantation as "a place of leisure of master as well as slave," became a major film genre; Ed Guerrero counts seventy-five features about the South between 1929 and 1941, including, of course, the blockbuster *Gone with the Wind* (1939).[102] For about a quarter, struggling Americans—or at least those who were white—could enter a darkened theater and spend a few hours with a fantasy of a gracious agrarian past in which all whites were wealthy and all blacks were house servants who affectionately served their masters.[103]

In creating more roles for black characters, Hollywood's escapist turn produced both challenges and opportunities for black actors. To be sure, the roles were socially circumscribed. *Hearts in Dixie*, for example, repeated many of the literary and stage stereotypes of the Negro, from Clarence Muse's submissive "Old Negro" patriarch to Stepin Fetchit's lazy buffoon, and it was set in a supposedly contemporary South that looked suspiciously like the Old South.[104] Yet black characters in 1930s films were often more humanized and complex than their precursors: "servants or foils who were faithful *and* flippant, mannered *and* casual, distant *and* familiar."[105] Moreover, with the popularity of these characters, a small group of black actors became successful in Hollywood, among them Stepin Fetchit, Eddie Anderson, Louise Beavers, Bill Robinson, Hattie McDaniel, and Clarence Muse. Many black Americans felt pride in this success and believed it boded well for the progress of the race.[106] Dismond, for one, suggested that talkies starring Negroes were already combating white prejudices and stimulating "race consciousness and self-respect" in the black community; through such films, black actors could "easily become a potent factor in our struggle for better race relations."[107] Nevertheless, she acknowledged the importance of "proper direction and sympathetic treatment." While black stars held great potential for influencing American race relations, their success did not automatically translate into positive influence. As a small group of black celebrities established itself in Hollywood, the stage was set for a more critical perspective on American film's racial patterns, and especially "Uncle Tom roles."

Uncle Tom's Rebellion

Hollywood became an increasingly politicized space for black activists during the 1930s and 1940s. With studios casting black performers in feature roles, the black press shifted its attention away from the slowing output of "race movies" made by and for the black community in favor of reporting on—and critiquing—opportunities for black performers in Hollywood studio films.[108] With the exception of *Birth of a Nation*, film was not a significant arena for civil rights activism during the silent film era. In the early 1930s, the smattering of black protests against films were limited to the use of racially offensive language, and particularly the N-word.[109] However, developing social scientific research on the social and psychological impact of film broadened the conversation. With greater awareness of the complex ways that racial patterns in film and radio contributed to the continuing denial of rights to black people in America, an increasingly sophisticated critique of "Uncle Tom roles" in film developed.

As with the earlier political transformation of "Uncle Tom," censure of Uncle Tom roles—which pictured black people as socially, intellectually, or morally inferior to whites—required the formation of a critical mass of successful individuals. In film, however, developments in the emerging social scientific disciplines of psychology and sociology played a significant role in the articulation of this critique. As moving pictures became an increasingly common part of American society, neighborhood social workers began to investigate their effects.[110] Psychologists, too, began to give serious consideration to film, suggesting that the unique vividness of the film medium gave it extra influence over audiences. "The more vividly the impressions force themselves on the mind," argued Hugo Munsterberg in *The Photoplay: A Psychological Study* (1916), "the more easily must they become starting points for imitation and other motor responses."[111] In 1933, the Payne Fund sponsored a twelve-book series of studies on the influence of motion pictures on children and youth, among them Herbert Blumer's *Movies and Conduct* and W. W. Charter's *Motion Pictures and Youth: A Summary*. What separated this research from earlier concerns about the effects of various forms of entertainment on youth was its sophisticated account of the interaction between a movie and its viewer. Where earlier critics suggested that movies were dangerous because they might inspire imitation, social scientists of the 1920s and 1930s showed their more subtle influence on how young people saw the world.

Research on film's psychological effects relied on the social scientific category of stereotype, a category introduced to American culture by Walter Lippmann in his influential *Public Opinion* (1922). Of course, long before the 1920s, "stereotype," a nineteenth-century printing technology based on reusable molds, became a figurative term either for something copied many times or for one of the copies.[112] And in the twentieth century, when elites used the term to criticize the banality of commonplace ideas, it gained a derogatory valence. But Lippmann gave the stereotype a new sociological meaning, one that has become so commonplace that it's hard to imagine that people ever thought differently.[113] And it paved the way for an understanding of the broad potential impact of black characters and images that were not exaggerated enough to be caricatures but were, it seemed, damaging to the race nevertheless. Before Lippmann's intervention, most psychologists and laypeople believed that human beings made choices on the basis of either rational thought or emotion. Rational thought came from knowledge and experience of the world (nurture), while emotion came from instinct (nature). Lippmann's idea was that human beings make choices in response not to the rational facts about who and what they encounter, but rather to their *perceptions* of those facts, perceptions shaped by the culture around them. For example, when a person witnessed a sunset in real life, what she really saw was mediated by all the images of sunsets she'd already seen. Lippmann called such culturally determined perceptions "stereotypes." And he argued that stereotypes were absolutely necessary to human function because the modern world was too complex for anyone to perceive all of the facts rationally. "Instead," he wrote, "we notice a trait which marks a well known type, and fill in the rest of the picture by means of the stereotypes we carry about in our heads."[114] Of course, this kind of perceptual process likely existed long before modernity. But there is a difference, as Ruth Amossy suggests, between holding a collective view (of a foreign group, for example) and recognizing that such views are not strictly rational. "That inherited views and group categorization should be regarded as misleading *a priori*," Amossy observes, "was by no means obvious to past centuries."[115]

Lippmann's conceptualization of stereotype encouraged social scientists to transition from a consensus that racial views were the rational result of a "natural" hierarchy of races to an understanding of "'race prejudice' as a fundamentally irrational attitude."[116] In their pioneering research, social psychologists Daniel Katz and Kenneth Braly surveyed views of racial and national groups and concluded that attitudes towards them were "stereotypes of our cultural pattern and are not based upon . . . any genuine qualities" of a group.[117] Having defined race prejudice as the result of irrational stereotypes, researchers began to identify these stereotypes and track their formation and consequences within society, especially in children.[118] Beginning with the now-classic research of Bruno Lasker in *Race Attitudes in Children* (1929), sociologists found that motion pictures were a major source for children's racial attitudes.[119]

With increasing scientific evidence of the harmful effects of film, the black press became less inclined to offer automatic approval to film performances by black actors. During the mid-1930s, contributors to black periodicals expressed concern that certain kinds of black screen images caused harmful racial attitudes in white Americans, international movie audiences, and even the race itself. Black film celebrities found themselves on the front lines of racial activism whether they wanted to be or not. In a remarkably penetrating essay on American film's racial patterns, published in *The Crisis* in 1934, the lawyer and activist Loren Miller reflected that there were "[u]nwritten, but iron clad rules in the movie industry" that made white characters "overlords" and relegated Negroes to "servant parts in which they are either buffoons or ubiquitous Uncle Toms," either comic or subservient.[120] Such roles were harmful not simply because they suggested that all black people were social inferiors but also because they normalized unequal power relations in the minds of both races. Moreover, Miller observed, if the neighborhood movie theater was the place where white Americans "confirm[ed] their beliefs about Negroes," it was also where "Negroes themselves fortif[ied] their inferiority complexes by seeing themselves always cast as the underdog to be laughed at or despised."[121] Repeated exposure to

American film's pattern of presenting black characters as comic, submissive, or savage conditioned black film audiences to, for example, cheer when a film's invariably blonde heroine got rescued from "the clutches of 'savage' Africans," thus unconsciously celebrating the triumph of "natural white virtue" over "black vice."[122] Miller believed that the race could challenge the damage done by the racial patterns of Hollywood films in two ways. For one, black filmmakers could produce films with better racial representations. With the exception of Oscar Micheaux, he observed, black moviemakers too closely mimicked white films, resulting in stories that may have avoided certain representational pitfalls but were no truer to black life than white studio films. After all, how many black Americans lived in mansions with butlers at their beck and call? Miller had greater hopes for the second option: in lieu of the puff pieces that usually filled their pages, black periodicals could engage in a robust critique of film and its implications for black life and rights. From there, the community could launch protests.

Whether or not spurred by Miller's suggestion that the race should "demand pictures that reflect their own lives and aspirations," the black press did indeed take a more critical approach to film and radio criticism in the following years, calling attention to the ways that Hollywood's circumscribed black roles impeded the race's progress.[123] Just as black political rhetoric used the figure of Uncle Tom to police acceptable forms of political representation, now activists invoked the Uncle Tom type of role to debate how the race should be depicted on film. "Why is it that our best colored actors only have parts as butlers or maids in white films?" asked John Tidwell of Norfolk, Virginia, in a 1936 letter to the editor of *The Afro-American*. He called for pictures that showed "the better class of our race instead of the Uncle Tom type."[124]

As the critique of black images in Hollywood developed, the category of "Uncle Tom roles" expanded from slave to servant to any part deemed contrary to the progress of the race. Some parts considered Uncle Tom roles, such as Bill Robinson's Uncle Billy in *The Littlest Rebel* (1935) and Hattie McDaniels' mammy in *Gone with the Wind* (1939), quite literally resurrected the old plantation days, while others transferred the power dynamic of slavery to modern contexts. Still other Uncle Tom roles were unrespectable types such as zoot-suited crap-shooters. A good year for black entertainment meant that Hollywood films were getting "away from the old 'Uncle Tom' parts."[125] Of course, black audiences were not unanimous about what counted as an "Uncle Tom" part, especially given the obviously limited roles available to black actors in Hollywood. For example, some derided Robinson for his work in the Shirley Temple vehicles *The Littlest Rebel* and *The Little Colonel* (1935) because they capitulated to Southern prejudices. "Both the movies and the radio are still the slaves of Dixie and its asinine racial prejudices, bowing to the crack of the Southland's whip like Uncle Tom before the lash of Simon Legree," wrote *The Afro-American's* Ralph Matthews.[126] Yet Robinson's professional success was novel enough that some nevertheless saw such roles positively. Defending Robinson in a letter to the editor, Rienzi B. Lemus pointed out that until recently *The Afro-American* had been complaining about producers hiring white actors who blacked up instead of casting black actors.[127] Indeed, not long before, Matthews himself had complained about stage productions of *Uncle Tom's Cabin* that used blackface instead of black actors.[128]

The trouble with Uncle Tom roles went beyond the ideas they would spread to whites. Such images could also damage black self-image, especially among impressionable children. In a 1934 open letter, a *Defender* reader named Helena Wilson recounted bringing two young boys "not yet quite old enough to understand race prejudice" to see the prison film *The Last Mile* (1932). She was disgusted by the film's "false and vicious characterization" of the race, especially in the form of an "'imbecile Negro' [who] remarks that his place in heaven is sure to be near the garbage pail"—prompting much laughter from the whites in the audience.[129] When the boys asked her "if it were really true that colored people would have to live in heaven near the garbage pail," Wilson was struck by how greatly film could impair racial pride. Describing *The Last Mile's* submissive character as "what enlightened members of my group term an Uncle Tom," she argued that, although such figures had once existed, the "period of humble, passive submission on the part of all Negroes has passed. . . . [T]hat specie of humanity known as the Uncle Tom Negro is rapidly being retired to the limbo of oblivion, and our only observation of his passing is, Father forgive him for he knew not what he was doing."[130] Even if Uncle Toms had once been an understandable element of the black community, they had no place in contemporary culture. Such characters reinforced slavery-era power dynamics and dissuaded black children from realizing their equality.

Frustration with the racial representations of popular performance prompted rejection of the Uncle Tom character type. During the early 1930s, black activism in Hollywood was for the most part limited to discussion within the black press, with some action directed against use of the N-word.[131] NAACP branches began protesting films in the mid-1930s, and toward the end of the decade, white Southerners' efforts to ban films that displayed "social equality" helped shift activists' attention to the limited scope of black film roles and Hollywood's reproductions of antebellum power dynamics.[132]

At first, this spirit of resistance found playful expression on the stage through satirical works by Langston Hughes and Duke Ellington in which the figure of Uncle Tom was central. In the late 1930s, Hughes wrote a series of skits satirizing popular white-authored accounts of black American life including *Imitation of Life*, Eugene O'Neill's *Emperor Jones*, and *Uncle Tom's Cabin*. Two or three of these would open performances of his political play *Don't You Want to Be Free?* at the leftist Harlem Suitcase Theatre. Hughes' comic send-up of *Uncle Tom's Cabin*, "Colonel Tom's Cabin" (also known as "Little Eva's End"), playfully challenged American popular culture's romanticized vision of the antebellum South by conjoining the characters of *Uncle Tom's Cabin* with symbols of modern black culture.[133] Upsetting the conventional cinematic coupling of a charmingly naive white child and a loyal black servant-cum-entertainer (often seen with Shirley Temple and Bill Robinson), Hughes' Eva, who has Shirley Temple's blond curls and child's clothing and the stage Topsy's dark skin and adult-sized body, is no angel: "petulant and naughty," she talks back to her father and insults Uncle Tom.[134] Instead of reciting the Bible, she is preoccupied with modern black culture: she sings Ella Fitzgerald's "A-Tisket, A-Tasket," "switches and hops" to "St. Louis Blues," and announces her love of the jazz musician Benny Goodman and Harlem's Cotton Club.

Set in a Southern mansion at a "relative" time, with several characters costumed "in the manner of the old South," "Colonel Tom's Cabin" puts the nostalgic view of the antebellum South into conflict with the liberating effects of jazz and blues.[135] Hughes' skit replaces the sharp-eyed Augustine St. Clare of Stowe's novel with "Mars Sinclair," a Southern sentimentalist who rhapsodizes about "the beautiful South" and its "cotton, mammies, and moonlight" but also ventriloquizes some of Simon Legree's most famous lines. Tom initially appears protective of Little Eva and faithful to Sinclair.

He obediently and quite literally plays the Uncle Tom role: when Sinclair tells Tom that he owns him, "body and soul," Tom gives the usual response, but punctuated by a jazz dance move: "My body may belong to you, Mars Sinclair! (*Switching*) But, oh! My soul!" With its modern twist, this interaction queers what was a sentimental center of the play, making it clear that the faithful slave is merely enacting a role.

"Colonel Tom's Cabin" is not a condemnation of *Uncle Tom's Cabin* as a novel or play. Indeed, several times Hughes praised new plays by comparing them to *Uncle Tom's Cabin*, and he oversaw a 1952 illustrated edition of *Uncle Tom's Cabin* that commended "[t]he love and warmth and humanity that went into its writing."[136] Rather, Hughes' skit defiantly celebrates modern black expression in the face of retrograde cultural images, using the character of Uncle Tom to mark the race's transition to modernity. Uncle Tom rebels against Sinclair's assumption that he is the stereotypical "perfect slave" through music and dance, countering the white man's suggestion that he sing a spiritual by crooning an aria from *Porgy and Bess* and then, following Eva's suggestion, a number from the "St. Louis Blues." (That the former comes from a white composer, George Gershwin, does not seem to be an issue.) This resistance to old musical forms reflects contemporaneous criticism of spirituals, which were sometimes called "'Uncle Tom' songs," for "preserv[ing] the memories of slavery, bring[ing] back to mind the field and fetter, and show[ing] the black man as a simple-minded praying and crooning creature utterly oblivious to the times and manners."[137]

Moreover, Hughes couples Tom's artistic rebellion with a political one. When Sinclair instructs him to "vote my way for my sake," Tom assertively refuses: "No! No! I may chop your cotton and cut your cane, but when I votes, (*to the audience*) I votes for Roosevelt!" Unlike the political Uncle Toms who stay loyal to the Republican Party despite its failure to help the race, this transformed character insists on voting for a Democrat for president. Announcing that "Uncle Tom is Mister Thomas now!" he refuses both the Uncle Tom character and the Uncle Tom behavioral model. Then, bolstered by his defiance, he uses a mask of kindness to do something he says he's "been wantin' to do ever since the Civil War . . . and that is slap Little Eva smack down." After doing so, he exits, "wiping his hands." As Eva bawls loudly, Sinclair calls after him, "You've broken Little Eva's wings." Uncle Tom has not injured or killed her but rather has fractured the angelic wings that tried to raise her above him. Having played the stereotypical role expected of him, Uncle Tom now asserts his own value and independence through jazz and blues. For Hughes, Uncle Tom embodies both restriction and liberation.

Following in Hughes' joyful spirit of rebellion against old performance models, Duke Ellington celebrated the deaths of Stephen Foster and Uncle Tom in his 1941 musical revue *Jump for Joy*, which played in Los Angeles for three months.[138] The insistently "modern and up-to-date" program, "sans any semblance of the plantation or Uncle Tom," took aim at stereotyped media images of the race and the white directors and producers who demanded them of black performers.[139] Ellington believed that every black artist found it challenging to maintain dignity while entertaining an American audience that has been "taught to expect a Negro on stage to clown and 'Uncle Tom,' that is, to enact the role of a servile, yet lovable, inferior."[140] The original script of *Jump For Joy*, Ellington told John Pittman of *People's World*, showed Uncle Tom on his deathbed with "a Hollywood producer on one side of the bed and a Broadway producer on the other side . . . trying to keep him alive by injecting adrenalin in his arms!"[141] Where an earlier African American discourse had presented Uncle Tom as a once-accurate but now outdated portrayal, Ellington saw this role as one enacted by the black performer in order to satisfy the desires of a white audience. Uncle Tom's time had come, but popular culture would not allow him to die a natural death.

Even as Ellington and Hughes challenged the performance conventions of Uncle Tom, both still relied on a history defined by this figure. Langston Hughes' 1941 poem "Epitaph" represents Uncle Tom as an ancestor whose methods are no longer valuable:

Uncle Tom,
When he was alive,
Filled the white folks
Full of jive.
But the trouble was
His jive was bad.
Now, thank God,
Uncle Tom
Is dead.[142]

Brief enough to carve on a tombstone, the poem announces the death of Uncle Tom in a way that calls more attention to his life than what comes after it. While the speaker expresses relief about Uncle Tom's death, the fact that two of the poem's nine lines read simply "Uncle Tom" gives the figure a looming presence. Indeed, despite declaring him dead, Hughes revisited Uncle Tom in future poetry. In two different poems titled "Uncle Tom," he engaged with this figure as a racial patriarch who needed to be remembered and even valued, but not emulated.[143]

Ellington's *Jump for Joy* similarly relied on a history defined by Uncle Tom. The first act ended with a number called "Uncle Tom's Cabin Is a Drive-In Now," in which a plantation cabin has become a Los Angeles restaurant. Challenging the racial restrictions of Hollywood, the number's lyrics herald a modern era in which the race produces—and makes money from—its own images: "Jemimah doesn't work no more for RKO / She's slinging hash for Uncle Tom and coinin' dough. / Just turn on your headlights, and she'll take a bow, / Cause Uncle Tom's Cabin is a drive-in now!"[144] In its celebration of a transformative change, the song holds on to Uncle Tom and *Uncle Tom's Cabin* in reimagined forms. Artists of this era could write off the Uncle Tom performance mode, but they could not remove Uncle Tom as a figure of the race's history. If Uncle Tom's cabin has become a drive-in, it nevertheless retains the same name.[145]

Hollywood's Uncle Toms

If some black Americans were optimistic about the end of "Uncle Tom roles," David O. Selznick's blockbuster *Gone with the Wind* (1939), with its Uncle Tom and Mammy character types, made it more than clear that Hollywood was interested in resurrecting the slavery past in grand fashion. Selznick, aware of growing attention to film in the black community, had solicited input from black leaders and journalists during the making of the film, resulting in changes including removal of the N-word.[146] Yet, as the NAACP's *Crisis* noted, Selznick's film still emphasized "the devotion and faithfulness (to their white folks) of the 'Uncle Tom' servant type."[147] With the film's release, the tangled rhetoric of Uncle Tom helped black Americans debate how the race should be represented on film and what forms of activism would most effectively counteract a picture with unfavorable black characters. *The Defender*, for example, denounced Selznick's film as "anti-Negro propaganda of the most vicious character" and urged a mass protest by the race.[148] In the first major black protest against a film since *Birth of a Nation*, incensed activists picketed *Gone with the Wind* with signs proclaiming "You'd Be Sweet Too under a Whip!" Recognizing the link between film's characterizations of black people and the continued oppression of black Americans, picketers of *Gone with the Wind* were part of a growing intervention in Hollywood by black civil rights activists at both the national and local levels. In what Ellen Scott calls "interpretive activism," critics and activists moved from pointing out obvious racial insults such as offensive language to more nuanced considerations of how the racial ideologies of film might impact American racial politics.[149]

Merging with the already-despised category of the "Uncle Tom Negro," "Uncle Tom roles" and their preponderance became a prominent concern for the black press, which began to censure those who accepted such roles. In a 1934 letter to *The Defender*, A. B. Johnson heaped responsibility for demeaning roles (the "modern version of 'Uncle Tom'") on the actors themselves rather than the studio system, asserting that change would come "when these actors realize the detrimental reflections which they cast on the entire Race" and "demand more intelligent parts."[150] By the time *Gone with the Wind* was set to be released, Clarence Muse proactively urged black Americans to recognize that, even though the film left much to be desired, its blacks stars were "victims like you of the American habit of Uncle Tom."[151] Indeed, established actors such as Muse and Hattie McDaniel worried that black protests of Uncle Tom roles would threaten their careers.

Nevertheless, local NAACP branches organized call campaigns and pickets against the studios and radio stations that featured Uncle Tom roles and the black actors who played them, finding fault both with a system controlled by whites and with the actors who contributed to it. Invoking the figure of Uncle Tom allowed them to blame the lack of equality in American film on those in the race not doing enough, repeating a rhetorical strategy long and still used in debates about leadership and protest strategies. According to the black press, Hollywood's "Uncle Tomism" posed a serious threat to American racial politics. Those who took Uncle Tom roles, such as Eddie Anderson's Rochester, were responsible for "increasing the nonsense of white racial supremacy" to fill

their own pockets.[152] Soldiers stationed abroad during World War II reported
feeling ashamed of the roles they saw on the screen, suggesting that "Uncle
Tom actors" made a "bad name for the race."[153] During the 1940s, actors were
expected to reject Uncle Tom roles or to convince producers to change them,
as Canada Lee did with *Lifeboat* (1944) when he successfully lobbied to cut
from the script "'Uncle Tom' phrases" such as "yessir" and "nosirr."[154]

Stung by the suggestion that their work harmed the race, established actors insisted that protesters didn't understand the difference between being
an Uncle Tom and playing an artistic role. When protesters organized
against *Stormy Weather* (1943), starring Bill Robinson and Lena Horne, the
entertainer, manager, and *California Eagle* editor Harry Levette defended
Robinson's artistry and maintained that protesters were "not sufficiently
qualified or versed in entertainment matters to know the difference between
pure comedy and Uncle Tomism."[155] At a 1943 roundtable conference on race
and Hollywood, Muse, who acknowledged that he was "accused more than
anyone else of playing what the NAACP calls 'Uncle Tom' roles," suggested
that the term was a weapon rather than an accurate description of a role.
"Just what do we mean by 'Uncle Tom' roles?" he asked. "The term 'Uncle
Tom' is all mixed up with all our problems, and is used to condemn anybody
whom we wish to destroy."[156]

Indeed, throughout the 1940s black Americans repeatedly used the rhetoric of Uncle Tom to reproach those who took roles seen as bad for the race,
censuring Uncle Tom roles as harshly as Uncle Tom leaders. "As long as our
actors and actresses are willing to sell their services in such degrading roles,"
wrote an *Afro* reader of Hattie McDaniel's turn in *Three Is a Family* (1944),
"so long will our progress be hindered."[157] By shifting some of the blame for
Hollywood's racial politics onto members of the race, activists could envision
having the power to change the situation through their own efforts. Even
Langston Hughes joined the criticism of black actors in Uncle Tom roles in
one of his Jess B. Simple stories, telling his skeptical "Simple Minded Friend"
that those who took Uncle Tom roles, and not Hollywood's Jewish producers, were to blame for Hollywood's portrayal of the race. In a comment that
reflected the range of forms possible for Uncle Tom roles, Hughes' narrator
points out to Simple that "Negroes are the ones who sport the outlandish
zoot-suits that out-zoot anything to be seen on land or sea . . . the ones who

out-dialect any dialect to be heard North or South. . . . Suppose it does happen to be a Jewish producer who tells said Negro to Uncle Tom. Couldn't that Negro say NO? Or is he tongue-tied?"[158] Given the cinema's acknowledged influence on American race relations, an actor who accepted an Uncle Tom role betrayed his race and thus became an "Uncle Tom" in more than one way.

Against Uncle Tom's Cabin

At the same time that black activists protested "Uncle Tom roles," they also continued to deploy the Uncle Tom slur in politics to criticize those whose attitude or behavior worked contrary to the race's progress. According to their opponents, Uncle Toms were reactionaries who opposed integration in education, transportation, and the military.[159] Uncle Toms steadfastly supported the Republican Party even though it had betrayed the race by, among other things, resegregating federal offices and failing to support anti-lynching legislation. They backed down from voting and serving on juries. When the race agitated for integration and equal treatment, Uncle Toms counseled patience or even publicly announced that the reforms demanded by fellow black activists were unnecessary.

Once Uncle Toms became a grave concern in popular culture as well as politics, some black Americans began to turn against *Uncle Tom's Cabin* itself. Individual readers, of course, continued to defend Stowe's novel. But many black Americans did not read it at all. By 1944, when Metro-Goldwyn-Mayer announced plans to produce a new adaptation of *Uncle Tom's Cabin* in Technicolor, starring Paul Robeson and Lena Horne, studio executives were surprised to encounter objections.[160] They hadn't realized that no matter the effect of Stowe's novel in the antebellum era, many African Americans did not want to revisit the memory of slavery, especially on the silver screen. Robeson and Horne soon announced that they would not accept the roles.[161] In a meeting with producer Arthur Hornblow, Leon H. Hardwick of the International Film and Radio Guild suggested that the proposed film would meet protests all over the country because it represented an aspect of American history better forgotten.[162] Moreover, by rehashing the days of slavery, the film perpetuated the idea that black folks belonged only in menial roles. "We tire of seeing ourselves as bootblacks, porters, maids and now—of all things—slaves," he explained.[163] Whether or not such roles accurately represented the slavery past or the occupations to which black people were often limited, they promoted a social structure in which black people were always subservient to whites. As *The Afro-American*'s E. B. Rea reflected, even though *Uncle Tom's Cabin* was an indictment of slavery, those days were still too recent to be shown on screen without "inflat[ing] racial antagonism": "the wound is not healed enough."[164] Another *Afro-American* article posited that "[t]he same ill will would meet any film set in the hated slavery period."[165]

While protesters responded to *Uncle Tom's Cabin* as a reminder of a painful history they did not want to see, those who defended it based their support on the text of the novel. NAACP head Walter White tried to discourage local branches from protesting by distributing a memo arguing that they were inaccurately connecting the politics of *Uncle Tom's Cabin* to the term "Uncle Tom" when the character was, in fact, "a revolutionary."[166] But while White's memo insisted on regarding *Uncle Tom's Cabin* as a literary work, protesters saw it as a dangerous prescription for American society. MGM soon responded to the "unprecedented barrage of protests from sources all over the country" by shelving the project.[167] In 1945, when a theater in Bridgeport, Connecticut, booked a stage adaptation of *Uncle Tom's Cabin*, the white press was mystified by the local NAACP's picketing of the performances. How, the *Chicago Sun* asked, could "a melodrama penned as an attack on slavery . . . hold the Negro up to ridicule"?[168] Writing in *The Defender*, Lucius C. Harper explained that representing slavery before white theatergoers was inherently dangerous because of the "peculiar tendency" of whites "to look at the Negro collectively, while he looks at himself and members of his own race individually." In Harper's view, whites would see the play as a document of "the entire pattern of Negro life, be it lived in 1865 or in 1945," viewing the forced hierarchies of the past as appropriate models for the present.[169]

To W. E. B. Du Bois, however, the Bridgeport protests were the "most idiotic" of all the "crack-pot protests against race prejudice" he had encountered.[170] In a passionate defense of Stowe's novel and its stage adaptations, he reminded readers of *The Defender* that Stowe's novel was in its time the world's most emotionally potent appeal for the anti-slavery cause. Even if the character's example was better suited to 1845 than to 1945, "Stowe's Uncle Tom was no hypocrite nor coward," Du Bois asserted. While Stowe's character submitted selflessly, in the vein of Socrates and Jesus Christ, the contemporary Uncle Tom was "a fawning, self-seeking coward, too selfish to fight and too ignorant to understand what submission is costing others." Reading *Uncle Tom's Cabin* in its historical and religious context, Du Bois concluded that it was not a libel on the Negro people but rather "on the whole a fine tribute to Negro character and a bitter attack on enslavement."

Inspired by the Bridgeport controversy, in 1946 the *Negro Digest* conducted a poll investigating "whether the popular, often-performed play *Uncle Tom's Cabin* is anti-Negro," with the results organized by race and region (see figure 6.3).[171] According to the poll, the majority of the race agreed that the play was indeed "anti-Negro." Even so, antagonism varied by region: in the South, 50 percent of blacks agreed that *Uncle Tom's Cabin* was anti-Negro, while 58 percent in the North and 61 percent in the West did. The poll also revealed striking differences between the attitudes of blacks and whites toward the play, especially in the South, where almost all white respondents (95 percent) did not believe it was anti-Negro. In an explanation of the study's findings, the *Negro Digest* reported that whites who believed that *Uncle Tom's Cabin* was pro-Negro equated "pro-Negro" with anti-slavery and that blacks supported the play as "a valid picture of the past which cannot be ignored" despite the race's progress. Respondents who deemed the play anti-Negro, however, based their judgment on its characterizations, and particularly on Uncle Tom. Believing that the play "presents the Negro in a submissive, docile, cringing role which portrays the Negro as less than a man," this group agreed that "the play was fine in its time, that it served as a valuable weapon in a past era but that with the new manhood and militancy of the Negro today, it has no place on the American stage." Despite the play's past contributions, modern values made the Uncle Tom character not only inaccurate to the times but also dangerous. In a nation that kept pushing black Americans down when they tried to climb the social, political, and economic hierarchy, performances of the slavery past would only add extra weight.

Yet the truth was that even if Uncle Tom could be banished from the stage and screen, this figure could not be erased from American history or cut out of black identity. Uncle Tom embodied the vast space between slavery and freedom and the inherent challenges of an identity rooted in historical and continuing oppression. So even though Hollywood finally figured out

NEGRO DIGEST POLL

Is 'Uncle Tom's Cabin' Anti-Negro?
By Wallace Lee
Director, Negro Digest Poll

SHARPLY divergent views separate Negro and white opinion in America in the controversy over whether the popular, often-performed play *Uncle Tom's Cabin* is anti-Negro.

Negroes themselves are pretty much on opposite sides of the fence, the January NEGRO DIGEST poll reveals. Only by a slight margin does the Negro population generally feel that the famous Abolitionist play by Harriet Beecher Stowe is a reflection on their race. On the other hand most whites expressed the belief that the play is for the Negro rather than against him.

Results in the poll on the query, "Is *Uncle Tom's Cabin* anti-Negro?" as tabulated among whites showed:

	Yes	No	Undecided
North	8%	81%	11%
West	10%	78%	12%
South	1%	95%	4%

General feeling among whites questioned is that the play which has been performed in America more than any other play is pro-Negro by virtue of its being anti-slavery. By showing how Negro slaves were mistreated and stirring up sympathy for them, the Harriet Beecher Stowe classic presented the case for the Negro's freedom and certainly should be welcomed with open arms by Negroes, the majority of whites believe.

A very small group agreed with the majority of Negroes who felt that *Uncle Tom's Cabin* presents the Negro in a submissive, docile, cringing role which portrays the Negro as less than a man.

These whites and Negroes agree that the play was fine in its time, that it served as a valuable weapon in a past era but that with the new manhood and militancy of the Negro today, it has no place on the American stage. They point out that the name "Uncle Tom" in Negro circles has become synonymous with any colored person who bows down to whites and will not fight for his full rights as an American.

The tabulation among Negroes showed the following results:

	Yes	No	Undecided
North	58%	36%	6%
West	61%	35%	4%
South	50%	41%	9%

Those Negroes who stated that *Uncle Tom's Cabin* was not anti-Negro based their opinion on the belief that the play today represents an era in history that is part of the heritage of the Negro and despite the changes that have given Negroes a new stature and new attitudes, it remains a valid picture of the past which cannot be ignored. Many objected to efforts to ban the play as not in line with free American expression.

68

Figure 6.3. "Is *Uncle Tom's Cabin* Anti-Negro?," in January 1946 issue of *Negro Digest*.

that making a new *Uncle Tom's Cabin* was more trouble than it was worth, Uncle Tom lived on: in popular culture, in political rhetoric, in memory and mind. White Americans continued to invoke this figure with nostalgia for the old type of Negro who knew his place. Black Americans lobbed the Uncle Tom slur at those they believed were impeding the race's progress. But as the twentieth century continued, it became increasingly clear that the race could not move on from the slavery past without more fully reckoning with, and perhaps reconsidering, its memory. As long as anyone remembered Uncle Tom, no one could forget him.

CONCLUSION

Twentieth-Century Uncle Toms

AT A TIME WHEN BLACK AMERICANS widely acknowledged the damage done by Uncle Tom types in politics and Uncle Tom roles in popular culture, Richard Wright titled his debut collection of fiction *Uncle Tom's Children* (1938). Clearly riffing on Stowe's novel, Wright's choice of title was audacious, even foolish. Why claim descent from Uncle Tom when no one wanted this figure to stick around? Why bring up this reminder of slavery when the embodiment of Uncle Tom on stage and screen seemed intrinsically dangerous? As the grim realities of the Depression punctured the jubilance of the 1920s, the New Negro conviction that the Old Negro could be easily plucked out of American life became increasingly untenable.[1] Where Alain Locke had breezily proclaimed that the days of Uncle Tom were over both historically and aesthetically, the emergence of modern protest literature in the late 1930s brought renewed attention to the ways that Uncle Tom and the past he signified continued to haunt black life and thought in the United States. In the nineteenth century, literature had created the cultural figure of Uncle Tom; in the twentieth, literature provided the most flexible space for considering his legacy. Beginning with Wright's *Uncle Tom's Children*, black American writers drew on the figure of Uncle Tom to explore a less dismissive, more instructive relationship with the past, one mindful both that time alone would not heal the damage of slavery and that this history held valuable insights for younger generations.

Uncle Tom's Children challenged the New Negro optimism of the 1920s by exploring just how heavily the social structures and psychology of slavery continued to affect black life, especially in the South. As such, the collection followed Wright's "Blueprint for Negro Writing" (1937), which contended that a revolutionary literature needed to move beyond simply portraying the details of an individual's life (especially bourgeois life) to explore the broader meanings of that individual's environment. In Wright's view, oppressed people could not become free without fully understanding the social and historical forces that produced their oppression, and it was the black writer's responsibility to represent those forces. "[A]t the moment a people begin to realize a meaning in their suffering," he suggested, "the civilization which engenders that suffering is doomed."[2] Wright distinguished himself from other black novelists by his commitment to representing the deep origins of black life in America; he claimed that other black writers had not been willing to go "with a deep and fearless will down to the dark roots of life."[3] "Blueprint" instructed black authors to "feel the meaning of the history of their race as though they in one lifetime had lived it themselves throughout all the long centuries," to tend to the historical experiences at the heart of modern life.[4]

With *Uncle Tom's Children*, Wright's point was not to show how far the race had come since the days of Uncle Tom but rather to depict the sources and the tragedy of its continued circumscription. Rather than pointing a finger at "Uncle Toms," Wright's collection uses this figure as a racially uniting "trope of relation."[5] Yet there are generational tensions in this common line of descent. While the title of *Uncle Tom's Children* suggests that Uncle Tom lives on in his descendants, the book opens with an epigraph that announces a dramatic break from the past: "The post Civil War household word among Negroes—'He's an Uncle Tom!'—which denoted reluctant toleration for the cringing type who knew his place before white folk, has been supplanted by a new word from another generation which says—'Uncle Tom is dead!'"[6] What does it mean for Uncle Tom to be dead? Even if the submissive historical type is gone, linguistically he's still alive; the epigraph posits a change in the language used to reference Uncle Tom—"a new word"—rather than a change in material conditions. Indeed, the somber contents of *Uncle Tom's Children* call the epigraph's triumphant tone into question. In the Jim Crow South of Wright's novellas, white men beat and kill black men for perceived crimes without trial, force them to labor "like slaves" simply because of the color of their skin, and rape black women with impunity.[7]

This inequality is sustained not only by those who perpetrate such injustice but also by black folks who believe that there is no possibility for survival outside of "the lived embodiment of deference" signified by Uncle Tom.[8] In "The Ethics of Living Jim Crow," the autobiographical essay that opens the 1940 edition of *Uncle Tom's Children*, the young Wright struggles against an older generation that tells him to keep his head down wherever white folks are concerned. His "Jim Crow lessons" begin when he and his friends get into a fight with white boys who have thrown bottles at them. Instead of comforting her crying son, Wright's mother scolds and beats him, telling him that he is "never, never, under any conditions, to fight *white* folks again."[9] In the Jim Crow South, her son's instinct to stand up for himself against whites must be nipped in the bud. Later, as a teenager working at a small optical factory, Wright's elders again rebuke him when they hear that white employees physically threatened him after he asked to take on greater professional responsibilities. For this, the relatives "called me a fool. They told me that I must never again attempt to exceed my boundaries. When you are working for white folks, they said, you got to 'stay in your place' if you want to keep working."[10] Failing to see beyond their current situation, the folks at home encourage him to be like the epigraph's Uncle Tom, who "knew his place before white folk."

What distinguishes Uncle Tom's children from their father? Several of the collection's novellas depict tensions between a younger generation ready to assert its humanity and an older one that does not dare step outside the strictures of Jim Crow. While their parents balk at even the slightest resistance to white dominance, the younger folks insist on asserting their rights as human beings, even if it means an early death. They are far more aggressive than Stowe's character. In Wright's account, Uncle Tom's children defy the demands of white town leaders, shoot white men who threaten them or their way of life, and lead protest marches even after being beaten severely. Despite their efforts, however, they are doomed. Wright's protagonists, unlike the author himself, do not successfully escape from the Jim Crow South. The closest any of them come is the ambiguous ending of "Big Boy Leaves Home," with the protagonist in the back of a truck headed toward Chicago. Moreover, three of the four remaining novellas end with the death of the protagonist, whose defiance cannot, in the end, save him or her. In Wright's collection, victory in the Jim Crow South often means nothing more than choosing how one dies.

Unlike the public condemnations of Uncle Toms in public life, *Uncle Tom's Children* offers not censure but sympathy for those caught in the social and psychological structures of slavery. Of course, the limitations of sympathy became obvious to Wright once *Uncle Tom's Children* was published. As he recalled in "How 'Bigger' Was Born" (1940), an essay reflecting on the process of writing his first novel, *Native Son* (1940), when reviews of his debut collection came out, he realized that he'd made "an awfully naive mistake" and "written a book which even bankers' daughters could read and weep over and feel good about."[11] For Wright, the problem with such sentiment was that it could make those who had only felt something feel as if they had done something. As a result, Wright recalled, "I swore to myself that if I ever wrote another book, no one would weep over it; that it would be so hard and deep that they would have to face it without the consolation of tears."[12] Indeed, *Native Son*'s protagonist, Bigger Thomas, is not an easy object of sympathy. He is, as Wright reflected, "resentful toward whites, sullen, angry, ignorant, emotionally unstable."[13] But he is "an American product" whose existence serves as both a symbol and a prophecy of a racist American culture.[14] The naturalist style of *Native Son* was motivated by Wright's conviction that in order to change the environment that made Bigger, the nation needed to confront that environment's shocking reality.

When one of Wright's mentees, James Baldwin, announced his own arrival on the literary scene, he did so by suggesting that Wright's account of Bigger was in the end just a replication of the forces that made him. In his 1949 essay "Everybody's Protest Novel," Baldwin enacted a particularly complicated manifestation of what Harold Bloom calls "the anxiety of influence" by suggesting that Wright's native form, the protest novel, was ultimately a reactionary genre.[15] Like the poets Bloom described, whose resistance to being derivative of their predecessors often worked through misreading them, Baldwin announced his emergence on the American literary scene by rejecting two literary precursors: Wright's *Native Son* and Stowe's *Uncle Tom's Cabin*. Baldwin framed his critique of Stowe and Wright as a consideration of the American protest novel and its unavoidable sentimentality, arguing that this genre had robbed black Americans of their essential humanity by reduc-

ing them to the status of social victims. Where Alain Locke had identified an
aesthetic offense in Stowe's sentimentalism, Baldwin saw something more sinister at work. *Uncle Tom's Cabin* was "a very bad novel," he wrote, flooded with
"self-righteous, virtuous sentimentality"—and sentimentalism, he suggested,
was "the signal of secret and violent inhumanity, the mask of cruelty."[16] The
failure of the protest novel lay in "its insistence that it is [the Negro's] categorization alone which is real and which cannot be transcended."[17] In reenacting
the traumas of slavery and racism, the protest novel defined blacks wholly by
these injustices, "so that the allegedly inferior are actually made so, insofar as
the societal realities are concerned."[18] Comparing *Native Son*'s Bigger Thomas
with Stowe's Uncle Tom, Baldwin played on the title of Wright's first book,
describing Bigger as "Uncle Tom's descendant, flesh of his flesh, so exactly
opposite a portrait that, when the books are placed together, it seems that the
contemporary Negro novelist and the dead New England woman are locked
together in a timeless, deadly battle; the one uttering merciless exhortations,
the other shouting curses."[19] To Baldwin, both Wright and Stowe were guilty
of creating black characters whose identities were defined entirely by their
race: one an appalling criminal, the other an idealized martyr. Because neither portrayal left room for a more complicated humanity, Wright's novel
was neither better nor truer than what a nineteenth-century white writer had
produced. Having helped Wright explore how history affected modern life,
the figure of Uncle Tom now activated Baldwin's consideration of how the
literary modes of the past continued to shape black literature.

Baldwin's influential essay is still probably the most extensive attack on
Harriet Beecher Stowe and *Uncle Tom's Cabin* ever written by an African
American author.[20] It has been aptly described as "less a careful reading of
Stowe's work than a personal manifesto, a gesture toward self-liberation"
from the shadows of both *Uncle Tom's Cabin* and *Native Son*.[21] However, in
the process of charging Wright with being Stowe's literary descendant, Baldwin reveals the great extent to which Stowe was also his predecessor. Indeed,
Baldwin felt the tremendous power of *Uncle Tom's Cabin* even as a child. In
"The Devil Finds Work" (1976), a book-length essay on the cultural influences of his youth, he recalled Stowe's novel as the means through which he
understood his place as a black man in American society. It was the first book
that he could remember reading, and he did so "obsessively," "compulsively,"

"over and over and over again."[22] His obsession with the book as a seven- or eight-year-old became so severe that his mother tried to hide the book high out of his reach. But he was somehow able to climb up and get it, and then, "my mother, as she herself puts it, 'didn't hide it anymore,'" and, indeed, from that moment, though in fear and trembling, began to let me go."[23] As an adult, he reflected that reading the novel so many times "was this particular child's way of circling around the question of what it meant to be a nigger. . . . I did not believe in any of these people so much as I believed in their situation, which I suspected, dreadfully, to have something to do with my own."[24] For Baldwin, Stowe's novel was not a historical document but a social one illuminating how whites saw him.

Whether or not *Uncle Tom's Cabin* was, as Baldwin suggested, "a very bad novel," its persistence in American culture continued to be crucial to black fiction for several decades, becoming a key text for black writers and artists seeking to explore how they should relate to the African American past. Ralph Ellison wrote that the shock of seeing a poster for a "Tom show" in a Vermont village in 1945 was part of his inspiration to write *Invisible Man* (1953). As Ellison reflected in his 1981 introduction to the novel, "what is commonly assumed to be past history is actually as much a part of the living present as William Faulkner insisted. Furtive, implacable and tricky, it inspirits both the observer and the scene observed, artifacts, manners and atmosphere and it speaks even when no one wills to listen."[25] *Uncle Tom's Cabin* was, inextricably, a part of the African American past, and it had influenced "both the observer and the scene observed": the way that whites looked at blacks as well as the way that blacks understood themselves—whether they wanted it to or not.

Like Wright's *Uncle Tom's Children*, Ellison's novel is interested in the ways that the slavery past haunts modern life. However, where Wright shows how the tragic environment created by American history shapes the people who live in it, *Invisible Man* offers a more dynamic account of a history that cannot be forgotten and might even be misremembered. If Wright sees the past as something to be understood in order to be overcome, Ellison, as Farrah Jasmine Griffin suggests, understands "the significance and importance" of ancestors.[26] Throughout *Invisible Man*, the invisible protagonist struggles mightily to advance from his humble origins. Yet as he wins a college scholarship, leaves home, and eventually becomes a communist organizer, he is haunted by a memory of his grandfather, a former slave regarded by his family as "the meekest of men." On his deathbed, the grandfather gathers his family around him and shocks them by announcing that his outward submissiveness to whites was not an indication of his faithfulness to them but a strategy of opposition that he hopes his descendants will continue:

> "Son, after I'm gone I want you to keep up the good fight. I never told you, but our life is a war and I have been a traitor all my born days, a spy in the enemy's country ever since I give up my gun back in Reconstruction. Live with your head in the lion's mouth. I want you to overcome 'em with yeses, undermine 'em with grins, agree 'em to death and destruction, let 'em swoller you till they vomit or bust wide open."... "Learn it to the younguns," he whispered fiercely; then he died.[27]

Offering a bleak vision of a nation divided along racial lines, the grandfather asserts that his treachery comes by virtue of his birth as a black man in a white nation. His last words recommend a seemingly paradoxical interpretation of submissive behavior: for him, smiling and agreeing are tactics of war, strategically aimed at destroying the white enemy. But how does this work? How can agreement lead to "death and destruction"? Surrounding family members encourage the young invisible man and his generation to forget the grandfather's puzzling advice. Yet his mind will not let him. The night of the horrific "battle royale," when the invisible man receives a shiny black briefcase containing a scholarship to a segregated state college, he dreams of his grandfather. In the dream, his grandfather tells him to open his briefcase. Inside is an envelope, and inside of that are many more, nested like Russian dolls. "Them's years," says the grandfather.[28] After working his way through these "years," the invisible man finds, at last, a short message that the grandfather tells him to read out loud: "To Whom It May Concern, Keep This Nigger-Boy Running." Waking from the dream "with old man's laughter ringing in my ears," the invisible man has "no insight into [the dream's] meaning." This dream periodically surfaces in *Invisible Man*, each time hinting that the old man was less complacent than his family remembers him.

The invisible man's memories also challenge the family's story about the grandfather's meekness. In one memory, his grandfather warned him that a black person should never let a white man "tell you his business" because the temporary closeness will exacerbate the white man's existing hatred for black people. In another, his grandfather tried to register to vote, and when "it was demanded that he quote the entire United States Constitution as test of his fitness," he "confound[ed] them all by passing the test although they refused him the ballot."[29] As these memories of resistance emerge in the novel, they hold the potential to be useful models and sources of insight. And yet, each time his grandfather comes to mind, the invisible man fails to interpret what he recounts properly. "What," he asks, "had an old slave to do with humanity?"[30]

Throughout the novel, the invisible man repeatedly finds that the past is not easily discarded. In a comic articulation of the difficulty of shedding the past, he finds himself unable to dispose of an item of early Americana, a bank shaped like a grinning black man with his palm stretched out, that he has broken in the process of berating his tenement neighbors for their uncivilized, "cottonpatch ways." After wrapping the shards, he throws the package into a trashcan on the street, but a woman from a nearby house yells at him until he takes it back. Then he purposely drops it in the road, but a man picks it up and brings it back to him. Consequently, the invisible man is forced to put the package in his briefcase along with other articles of black history he has unwillingly collected. He must tote around the past even as he tries to step away from it. It is only at the end of the novel, when the invisible man is sequestered underground, that he unearths the real meaning of his grandfather's advice to "agree 'em to death and destruction." What this advice means, the invisible man realizes, is not that he should submit to injustice but that he should affirm the principles of American democracy even, or especially, where they are not practiced. The invisible man never describes his grandfather as an Uncle Tom; the term appears in the novel only as a slur, used twice by black nationalists who censure the invisible man for his association with white communist organizers. Nevertheless, Ellison's novel challenges the American vision of the faithful slave, suggesting that the Uncle Tom type might not have been as submissive as he seemed.

Ellison's understanding of the importance of reevaluating the slavery past helped open the door for a renewed consideration of this topic in both history and literature. Beginning with Kenneth Stampp's *The Peculiar Institution* (1956), in the mid-twentieth century a new historiography of slavery addressed the suffering of enslaved people, incorporating previously ignored records such as ex-slave interviews and nineteenth-century slave narratives. When William Styron appropriated the slave narrative form in *The Confessions of Nat Turner* (1967), black authors challenged Styron's portrayal by developing what Ishmael Reed would term the neo–slave narrative, which used the form, topics, literary conventions, and first-person voice of the antebellum slave narrative to address contemporary questions of racial formation.[31] Perhaps unsurprisingly, this creative attention to slavery sometimes drew on *Uncle Tom's Cabin*; Reed's neo–slave narrative *Flight to Canada* (1976) is in part a send-up of Stowe's novel.

This greater attention to the historical realities of American chattel slavery also shaped the vision of America articulated by black radicals during the 1960s. While for decades the Uncle Tom slur had been used to criticize behavior and images that belonged in the past, now this figure helped black nationalists diagnose an ever-present division within the race. In the contest between the integrationism of major civil rights groups including the NAACP and the radical separatism of the Black Muslim movement, Malcolm X repeatedly described the contemporary United States as an extension of the slavery era. "This is a white man's country," he told Louis Lomax in a 1963 interview, "and the Negro is nothing but an ex-slave who is now trying to get himself integrated into the master's house."[32] Approaching the historical structures of slavery as a contemporary problem, Malcolm X connected Martin Luther King, Jr., and his strategy of nonviolent resistance to the antebellum religious leaders who, he charged, kept slaves from resisting. Deploying a slur that he would use repeatedly, Malcolm accused King of being "just a twentieth-century or modern Uncle Tom or religious Uncle Tom, who is doing the same thing today to keep Negroes defenseless in the face of attack that Uncle Tom did on the plantation to keep *those* Negroes defenseless in the face of the attack of the Klan in that day."[33] Similarly, in a 1963 speech at Michigan State University, Malcolm X compared the "twentieth-century Uncle Tom" and his allegiance to white America to the "house Negro" of the antebellum South.[34] To Malcolm X, "Uncle Tom Negroes" reflected not so much a problem of the past but an enduring intraracial division between those who aligned themselves with whites and those who were loyal to the race. Time alone, he insisted, would not create the change the race needed.

While Malcolm X's invocation of "Uncle Tom" addressed a specifically racial context, his articulation of group loyalty through this figure became—and remains—useful for the variety of protest movements modeled after civil rights and black pride. Social and political movements of the 1960s and 1970s from feminism to gay rights incorporated the figure of Uncle Tom in order to police the boundaries of loyalty and authenticity. Feminists derided "Aunt Toms" such as Helen Gurley Brown—deemed "Aunt Tom of the Month" in the New York Radical Women's first broadside, *Notes from the First Year* (1968)[35]—who supported patriarchal values. Lesbians compared the expectations of a smiling, submissive heterosexual femininity to Uncle Tom and his "big ingratiating smile at massa."[36] In the United States today, the figure of Uncle Tom is invoked primarily in an African American context, but it also appears in a variety of intragroup critiques, among them "Uncle Tomahawk" for Native Americans and "Uncle Tom's Cabin Republicans," a play on the gay conservative group "Log Cabin Republicans," for gay Americans who support the GOP. In Eddie Huang's memoir *Fresh off the Boat* (2013), recently adapted for network television, he criticizes the "Uncle Chans" who "convinced us to assimilate, shut the fuck up, and play the part" of the Asian model minority.[37]

When the Uncle Tom slur is used in political and cultural commentary today, it is common for someone, somewhere in the online comments section, to point out that its usage does not accurately represent Stowe's novel. (Almost invariably, the figure's transformation is blamed on the stage adaptations.) Can *Uncle Tom's Cabin* ever shed its association with Uncle Tom's contemporary meaning? Perhaps it shouldn't. As much as this figure's long and controversial life reveals the intensity of racial divisions in America, there is also something heartening in the tenacity with which we have held on to Stowe's character and molded it for our own use. As many contemporary commentators have observed, *Uncle Tom's Cabin* is a reminder of the immense power of literature to help societies work through their most complex problems. But it is also evidence of the central role that characters can take in activating that use. In a starkly divided nation, we need another work of literature as transformative as *Uncle Tom's Cabin*. But we also need another character as shocking, as familiar, as vital as Uncle Tom.

ACKNOWLEDGMENTS

I could not have written this book without the resources provided by libraries and archives all over the country. I am thankful for the assistance of librarians, curators, and support staff at the American Antiquarian Society in Worcester, Massachusetts; the Beinecke Rare Book and Manuscript Library, at Yale University; the Boston Athenaeum; the Boston Public Library; the Harry Ransom Center, at the University of Texas at Austin; Houghton Library, at Harvard University (especially James Capobianco and Micah Hoggatt); the Moorland-Spingarn Research Center, at Howard University; the Museum of the City of New York; the New-York Historical Society; the New York Public Library's Main Branch, Library for the Performing Arts, and Schomburg Center for Research in Black Culture; and Stanford University Library's Special Collections (especially Rebecca Wingfield, John Mustain, and Tim Noakes). I'm particularly grateful to Katherine Kane and Beth Burgess, at the Harriet Beecher Stowe Center in Hartford, Connecticut, for going above and beyond in their support of my research and of this project as a whole. Thanks also to the Gilder Lehrman Institute at the New-York Historical Society, Harvard University's Graduate School of Arts and Sciences, and Stanford's Andrew W. Mellon Fellowship for funding archival research.

Over the years this project developed, I benefited from the valuable feedback of colleagues and friends who read drafts, suggested sources, discussed ideas, and gave advice that I occasionally had the good sense to take. Thank you to Chris Barrett, Robin Bernstein, Larry Buell, Leo Cabranes-Grant, Glenda Carpio, Tess Chakkalakal, Amanda Claybaugh, Nick Donofrio, Michele Elam, John Frick, Lesley Goodman, Evelyn Brooks Higginbotham, Brian Hochman, Hannah Doherty Hudson, Gavin Jones, Michelle Karnes, Randy Kennedy, Eitan Kensky, Paul Lucas, Liz Maynes-Aminzade, Lisa New, Martin Puchner, Arnold Rampersad, Shirley Samuels, Karen Sánchez-Eppler, Augustine Sedgewick, Elaine Showalter, Werner Sollors, Blakey Vermeule, Alex Woloch, and Arielle Zibrak. Thanks also to members of the Americanist Colloquium and the Sollors/Carpio Colloquium, who provided astute comments on the initial stages of this project. I am especially grateful to John Stauffer for his generosity of mind and spirit and to Skip Gates, whose incisive, energetic guidance has sustained my belief that scholarship can have meaning outside the academy. I am also indebted to J. P. Daughton, Lanier Anderson, and my co-fellows at Stanford for creating a rich and warm interdisciplinary intellectual community, and to the colleagues and administrators in the English Department who made me feel welcome and supported.

Thank you to my communities in Cambridge, the Bay Area, and beyond—Maria Antonia Albanes, Joni Angel, Brittany Blockman and Josh Pelletier, Brigid Boyle, Kate Courteau, Amanda Dennis, Nicole Deterding, Anna Evans, Molly Farneth, Leigh Ferrara, Eliza Gregory, Rebecca (Johnson) Kameny and Xander Kameny, Caitlin Kolb, Danielle Li, Lauren Nelson, Simone Schaner and Jed Farlow, Yoni Schneller, and Dalia Spingarn and Kristin Rasmussen—for sustaining me in mind, body, and spirit. I give special thanks to Claire Jarvis and Kathleen Fredrickson for their wisdom and humor and to Sarah Wagner-McCoy, whose insights, imagination, and cooking have nourished me throughout the process of researching and writing this book. In New York, Howard Goldwasser, Jaemin Kim, and Noah Kim Goldwasser consistently provided a base for my New York research and a home away from home.

Finally, I am forever grateful for the unwavering support of Neil Spingarn and Dvora Cyrlak, who raised me to follow my intellectual curiosity even when that didn't lead to law school and cheered my progress on this book every step of the way. As this decade-long project comes to a close, I owe my deepest gratitude to Didi Rissman for believing in this book as much as she believes in me, and for believing in me with more bigheartedness and understanding than I ever dared imagine. You make everything better.

NOTES

Introduction

1. From a typescript of Chesnutt's speech to the Bethel Literary and Historical Association in Washington, DC, November 21, 1899, in *Charles W. Chesnutt: Essays and Speeches*, ed. Joseph R. McElrath, Jr., Robert C. Leitz III, and Jesse S. Crisler (Stanford, CA: Stanford University Press, 1999), 114.

2. Arnold Rampersad, *Ralph Ellison: A Biography* (New York: Knopf, 2007), 440.

3. Henry Louis Gates, Jr., "Cabin Fever," *New York Times*, October 22, 2006.

4. "The Break-Up," *30 Rock*, season 1, episode 8 (2007).

5. For example, the Grammy-nominated rapper Nas references Uncle Tom in the "American Way" track from his platinum-selling album *Street's Disciple* (2002). Criticizing black leaders for failing the race, Nas reserves special censure for Condoleeza Rice as "just another coon Uncle Tom fool." And the rapper Ice Cube, in "True to the Game" (*Death Certificate*, 1992), viciously attacks those who abandon black neighborhoods as soon as they make money. He raps, "Stop being an Uncle Tom, you little sell-out / House nigga scum / Give something back to the place where you made it from."

6. "Another Word about Uncle Tom," unsigned reprint, *The Independent*, September 2, 1852, in *"Uncle Tom's Cabin" and American Culture*, ed. Stephen Railton, accessed July 25, 2010, http://utc.iath.virginia.edu (henceforth UTCAC).

7. Harriet Beecher Stowe, *Uncle Tom's Cabin* (1852; New York: Norton, 2010), 19.

8. Frederick Douglass, *My Bondage and My Freedom* (1855; repr., Urbana: University of Illinois Press, 1987), 115; Frederick Douglass, *The Life and Times of Frederick Douglass* (Boston: De Wolfe and Fisk, 1892), 124.

9. Douglass, *My Bondage*, 105–106. In his 1892 autobiography, however, Douglass described the influence of Lawson's message somewhat more mildly: "This advice and these suggestions were not without their influence on my future character and destiny." Douglass, *Life and Times*, 112.

10. Indeed, Uncle Tom would maintain his appeal for Douglass throughout his life. In 1893, Douglass was reported to have asked to pose as Uncle Tom in the Stowe exhibit at the World's Columbian Exposition in Chicago, opposite a bust of Stowe created for

the occasion. "Fred Douglass as Uncle Tom," *Chicago Record*, May 25, 1893; *New York Times*, May 26, 1893; Indianapolis *Freeman*, June 3, 1893.

11. Thomas P. Riggio, "*Uncle Tom* Reconstructed: A Neglected Chapter in the History of a Book," *American Quarterly* 28.1 (1976): 57.

12. In 2010, the Metropolitan Playhouse in New York City's East Village staged a minimalist presentation of George L. Aiken's 1850s adaptation, to positive reviews. Rachel Saltz, covering the production for the *New York Times*, concluded her review by reflecting that *Uncle Tom's Cabin* "shouldn't be a stranger on our stages." Rachel Saltz, "Familiar Americana, but Still Full of Life," *New York Times*, November 29, 2010, C3.

13. According to David Reynolds, Uncle Tom "was often presented as a stooped, obedient old fool, the model image of a submissive black man preferred by post–Reconstruction, pre–civil rights America. It was this Uncle Tom, weakened both physically and spiritually, who became a synonym for a racial sellout by the mid-20th century." David Reynolds, "Rescuing the Real Uncle Tom," *New York Times*, June 13, 2011. This op-ed coincided with the publication of Reynolds' *Mightier Than the Sword: "Uncle Tom's Cabin" and the Battle for America* (New York: Norton, 2011), which similarly argues that the Uncle Tom dramas stripped Stowe's novel of its progressive politics.

14. Thomas F. Gossett, *"Uncle Tom's Cabin" and American Culture* (Dallas: Southern Methodist University Press, 1985), 387.

15. M. M. Manring, *Slave in a Box: The Strange Career of Aunt Jemima* (Charlottesville: University Press of Virginia, 1998), 16.

16. Leslie Fiedler describes *Uncle Tom's Cabin* as the inaugural text in what became a "Popular Epic" created by multiple authors and across media. He argues that Thomas Dixon's anti-Tom novels, *Birth of a Nation*, *Gone with the Wind*, and *Roots* all descend from Stowe's novel and collectively form "a myth of our history unequalled in scope or resonance by any work of high literature." Fiedler, *The Inadvertent Epic* (Toronto: CBC Merchandising, 1979), 17.

17. John William DeForest, "The Great American Novel," *The Nation* 6.132 (1868): 28. On the enduring appeal of this concept, see Lawrence Buell, *The Dream of the Great American Novel* (Cambridge, MA: Harvard University Press, 2014).

18. "Amusements," *Inter Ocean* (Chicago), April 27, 1896.

19. Archives consulted include: American Antiquarian Society; Beinecke Rare Book and Manuscript Library, Yale University; Boston Athenaeum; Boston Public Library; Harry Ransom Center, University of Texas at Austin; Harriet Beecher Stowe Center; Houghton Library, Harvard University; Moorland-Spingarn Research Center, Howard University; Museum of the City of New York; New-York Historical Society; New York Public Library for the Performing Arts; and Stanford University Library's Special Collections.

A set of such adaptations by Eslanda Robeson, the wife of movie star Paul Robeson, is not discussed in this book, but certainly invites further scholarly analysis. A 1932 revision, "Uncle Tom An' His Cabin," makes Tom the head of a touring Harlem jazz band. Robeson's 1943 play, significantly revised in 1952, more faithfully adapts Stowe's novel, adding scenes after each act in which Tom explains the relevance of the play's themes for a modern day audience.

20. See Harry Birdoff, *The World's Greatest Hit* (New York: S. F. Vanni, 1947).

21. Frick occasionally relies on Birdoff's account despite its lack of citations or bibliography, and he argues that "much of [Birdoff's] book is based upon primary materials currently housed in the archive of the Harriet Beecher Stowe Center in Hartford, Con-

necticut." My own research in this archive suggests that the Birdoff collection fails to back up a number of the claims in *The World's Greatest Hit*. John W. Frick, *"Uncle Tom's Cabin" on the American Stage and Screen* (New York: Palgrave, 2012), xv.

22. "Uncle Tom's Cabin" (Globe Theatre, Boston, May 26, 1877), Uncle Tom's Cabin Playbills, Harvard Theatre Collection, Houghton Library, Harvard University.

23. J. Harry Jackson, "The Stage," *The Freeman* (Indianapolis), March 4, 1899.

24. Eric Lott, *Love and Theft: Blackface Minstrelsy and the American Working Class* (New York: Oxford University Press, 1993), 4.

25. Even Frederick Douglass, who publicly censured white blackface minstrels as "the filthy scum of white society" and criticized black minstrels for following in their stead, reflected that there was "something to be gained, when the colored man in any form can appear before a white audience," and that such a company, "with industry, application, and a proper cultivation of their taste, may yet be instrumental in removing the prejudice against our race." Lott, *Love and Theft*, 15, 37. I see a contemporary parallel with LGBTQ characters in popular culture. It was not all that long ago that, according to Hollywood, the LGBTQ community essentially did not exist; indeed, for many decades the regulations of the Production Code Administration made sure of that. Today, a viewer revisiting the LGBTQ characters who seemed revolutionary in the 1980s and 1990s is likely to find them disappointingly essentialist. But for a marginalized group, the very fact of representation means something. There's a reason why, at least for my generation, the process of coming out often involves a personal movie marathon.

26. Jane P. Tompkins, "Sentimental Power: Uncle Tom's Cabin and the Politics of Literary History," in *Harriet Beecher Stowe's "Uncle Tom's Cabin": A Casebook*, ed. Elizabeth Ammons (New York: Oxford University Press, 2007), 73.

27. George Sand, "Review of *Uncle Tom's Cabin*," *La Presse*, December 17, 1852.

28. This anecdote is often repeated but is probably apocryphal, as there was no report of such an exchange until much later, in Charles Edward Stowe's 1889 biography, *A Life of Harriet Beecher Stowe*. Nevertheless, Americans of all political affiliations frequently invoked the precipitous influence of *Uncle Tom's Cabin* on the Civil War.

29. George Eliot, "Review of *Dred*" (1856), in *Critical Essays on Harriet Beecher Stowe*, ed. Elizabeth Ammons (Boston: G. K. Hall, 1980), 43.

30. Philip K. Fisher, *Hard Facts: Setting and Form in the American Novel* (New York: Oxford University Press, 1985), 98.

31. See Claire Parfait, *The Publishing History of "Uncle Tom's Cabin," 1852–2002* (Aldershot, Hampshire, UK: Ashgate, 2007). The appendix offers an extensive list of the American editions.

32. Stephen Railton, "Readapting *Uncle Tom's Cabin*," in *Nineteenth-Century American Fiction on Screen*, ed. R. Barton Palmer (Cambridge: Cambridge University Press, 2007), 62. John Frick estimates that the total cost for the 1927 Universal picture was $2,600,000. Frick, *"Uncle Tom's Cabin" on the American Stage and Screen*, 209.

33. Ying Wong and Jeanne Tsai, "Cultural Models of Shame and Guilt," in *Handbook of Self-Conscious Emotions*, ed. Jessica Tracy, Richard Robins, and June Tangney (New York: Guilford Press, 2007), 211.

34. Ron Eyerman, *Cultural Trauma: Slavery and the Formation of African American Identity* (Cambridge: Cambridge University Press, 2001), 120.

35. "The Uncle Tom Epidemic," *Literary World* (New York), December 4, 1852, 355.

36. André Schiffrin, *The Business of Books* (London: Verso, 2001), 8.

37. "Uncle Tom's Cabin," *Christian Parlor Magazine*, May 1, 1852, UTCAC.

38. "Uncle Tom's Cabin and the London Times," *New York Evangelist*, September 23, 1852, UTCAC.

39. For more on the enactment and enforcement of the Fugitive Slave Act, see Stanley Campbell, *The Slave Catchers: Enforcement of the Fugitive Slave Law, 1850–1860* (Chapel Hill: University of North Carolina Press, 1968).

40. Joan D. Hedrick, *Harriet Beecher Stowe: A Life* (New York: Oxford University Press, 1994), 204.

41. Ibid., 207.

42. See Ronald J. Zboray, *A Fictive People: Antebellum Economic Development and the American Reading Public* (New York: Oxford University Press, 1993), 5–11.

43. Ibid., 13.

44. Claire Parfait, *The Publishing History of "Uncle Tom's Cabin,"* 34.

45. See ibid., 47–66.

46. In the insider's world of mid-nineteenth-century American publishing, magazines and newspapers usually gave positive notices to publishers and authors who had influence, paid for advertisements, or sent handsome review copies. Those who did not were punished with negative reviews or total silence. See William Charvat, "James T. Fields and the Beginnings of Book Promotion, 1840–1855," in *The Profession of Authorship in America, 1800–1870: The Papers of William Charvat*, ed. Matthew J. Bruccoli (Columbus: Ohio State University Press, 1968).

47. Parfait, *The Publishing History of "Uncle Tom's Cabin,"* 53.

48. "Extraordinary Demand for 'Uncle Tom's Cabin,'" *The Liberator*, April 9, 1852, UTCAC.

49. "Uncle Tom's Cabin." *The Independent*, May 13, 1852, UTCAC.

50. "Literary," *The Independent*, June 10, 1852, UTCAC.

51. "Uncle Tom's Cabin," *National Anti-Slavery Standard*, August 19, 1852, UTCAC.

52. See Katharine Q. Seelye, "Lurid Numbers on Glossy Pages! (Magazines Exploit What Sells)," *New York Times*, February 10, 2006.

53. Parfait, *The Publishing History of "Uncle Tom's Cabin,"* 80.

54. "Eva's Parting," *Dwight's Journal of Music*, July 31, 1852, UTCAC.

55. "The Anti-Christian Influence of *Uncle Tom's Cabin*," repr. *Frederick Douglass' Paper*, April 15, 1853, UTCAC.

56. Henry James, *A Small Boy and Others* (New York: Scribner's, 1913), 159–160.

57. "Novels and Their Influences," *The Liberator*, June 11, 1852, UTCAC. In this article *The Liberator* quotes and responds to an article from the *New York Mirror*, which in turn quotes an article from the *Pittsburgh Gazette*.

58. "Uncle Tom Literature," *The Independent*, September 30, 1852, UTCAC.

59. William R. Taylor, *Cavalier and Yankee: The Old South and the American National Character* (Cambridge, MA: Harvard University Press, 1979), 307.

60. "'Uncle Tom' on the Stage," *Illustrated News* (New York), January 22, 1853, UTCAC.

61. "France," *New York Times*, February 23, 1853.

62. *The Liberator*, March 4, 1853, UTCAC.

63. "Notices of New Works," *Southern Literary Messenger*, October 1852, UTCAC.

64. Unsigned reprint, "The Effect of Uncle Tom in Europe," *Circular* (Brooklyn), May 7, 1853, UTCAC. In truth, however, Stowe's novel offers a critique of the English labor system: As St. Clare tells Ophelia, his travels in England convinced him of the truth of his pro-slavery brother Alfred's claim that his slaves are better off than many English laborers.

65. "From the British Slave System," *Graham's Magazine*, March 1853, UTCAC. Using eerily similar language more than 150 years later, former presidential candidate Ralph Nader suggested to a Fox newscaster that the newly elected President Obama faced a choice between being "an Uncle Sam for the people of this country, or Uncle Tom for the giant corporations." Nader seemed to think that there was nothing wrong with his choice of words, but the newscaster balked at the racially loaded term. FOX news, November 4, 2008, http://www.youtube.com/watch?v=7IshiClQqCM, accessed May 6, 2012.

66. "Uncle Tomitudes," *Putnam's Monthly Magazine*, January 1853, 100.

67. "The Uncle Tom Epidemic," 355.

68. On the cultural history of Frankenstein in the United States in relation to race and nation, see Elizabeth Young, *Black Frankenstein: The Making of an American Metaphor* (New York: New York University Press, 2008).

69. John Frow, "Spectacle Binding: On Character," *Poetics Today* 7.2 (1986): 227. See also John Frow, *Character and Person* (Oxford: Oxford University Press, 2014).

70. Alex Woloch, *The One vs. the Many: Minor Characters and the Space of the Protagonist in the Novel* (Princeton, NJ: Princeton University Press, 2003), 17.

71. Deidre Lynch, *The Economy of Character: Novels, Market Culture, and the Business of Inner Meaning* (Chicago: University of Chicago Press, 1998); Woloch, *The One vs. the Many*; David A. Brewer, *The Afterlife of Character, 1726–1825* (Philadelphia: University of Pennsylvania Press, 2005).

72. Woloch, *The One vs. the Many*, 30.

73. Lynch, *The Economy of Character*, 5.

74. Brewer, *The Afterlife of Character*, 14.

75. Joshua Landy, *How to Do Things with Fictions* (Oxford: Oxford University Press, 2012), 9.

76. E. M. Forster, *Aspects of the Novel* (1927), 103–105.

Chapter 1: A Manly Hero

1. "Judge Tourgée," *Freeman* (Indianapolis), August 22, 1896.

2. Elizabeth Ammons, "Heroines in *Uncle Tom's Cabin*," in *Critical Essays on Harriet Beecher Stowe* (Boston: G. K. Hall, 1980), 153.

3. See Ann Douglas, *The Feminization of American Culture* (New York: Knopf, 1977); Jane Tompkins, *Sensational Designs: The Cultural Work of American Fiction 1790–1860* (New York: Oxford University Press, 1985).

4. George Fredrickson, *The Black Image in the White Mind* (Middletown, CT: Wesleyan University Press, 1987).

5. See Lawrence Buell, *New England Literary Culture: From Revolution through Renaissance* (Cambridge: Cambridge University Press, 1986); Kenneth Lynn, *Visions of America: Eleven Literary Historical Essays* (Westport, CT: Greenwood Press, 1973); Stephen Railton, *Authorship and Audience: Literary Performance in the American Renaissance* (Princeton, NJ: Princeton University Press, 1991); Arthur Riss, *Race, Slavery, and Liberalism in Nineteenth-Century American Literature* (Cambridge: Cambridge University Press, 2006); Ezra Tawil, *The Making of Racial Sentiment: Slavery and the Birth of the Frontier Romance* (Cambridge: Cambridge University Press, 2006); Robyn Wiegman, *American Anatomies: Theorizing Race and Gender* (Durham, NC: Duke University Press, 1995); Richard Yarborough, "Strategies of Black Characterization in *Uncle Tom's Cabin* and the Early Afro-American Novel," in *New Essays on "Uncle Tom's Cabin,"* ed. Eric

Sundquist (Cambridge: Cambridge University Press, 1986); Jean Fagan Yellin, *The Intricate Knot: Black Figures in American Literature 1776–1863* (New York: New York University Press, 1972).

6. See, for example: Tompkins, *Sensational Designs*; Fredrickson, *The Black Image in the White Mind*; and James Baldwin, "Everybody's Protest Novel," *Partisan Review* 16.6 (June 1949): 578–585.

7. See Fredrickson, *The Black Image in the White Mind*.

8. As Fredrickson notes, the romantic racialist belief in the natural docility of blacks, which developed in the 1830s, would not have been possible if there had been any major slave uprisings after the Nat Turner rebellion in 1831.

9. Jesus tells his followers, "Whosoever shall humble himself as this little child, the same is the greatest in the kingdom of heaven" (Matthew 18:4), and "Whosoever shall not receive the kingdom of God as a little child shall in no wise enter therein" (Luke 17:17). All references to the Bible are to the King James version.

10. Fredrickson, *The Black Image in the White Mind*, 110.

11. Ibid., 118.

12. Ibid., 113.

13. The novel's romantic racialism is most notable in its vision of a millennial African future, in which Stowe's narrator digresses from the action of the novel to offer an expansive vision of a day when naturally gentle and simple Africans will offer glorious spiritual revelations. As Fredrickson points out, this moment bears a striking similarity to the millennial vision of Alexander Kinmont, who lectured in Cincinnati while Stowe lived there.

14. Thomas Graham describes the novel's "environmentalist explanation" of racial traits in "Harriet Beecher Stowe and the Question of Race," *New England Quarterly* 46.4 (1973): 618.

15. Harriet Beecher Stowe, *Uncle Tom's Cabin* (1852), ed. Elizabeth Ammons (New York: W. W. Norton, 1994), 81. All further references to *Uncle Tom's Cabin* are to this edition and will be cited parenthetically in the text.

16. Topsy's canny performance of race finds a complement in the St. Clare family's cook, Dinah, "the perfect mistress of that diplomatic art which unites the utmost subservience of manner with the utmost inflexibility as to measure" (180). Dinah performs subservience to keep the peace but maintains an almost preposterously messy kitchen regardless, thereby cordoning off the one space in the house that is, through its disorder, entirely hers. In the rift between Dinah's subservient appearance and her stubborn behavior, Stowe suggests that black people can shrewdly perform certain racialized roles for their own advantage.

17. *The Liberator*, July 2, 1852, in *"Uncle Tom's Cabin" and American Culture*, ed. Stephen Railton, accessed July 25, 2010, http://utc.iath.virginia.edu (henceforth UTCAC).

18. "Another Word about Uncle Tom," unsigned reprint, *The Independent*, September 2, 1852, UTCAC.

19. "Notices of New Works," *Southern Literary Messenger* 18 (October 1852): 633.

20. Ibid., 637.

21. Thomas Wentworth Higginson, "The Maroons of Surinam," *Atlantic Monthly*, May 1860, 553.

22. Henry C. Wright, "Uncle Tom's Cabin—Objectionable Characteristics," *The Liberator*, July 9, 1852, UTCAC.

23. "Fair Play," *The Liberator*, September 17, 1852, UTCAC. While in theory Wright opposed violence, in actuality he condoned violent escapes from slavery.

24. "Uncle Tom's Cabin; or, Life among the Lowly," *The Liberator*, March 26, 1852, UTCAC.

25. Ibid.

26. Jo-Ann Morgan, *"Uncle Tom's Cabin" as Visual Culture* (Columbia: University of Missouri Press, 2007), 26.

27. Cynthia Griffin Wolff, "'Masculinity' in *Uncle Tom's Cabin*," *American Quarterly* 47.4 (1995): 595–618.

28. The late Mrs. St. Clare was, as her son describes her, "a direct embodiment and personification of the New Testament," a woman with "no trace of human weakness or error" (195). Tom, too, embodies scripture, which "seemed so entirely to have wrought itself into his being, as to have become a part of himself, and to drop from his lips unconsciously" (26).

29. At the same time, however, St. Clare's heart without manliness is still morally preferable to Alfred's manliness without heart. We can see this in the differences between their respective children: Eva is infinitely loving and generous to all, but Henrique is selfish and cruel to the young slave who serves him.

30. Richard Yarborough characterizes their difference as a racial one: "If Harris is the articulate mulatto, correct in speech, rational, and initially impatient with religion, Tom is the passive, full-blood black, simple in expression, solicitous of all around him, gentle, and rarely shaken in his Christian faith." Yarborough, "Strategies of Black Characterization." Similarly, Joshua D. Bellin contrasts "the explosive rage of George Harris and the saintly mortification of Uncle Tom." Bellin, "Up to Heaven's Gate, Down in Earth's Dust: The Politics of Judgment in *Uncle Tom's Cabin*," *American Literature* 65.2 (1993): 280. See also Thomas Gossett, *"Uncle Tom's Cabin" and American Culture* (Dallas: Southern Methodist University Press, 1985); and Fredrickson, *The Black Image in the White Mind*.

31. "Judge Tourgée."

32. See John Stauffer, *The Black Hearts of Men: Radical Abolitionists and the Transformation of Race* (Cambridge, MA: Harvard University Press, 2002).

33. Yarborough, "Strategies of Black Characterization," 55.

34. The passage is Isaiah 43:2–3: "When thou passest through the waters, I will be with thee, and the rivers they shall not overflow with thee; when thou walkest through the fire, thou shalt not be burned, neither shall the flame kindle upon thee, for I am the Lord thy God, the Holy One of Israel, thy Saviour."

35. Tompkins, *Sensational Designs*, 127–128.

Chapter 2: Uncle Tom on the American Stage

1. Thomas Gossett, *"Uncle Tom's Cabin" and American Culture* (Dallas: Southern Methodist University Press, 1985), 260.

2. This letter has been quoted frequently and at length but I have been unable to locate it in any archive. A recent study of the Hutchinson Family Singers as cultural reformers mentions the letter but does not cite a source. See Scott Gac, *Singing for Freedom: The Hutchinson Family Singers and the Nineteenth-Century Culture of Reform* (New Haven, CT: Yale University Press, 2007).

3. See Eric Gardner, "Stowe Takes the Stage: Harriet Beecher Stowe's *The Christian Slave*," *Legacy* 15.1 (1998): 78–84.

4. Authors also had no control over the publication of translations. When Stowe sued a German publisher for translating *Uncle Tom's Cabin* without her permission (*Stowe v. Thomas*, 1853), the court ruled that translation was not a violation of an author's

copyright because the author had legal rights only to his (or her, in this case) exact language, and not the ideas behind it. Writing for the majority, Justice Robert C. Grier held that: "By the publication of Mrs. Stowe's book, the creations of the genius and imagination of the author have become as much public property as those of Homer or Cervantes. Uncle Tom and Topsy are as much *publici juris* as Don Quixote and Sancho Panza. . . . All that now remains is the copyright of her book; the exclusive right to print, reprint, and vend it, and those only can be called infringers of her rights, or pirates of her property, who are guilty of printing, publishing, importing or vending without her license, 'copies of her book.'"

   5. Gossett, *"Uncle Tom's Cabin" and American Culture*, 261.

   6. According to David Reynolds, the most recent chronicler of the cultural history of *Uncle Tom's Cabin*, the Uncle Tom of the American stage "was often presented as a stooped, obedient old fool, the model image of a submissive black man preferred by post-Reconstruction, pre–civil rights America. It was this Uncle Tom, weakened both physically and spiritually, who became a synonym for a racial sellout by the mid-20th century." Reynolds, "Rescuing the Real Uncle Tom," *New York Times*, June 13, 2011. This op-ed coincided with the publication of Reynolds' *Mightier Than the Sword: "Uncle Tom's Cabin" and the Battle for America* (New York: Norton, 2011), which similarly argues that the Uncle Tom dramas are responsible for the name's derogatory meaning.

   7. Charles Edward Stowe and Lyman Beecher Stowe, *Harriet Beecher Stowe: The Story of Her Life* (Boston: Houghton Mifflin, 1911), 148.

   8. See Sarah Meer, *Uncle Tom Mania: Slavery, Minstrelsy, and Transatlantic Culture in the 1850s* (Athens: University of Georgia Press, 2005).

   9. Ibid., 129.

   10. On George C. Howard and Caroline Howard, see John W. Frick, *"Uncle Tom's Cabin" on the American Stage and Screen* (New York: Palgrave, 2012), 34–38.

   11. Walter Scott Howard, "From Slavery to Prohibition: A History of the Drama of 'Uncle Tom's Cabin'" (unpublished manuscript, 1931), 46, George C. Howard Collection, Harry Ransom Center, University of Texas at Austin.

   12. According to Owens' wife and biographer, when the Baltimore production of *Uncle Tom's Cabin* was announced, the theater manager's lawyer begged him to retract the play, telling him, "You will ruin yourself with the 'South,' and get into all sorts of trouble; the people will tear the theatre down or do you a personal injury." But Owens, who himself apparently had "no sectional feeling in regard to the play," pressed on, proceeding to take the role of Uncle Tom himself (even though he did not typically black up) so that he could "be on the spot should any trouble take place." The play was a hit with Baltimore audiences. Mary C. Stevens Owens, *Memories of the Professional and Social Life of John E. Owens* (Baltimore: John Murphy, 1892), 74–76.

   13. Probably because of the lowly status of a "house playwright," little is known about Conway. For what is known about him, see Frick, *"Uncle Tom's Cabin" on the American Stage and Screen*, 84–86.

   14. In a letter to Kimball, Conway detailed two "difficulties of magnitude," neither of which involved the play's politics: the first was working out the complicated plot's time line, and the second was effectively combining the characters of Eliza and Emmeline in order to focus the audience's sympathy and avoid adding an extra actor to the cast. H. J. Conway to Moses Kimball, June 1, 1852, Moses Kimball Papers, Boston Athenaeum. For further discussion of correspondence related to the Boston Museum's staging of *Uncle Tom's Cabin*, see Bruce McConachie, "H. J. Conway's Dramatization

of 'Uncle Tom's Cabin': A Previously Unpublished Letter," *Theatre Journal* 34.2 (1982): 149–154; Edward Kahn, "Creator of Compromise: William Henry Sedley Smith and the Boston Museum's *Uncle Tom's Cabin*," *Theatre Survey* 4.2 (2000): 71–82.

15. William Henry Sedley Smith diary, November 20, 1852, Rare Books Department, Boston Public Library. My analysis of Smith's diary is indebted to Edward Kahn, but while Kahn begins from the premise that Conway's play compromised Stowe's antislavery politics and concludes that Smith's political views must have made him effect this compromise since neither Conway nor Kimball would have been likely to do so, I read Conway's script as anti-slavery rather than compromise and see no evidence in the diary or letters of Smith's intervention in the Conway script's politics. See Kahn, "Creator of Compromise."

16. Smith diary, January 22, 1853, Rare Books Department, Boston Public Library.

17. Smith diary, March 12, 1854, Rare Books Department, Boston Public Library.

18. Ethiop [William J. Wilson], "From Our Brooklyn Correspondent," *Frederick Douglass' Paper*, June 17, 1852, in *"Uncle Tom's Cabin" and American Culture*, ed. Stephen Railton, accessed July 25, 2010, http://utc.iath.virginia.edu (henceforth UTCAC).

19. "Uncle Tom's Cabin" playbills (National Theatre, Philadelphia, September 28, 1853; Chestnut Street Theatre, Philadelphia, November 21, 1853), Harvard Theatre Collection, Harvard University.

20. *Spirit of the Times* (New York), March 11, 1854, UTCAC.

21. There was one report of a show in Cleveland in 1852 (*Plain Dealer*, August 13, 1852) and another, by Anna Marble, in Chicago ("Uncle Tom's at the Theatre," *Chicago Daily Tribune*, December 20, 1852). While producers claimed that the show ran for one hundred nights and many scholars have accepted that number, a 1968 dissertation by William Jackson Kesler counts seventy-nine total performances at Troy, not one hundred. See William Jackson Kesler II, "The Early Production of the Aiken-Howard Versions of *Uncle Tom's Cabin*," PhD diss., University of Texas at Austin, 1968.

22. After New York, Western's version made appearances in Philadelphia; Boston; Worcester, Massachusetts; and Cleveland.

23. In the Taylor adaptation, George and Eliza were called Edward and Morna Wilmot; the names probably referenced the failed Wilmot Proviso, which would have prevented the spread of slavery into new territories. First added to an 1846 appropriations bill by Congressman David Wilmot of Pennsylvania, the Wilmot Proviso would have banned slavery from all territories to be acquired from Mexico as part of the Mexican-American War. It twice passed in the House but failed in the Senate. Despite this failure, the Wilmot Proviso contributed to the coming of the Civil War by deepening sectional tensions in the legislature.

24. "Uncle Tom's Cabin" broadside (1852), National Theatre, New York, Harry Birdoff Collection, Harriet Beecher Stowe Center. As there is no extant script, all information about Western's *Uncle Tom's Cabin* comes from the playbill's detailed synopsis and contemporaneous reviews.

25. "Uncle Tom's Cabin," *New York Herald*, September 3, 1852.

26. Robert Toll, *Blacking Up: The Minstrel Show in Nineteenth Century America* (New York: Oxford University Press, 1974), 162.

27. *Plain Dealer* (Cleveland), May 10, 1853.

28. Les Harrison, *The Temple and the Forum: The American Museum and Cultural Authority in Hawthorne, Melville, Stowe, and Whitman* (Tuscaloosa: University of Alabama Press, 2007), 135.

29. In Troy, when a local Baptist minister called a special meeting to reprimand his flock for going to see *Uncle Tom's Cabin,* he found that fully two thirds had already attended. Laurence Senelick, *The Age and Stage of George L. Fox 1825–1877* (Iowa City: University of Iowa Press, 1999), 271.

30. Richard Moody, ed., *Dramas from the American Theater 1762–1909* (Cleveland: World Publishing Company, [1966]), 354.

31. Gossett, *"Uncle Tom's Cabin" and American Culture,* 270.

32. Senelick, *The Age and Stage of George L. Fox,* 69.

33. "'Podgers' in New York," *Daily Placer Times and Transcript* (San Francisco), February 28, 1854.

34. Recalling his early attendance of the *Uncle Tom's Cabin* plays, James wrote, "It was a great thing to have a canon to judge by—it helped conscious criticism, which was to fit on wings (for use ever after) on the shoulders of appreciation." Henry James, *A Small Boy and Others* (New York: Scribner's, 1913), 162.

35. "H.," "'Uncle Tom' among the Bowery Boys," *New York Daily Times,* July 27, 1853.

36. *New York Atlas,* October 16, 1853, cited in Gossett, *"Uncle Tom's Cabin" and American Culture,* 270.

37. "The Theatre in New-York," *New York Daily Times,* October 25, 1853.

38. [From a New York Correspondent], "'Uncle Tom' on the Stage, *The Liberator,* September 9, 1853, UTCAC. Although the review is sometimes attributed to Garrison because it was published in his paper, it was unsigned.

39. See Toll, *Blacking Up.*

40. Emmett King, "The Great American Drama," *Metropolitan Magazine* 31 (1909): 327. An important exception to the comic minstrel role was the sentimental songs of the famous minstrel songwriter Stephen Foster, which became popular around the time that *Uncle Tom's Cabin* did. In compositions such as "The Old Folks at Home" and "Massa's in the Cold Ground," Foster depicted the yearning of Southern blacks for happy homes in the South or for departed lovers and family members.

41. Ibid.

42. Topsy was also a marked departure from previous racial representations. In fact, Aiken's script originally made Topsy a boy, as no woman would consent to "blacking up." But George C. Howard's wife, Caroline Fox Howard, did so much with the role of Topsy that she became famous for it and played it frequently for the rest of her career.

43. The text used here comes from an 1852 script held in the George C. Howard Collection, Harry Ransom Center, University of Texas at Austin.

44. George Aiken, "Uncle Tom's Cabin," [1852], George C. Howard Collection, Harry Ransom Center, University of Texas at Austin.

45. The published 1858 script trims even more than the 1852 script, offering no mention of Tom's involvement in Cassy and Emmeline's escape or his reasons for not joining them and instead mentioning the escape only after it has happened. See George L. Aiken, *Uncle Tom's Cabin* (New York: Samuel French, 1858).

46. Harrison, *The Temple and the Forum,* 162.

47. Jeffrey D. Mason, *Melodrama and the Myth of America* (Bloomington: Indiana University Press, 1993), 124.

48. My understanding of dignity is indebted to Michael Rosen's *Dignity: Its History and Meaning* (Cambridge, MA: Harvard University Press, 2012).

49. Bruce McConachie, the first scholar to publish on the recovered 1876 Conway-Aiken script, compared it to the 1852 playbills and concluded that the 1876 version

seemed to match the original Conway play (except, of course, where it is replaced by the Aiken text). Prior to the script's recovery, Robert Toll's description of the play as "pro-Southern," a judgment largely based on Birdoff's assessment, was generally accepted. With the discovery of the 1876 script, this understanding of Conway's play was somewhat amended to, as McConachie described it, "mildly anti-slavery," or, according to Eric Lott, a work of "relatively complacent politics." Recent scholarship has begun to complicate this reading of Conway: Sarah Meer describes the Conway *Uncle Tom's Cabin* as "more muddled in its politics than calculating," and Les Harrison, contesting the notion of Aiken's play as authentic in regard to Stowe's novel and Conway's as inauthentic, notes the preponderance of debate in Conway's play, a dramatic strategy that embraces a part of Stowe's novel that Aiken's script largely ignores. While David Reynolds highlights the play's "biting comments on slavery and the institutions that support it," John Frick argues that each of these "supposedly subversive examples . . . was, in some way, compromised and hence rendered ambiguous." See Bruce McConachie, "Out of the Kitchen and into the Marketplace: Normalizing *Uncle Tom's Cabin* for the Antebellum Stage," *Journal of American Drama and Theatre* 3.1 (1991): 5–28; Toll, *Blacking Up*; Eric Lott, *Love and Theft: Blackface Minstrelsy and the American Working Class* (New York: Oxford University Press, 1993); Meer, *Uncle Tom Mania*; Harrison, *The Temple and the Forum*; Reynolds, *Mightier Than the Sword*, 143; Frick, *"Uncle Tom's Cabin" on the American Stage and Screen*, 89.

50. William Lloyd Garrison to Helen E. Garrison, September 5, 1853. Louis Ruchames, ed., *The Letters of William Lloyd Garrison: From Disunionism to the Brink of War, 1850–1860* (Cambridge, MA: Belknap Press of Harvard University Press, 1975), 247–248.

51. "Boston Museum: 'Uncle Tom's Cabin,'" *Frederick Douglass' Paper*, December 3, 1852. Reprinted from the *Boston Commonwealth*.

52. H. J. Conway, "Uncle Tom's Cabin: A Drama in Five Parts," 2.3, unpublished MS, Boston, 1852. The Conway script has not been published in print, but it is available on the University of Virginia's *"Uncle Tom's Cabin" and American Culture* website, on a page titled "H. J. Conway's Uncle Tom," accessed May 6, 2012, http://utc.iath.virginia .edu/onstage/scripts/conwayhp.html. This transcription of the play was extracted from a manuscript version of the promptbook that was used in an 1876 production at the Boston Museum and is housed at the Howard Collection, Performing Arts Collection, Harry Ransom Center, University of Texas at Austin.

53. Parker Pillsbury, "'Uncle Tom's Cabin' at a Boston Theatre," *The Liberator*, December 24, 1852, 1.

54. "'Uncle Tom's Cabin' Abroad," *The Liberator*, January 7, 1853, 1. Reprinted from the *Quincy Patriot's* Boston correspondent.

55. On Barnum's career-spanning engagement with images of race, see Benjamin Reiss, *The Showman and the Slave: Race, Death, and Memory in Barnum's America* (Cambridge, MA: Harvard University Press, 2001).

56. This was not the first time that Barnum borrowed one of Kimball's productions. The two sustained a decades-long friendship, during which Barnum often wrote to Kimball asking to share scripts and exhibits (such as *The General* in 1847 and William Henry Sedley Smith's *The Drunkard* in 1848) and recommendations (a good naturalist for the museum exhibitions in 1849, an extra Egyptian mummy in 1870). See Phineas Taylor Barnum Papers, Manuscripts and Archives Division, New York Public Library.

57. I address the series of responses and republications that have encouraged literary

critics to identify a concessionary attitude toward slavery in Conway's play, and especially Barnum's production of it, in Spingarn, "When Uncle Tom Didn't Die: The Anti-
slavery Politics of H. J. Conway's *Uncle Tom's Cabin,*" *Theatre Survey* 53.2 (2012): 203–218.

58. A slave-owner earlier in his life, by 1855 Barnum wrote to the Unitarian minister and abolitionist Thomas Wentworth Higginson, "I have traveled much in the
southern states & have got to abhor the curse from witnessing its fruits. I have spent
months on the cotton plantations of Mississippi, where I have seen more than one
'Legree.'" Ten years later, he gave an impassioned speech to the Connecticut legislature
arguing that the right to vote should be "extended to every educated and moral man
within our state, *regardless of color.*" Letter from Barnum to Rev. Thomas Wentworth
Higginson, ca. April 1855, in *Selected Letters of P. T. Barnum,* ed. A. H. Saxon (New York:
Columbia University Press, 1983), 86; "Connecticut Legislature," *Hartford Daily Cou-
rant,* May 25, 1865, 2.

59. "Uncle Tom at Barnum's," *New-York Daily Tribune,* November 15, 1853, 7.

60. Dramatized "from the popular and world-renowned work of Mrs. HAR-
RIET BEECHER STOWE," this production, the ads proclaimed, featured "ORIG-
INAL MUSIC, CHORUSES, a MOVING PANORAMIC DIORAMA, and other
expensive and highly effective auxillaries [*sic*]." Advertisement for Barnum's American Museum, *New-York Daily Tribune,* November 7, 1853. The same text appears in
advertisements from November 8, 9, 10, 11, 12, 14, and 15 in both the *Tribune* and the
Times.

61. Advertisement for Barnum's American Museum, *New-York Daily Tribune,* November 16, 1853. Probably because of the two-page layout of the reproduced advertisement in Birdoff's *The World's Greatest Hit,* this advertisement is misquoted in Meer's
Uncle Tom Mania in a manner that suggests a radically different reading: the key phrase
"SLAVERY AS IT IS" is overlooked so that the advertisement seems to argue that
"Southern Negro"—and not "Southern Negro SLAVERY AS IT IS"—is abhorrently
deformed, cruel, and barbaric.

62. "Uncle Tom at Barnum's," *New-York Daily Tribune,* December 7, 1853.

63. For more on the anti-slavery politics of Conway's *Uncle Tom's Cabin,* see Spingarn, "When Uncle Tom Didn't Die."

64. "Uncle Tom at Barnum's," *New-York Daily Tribune,* December 7, 1853.

65. Richard Yarborough, for example, describes Uncle Tom's death as one of the
novel's political failings, writing that for Stowe, "[h]eavenly salvation might indeed be
possible for blacks, but a truly just interracial society was inconceivable." Yarborough,
"Strategies of Black Characterization in *Uncle Tom's Cabin* and the Early Afro-American Novel," in *New Essays on "Uncle Tom's Cabin,"* ed. Eric Sundquist (Cambridge:
Cambridge University Press, 1996), 65.

66. Harriet Beecher Stowe, *Uncle Tom's Cabin* (1852), ed. Elizabeth Ammons (New
York: W. W. Norton, 1994), 365.

67. Ibid., 388.

68. *Oxford English Dictionary,* June 2017, s.v. "down, adv.," OED Online, accessed
July 20, 2017, http://www.oed.com/view/Entry/57211?redirectedFrom=down+east.

69. James, *A Small Boy,* 162.

70. Ibid., 160.

71. Ibid., 159.

72. A. M. Drummond and Richard Moody, "The Hit of the Century: *Uncle Tom's
Cabin,* 1852–53," *Educational Theatre Journal* 4 (1952): 319.

73. Ibid.

74. "H.,"" 'Uncle Tom' among the Bowery Boys," *New York Daily Times*, July 27, 1853.

75. "Uncle Tom's Cabin," *Daily Cleveland Herald*, November 11, 1853.

76. "City Items," *New-York Daily Tribune*, December 15, 1858.

77. "Uncle Tom's Cabin," *Plain Dealer*, November 27, 1854.

78. "A Dramatic Treat in Preparation," *Daily Evening Bulletin* (San Francisco), October 7, 1858.

79. "Amusements," *Daily National Intelligencer* (Washington, DC), May 11, 1865.

80. "Local Items," *Albany Journal*, March 14, 1854.

81. Meer, *Uncle Tom Mania*, 61.

82. *Uncle Tom's Cabin; or, Hearts and Home* playbill, Minstrel Hall, New York, May 15, 1855, Harvard Theatre Collection, Harvard University.

83. "Happy Uncle Tom," *Frank Brower's Black Diamond Songster* (New York: Dick and Fitzgerald, n.d.).

84. "Uncle Tom's Cabin," *National Era*, October 27, 1853. This production, at Philadelphia's National Theatre, was advertised as being written by S. E. Harris but appears to have been a rip-off of Aiken, with "Deacon Jeroboam Pettibone" and "Sampson Skinner" replacing Aiken's characters Deacon Perry and Gumption Cute. Interestingly, the cast list includes the surnames of three key persons from the production at New York's National, with Mr. Howard playing "Adolph, a slave," Mr. Purdy as "Sambo, a slave," and Mr. Aiken "the auctioneer." *Uncle Tom's Cabin* playbill, National Theatre, Philadelphia, September 28, 1853, Harvard Theatre Collection, Harvard University.

85. *Daily Commercial Register* (Sandusky, OH), January 28, 1854.

86. W., "The Past, the Present, and the Future," *Frederick Douglass' Paper*, January 27, 1865.

87. Several productions shared this subtitle: Joseph M. Fields' *Uncle Tom's Cabin; or Life in the South as It Is*, George Jamieson's *The Old Plantation; or Uncle Tom as He Is*, and Sam Sanford's *Happy Uncle Tom's Cabin: or Real Life in Old Virginia*. See Joseph P. Roppolo, "Uncle Tom in New Orleans: Three Lost Plays," *New England Quarterly* 27.2 (1954): 213–226. Sanford's adaptation is referenced in James Dormon, *Theatre in the Antebellum South, 1815–1861* (Chapel Hill: University of North Carolina Press, 1967), 279, n. 66; *Lynchburg Daily Virginian*, January 10, 1854.

88. The other two included one by Dan Rice (not to be confused with T. D. Rice) and a third called *The Old Plantation, or Uncle Tom as He Is*.

89. "Mr. George Jamison's 'Uncle Tom' Drama," *Daily Picayune*, April 3, 1854.

90. *The Old Plantation; or The Real Uncle Tom* playbill, Bowery Theatre, New York, March 5, 1860, Harvard Theatre Collection, Harvard University.

91. *The Old Plantation; or The Real Uncle Tom* playbill, Bowery Theatre, New York, March 1, 1860, Harvard Theatre Collection, Harvard University; advertisement for *The Old Plantation; or The Real Uncle Tom* at Winter Garden Theatre, June 22, 1860.

92. *The Old Plantation; or The Real Uncle Tom* playbill, Bowery Theatre, New York, March 1, 1860, Harvard Theatre Collection, Harvard University.

93. *The Barre Patriot* (Massachusetts), March 24, 1854, reprinted from *The Delta*.

94. "Our New York Letter," *Philadelphia Inquirer*, March 3, 1862.

95. *Lowell Daily Citizen*, March 7, 1862.

96. "Dramatic, Musical, &c.," *North American and United States Gazette*, March 17, 1862.

97. "Uncle Tom's Cabin," *New-York Daily Tribune*, February 26, 1862, 8.

Chapter 3: Uncle Tom and Jim Crow

  1. Leslie A. Fiedler, *The Inadvertent Epic: From "Uncle Tom's Cabin" to "Roots"* (Toronto: Canadian Broadcasting Corporation, 1979), 26.

  2. "The Emancipation Slaves," *New York Times*, July 13, 1865.

  3. *Boston Daily Advertiser*, July 30, 1867.

  4. John William DeForest, "The Great American Novel," *The Nation* 6.132 (1868): 28.

  5. "The Proclamation an[d] Its Effects," *Chicago Tribune*, May 31, 1865.

  6. *Pomeroy's Democrat* (New York), November 21, 1874, 7.

  7. Thomas Nelson Page, "Scenes in Old Virginia," *Baltimore Sunday Herald*, April 2, 1893, 19.

  8. "Political Movements of the Day," *New York Herald*, June 23, 1871.

  9. In a speech on "The Probable Destiny of the African Race in America," the Reverend David Wills told a meeting of the National Educational Institute that "there was a time when Uncle Tom had a cabin, but out of the confusion since the war Uncle Tom had come without a cabin." "The National Institute," *Philadelphia Inquirer*, August 11, 1876. Other instances of the "Uncle Tom without a cabin" rhetoric include "Our Ebony Idol," *New York Herald*, October 11, 1874; *Wheeling Daily Register* (Wheeling, WV), November 24, 1876; "Uncle Tom without a Cabin," *Telegraph and Messenger* (Macon, GA), March 25, 1884.

  10. "Literary Notes," *Cincinnati Commercial*, June 5, 1876.

  11. "The Aguilar Free Library," *New York Times*, July 5, 1896.

  12. John Frick, citing George Odell's fifteen-volume *Annals of the New York Stage* (1927–1941) suggests that after the Civil War, *"Uncle Tom's Cabin"* was even more ubiquitous on New York's stages than it had been before the war." Frick, *"Uncle Tom's Cabin" on the American Stage and Screen* (New York: Palgrave, 2012), 111.

  13. For example, an advertisement for an *Uncle Tom's Cabin* show at Washington, DC's National Theatre trumpeted its "Realistic Cascade of Real Water," among other features. Advertisement for "Uncle Tom's Cabin," *Washington Post*, October 87, 1878, 4.

  14. Frick, *"Uncle Tom's Cabin" on the American Stage and Screen*, 120.

  15. "Theatrical," *Salt Lake Daily Telegraph*, October 5, 1867.

  16. "Great Events," *Jackson Citizen Patriot* (Jackson, MS), May 3, 1865; "Maguire's Opera House," *Evening Bulletin* (San Francisco), July 27, 1866; "'Uncle Tom's Cabin' at the Museum," *Boston Globe*, May 2, 1876, 4; "The Olympic," *Daily Inter Ocean*, January 3, 1882; "'Uncle Tom's Cabin' and Variety at the Howard," *Boston Daily Advertiser*, January 30, 1877.

  17. "New York Letter," *Evening Bulletin* (Baltimore), May 27, 1876.

  18. "Amusements," *Boston Daily Globe*, June 19, 1888.

  19. "Lothrop's Opera House," *Worcester Daily Spy*, November 9, 1894; "The Passing Show," *Boston Morning Journal*, May 2, 1894.

  20. "Amusements," *Minneapolis Journal*, May 29, 1900.

  21. George Fawcett Rowe, *Uncle Tom's Cabin* (1878), accessed May 6, 2012, http://utc.iath.virginia.edu/onstage/scripts/rowehp.html.

  22. Charles Townsend, *Uncle Tom's Cabin: A Melodrama in Five Acts*, Roorbach's American Edition Acting Plays (New York: Harold Roorbach, 1889); William A. Brady's *Uncle Tom's Cabin* (1901), Museum of the City of New York. A prefatory note in the Roorbach edition, emphasizing the adaptation's need for only twelve actors, with "no re-changes of costumes or make-up" and simple scenery and sets, suggests that this adaptation was meant for smaller traveling troupes.

23. Advertisement for Sam Sanford's *Uncle Tom's Cabin* at Washington Theatre Comique, *The Critic* (Washington, DC), September 25, 1872.

24. "Amusements," *Cincinnati Daily Enquirer*, December 27, 1865. During the same period, the blackface comedian Frank Brower had his own "Happy Uncle Tom" skit, though as discussed in the previous chapter, it had nothing in common with Stowe's work except the name.

25. "Uncle Tom's Cabin," *Pomeroy's Democrat*, October 6, 1869.

26. "Letter from New York," *Galveston Daily News*, January 6, 1881.

27. Ibid.

28. "Uncle Tom's Cabin for the Southern Market," *Baltimore Sun*, October 26, 1853. Similarly, in the late 1860s Kunkel played Uncle Tom as "contented and faithful" in "a modified dramatization" of *Uncle Tom's Cabin* staged in Baltimore, which was advertised as reveling "in the true attachment of the Slave to his Master and Family." Advertisement for *Uncle Tom's Cabin* at Maryland Institute, *Baltimore Sun*, September 24, 1868; advertisement for *Uncle Tom's Cabin* at Maryland Institute, *Baltimore Sun*, July 1, 1867; advertisement for *Uncle Tom's Cabin* at Maryland Institute, *Baltimore Sun*, June 24, 1867.

29. "The Drama," *New York Herald-Tribune*, February 19, 1878; "'Uncle Tom's Cabin' at the Boston," *Boston Globe*, April 4, 1876. Similarly, a Philadelphia critic commented that Kunkel "endowed the character with all due manliness and tenderness, and played throughout with rare pathetic power." "The Theatre," *Philadelphia Inquirer*, December 25, 1877.

30. In his later accounts of his career, Kunkel revised his own Uncle Tom origins, describing the unabashedly pro-slavery show he performed in Charleston in 1853 as a daring adaptation of Stowe's novel for which the city passed an ordinance banning any black person from attending. According to Kunkel, "Negroes came secretly to us and offered as much as $5 and $10 in gold, fortunes to them, you may believe, for a peep at the performance. Some we did slip into the 'flies,' but it finally got too warm for us, and at Savannah we had to give it up." "Uncle Tom's Cabin," *Cincinnati Commercial Gazette*, May 27, 1883.

31. "Uncle Tom's Cabin," *New Haven Evening Register*, April 29, 1879.

32. "Amusements," *Chicago Tribune*, September 5, 1879.

33. The group chose *Uncle Tom's Cabin* for its first production in 1871. Other black companies assembled in Pittsburgh (in 1878) and in Nashville, Tennessee (1887), the latter earning praise from the *Western Appeal*, a black newspaper founded in St. Paul, Minnesota. "The Northwest," *Chicago Tribune*, December 28, 1871; "Amusements," *Plain Dealer*, December 7, 1878; *Western Appeal*, September 24, 1887; *Western Appeal*, December 31, 1887.

34. *Cleveland Gazette*, June 7, 1884.

35. "Amusements," *Cincinnati Enquirer*, March 8, 1876.

36. "Latest News Items," *Evening Bulletin* (San Francisco), November 8, 1878.

37. "Society Notes," *The Freeman* (Indianapolis), June 29, 1895.

38. Bob Cole, "The Negro and the Stage," *Colored American Magazine* 4 (1902): 303.

39. Andrew Ward, *Dark Midnight When I Rise: The Story of the Jubilee Singers Who Introduced the World to the Music of Black America* (New York: Farrar, Straus and Giroux, 2000), xiii. Some have described the Fisk Jubilee Singers and their songs as "mere white crowd pleasers, anthems of helplessness and resignation, vestiges of bondage whose authenticity was muddled by the intercessions of white arrangers and composers" (ibid., xiv). But as Ward's account suggests, in the context of American racial politics during

the times, both the singers and their songs were far more militant, autonomous, and progressive than they seem today.

40. Dena J. Epstein notes the "dual role" of the Fisk group "as children of slaves who were also harbingers of what education could do for black youth." Epstein, "Black Spirituals: Their Emergence into Public Knowledge," *Black Music Research Journal* 10.1 (1990): 60.

41. According to Lynn Abbot and Doug Seroff, "[t]hrough the 1870s and 1880s, there were probably more African American entertainers gainfully employed as jubilee singers than in any other branch of professional entertainment." Lynn Abbot and Doug Seroff, *Out of Sight: The Rise of African American Popular Music 1889–1895* (Jackson: University Press of Mississippi, 2002), 119. More work remains to be done on the role of this significant body of black cultural production in American history.

42. In Indianapolis in 1787, "more than one was heard to remark last evening at the close of some particularly fine passage, 'That of itself is more than worth the cost of my ticket.' Those that care nothing for the play should attend for the music." "The Local Stage," *Indianapolis Sentinel*, March 27, 1878.

43. "The Theatre," *Philadelphia Inquirer*, December 25, 1877.

44. David S. Reynolds, *Mightier Than the Sword*, 181.

45. *Cleveland Gazette*, November 10, 1883.

46. *Cleveland Gazette*, September 5, 1885.

47. In John O. Griffith's short story "The Black Thread," set thirty years after Emancipation, an *Uncle Tom's Cabin* troupe comes to the fictional town of Rillville. The show is eagerly anticipated by both whites and blacks, including the story's central family, the Shoffers. At the show, it turns out that the man who plays Uncle Tom is the long-lost son of Grandma Shoffer, and the two are happily reunited. Here, *Uncle Tom's Cabin* serves as a mechanism of connection between generations. Griffith, "The Black Thread," *Half-Century Magazine*, November 1917–March 1918.

48. Cole, "The Negro and the Stage," 304.

49. William L. Andrews, "The Representation of Slavery and Rise of Afro-American Literary Realism, 1865–1920," in *Slavery and the Literary Imagination*, ed. Deborah E. McDowell and Arnold Rampersad (Baltimore: Johns Hopkins University Press, 1989), 69.

50. See August Meier, *Negro Thought in America 1880–1915: Racial Ideologies in the Age of Booker T. Washington* (1966; repr., Ann Arbor, MI: Ann Arbor Paperbacks, 1988).

51. David W. Blight, *Beyond the Battlefield: Race, Memory, and the American Civil War* (Amherst: University of Massachusetts Press, 2002); Nina Silber, *The Romance of Reunion: Northerners and the South, 1865–1900* (Chapel Hill: University of North Carolina Press, 1993).

52. See Kimberly Wallace-Sanders, *Mammy: A Century of Race, Gender, and Southern Memory* (Ann Arbor: University of Michigan Press, 2008).

53. *Uncle Tom's Cabin* playbill, Booth's Theatre, New York, March 5, 1878, Harvard Theatre Collection, Harvard University.

54. Classified job ad, *New York Herald*, February 6, 1878; "Artists in the Shade," *New York Herald*, February 14, 1878.

55. Unidentified clipping, February 23, 1878, Harvard Theatre Collection, Harvard University.

56. H. W. G., "The Stage," *Atlanta Daily Constitution*, January 12, 1881.

57. An 1878 New Orleans production received some positive press attention, but

the New Orleans *Times* suggested that no self-respecting Southerner would attend: "The only emotion appropriate with reference to Uncle Tom's Cabin, at this late day, is one of surprise that there should be bad taste enough to prompt its production in a Southern City and so little intelligence as to suppose that Southern audiences will be attracted by a performance which is an organized libel upon Southern people and Southern traditions." Despite this objection, the Academy of Music had a full house for the performance, particularly in the cheaper seats and the "colored gallery." "Uncle Tom's Cabin," *Times* (New Orleans), April 16, 1878; "Amusements," *Times* (New Orleans), April 16, 1878.

58. *Cincinnati Daily Gazette*, December 15, 1870.

59. "A Chivalric Howl," *Daily Republican* (Little Rock), November 12, 1973. Positive responses to the successful production of *Uncle Tom's Cabin* at New Orleans' Academy of Music include: "By Telegraph and Mail," *North American and United States Gazette* (Philadelphia), October 25, 1873; *New-York Daily Tribune*, November 1, 1873.

60. "Uncle Tom's Cabin," *Atlanta Constitution*, April 8, 1881; "Uncle Tom's Cabin," *Augusta Chronicle*, April 15, 1881.

61. Ibid. Similarly, a Georgia newspaper assured its readers that "there is nothing whatever objectionable in the play." "Uncle Tom's Cabin," *Augusta Chronicle*, February 22, 1881.

62. "Uncle Tom's Cabin," *Atlanta Constitution*, April 9, 1881.

63. "A Shower of Eggs," *Daily Arkansas Gazette*, April 16, 1881.

64. "All Around," *Atlanta Constitution*, April 14, 1881.

65. "Uncle Tom's Cabin in the South," *Daily Inter Ocean*, April 23, 1881.

66. *Vicksburg Daily Commercial* (Vicksburg, MS), June 21, 1882.

67. Reprinted from *The Vicksburg Herald*. "'Uncle Tom's Cabin' in the South," *Cincinnati Commercial*, March 26, 1883.

68. "'Uncle Tom's Cabin' Blacklisted," *Charlotte Daily Observer*, April 25, 1903.

69. *The Appeal* (St. Paul, MN), May 9, 1903.

70. "No Uncle Tom's Cabin Wanted," *Dallas Morning News*, February 19, 1892.

71. "Uncle Tom's Cabin at Bryan," *Dallas Morning News*, February 21, 1892.

72. Reprinted from *The Houston Daily Post*. "Abolitionist Trash," *Cleveland Gazette*, March 12, 1892.

73. According to the *New York Times*, Douglass endorsed Cook's production as a way to provide at least some evidence of African American progress at a fair that otherwise ignored it. "An Opera by Colored People," *New York Times*, January 7, 1893.

74. "The South at Chicago," *Atlanta Constitution*, February 17, 1893.

75. "Colored People's Day," *Baltimore Sun*, August 25, 1893.

76. "'Uncle Tom' and 'The Clansman,'" *Macon Daily Telegraph*, October 19, 1906.

77. Jerome interprets the biblical story of the Ethiopian eunuch's conversion (Acts 8:27–38) as proof of the power of submission to God.

78. As Scott Romine notes, Dixon's chapter titled "The Old and the New Negro" replaces the loyal, ineffectual old Nelse with Dick, who was once Charlie Gaston's devoted childhood pal but has now returned after a long absence and raped white Tom Camp's daughter. He is subsequently lynched. Scott Romine, "Dixon and the Literary Production of Whiteness," in *Thomas Dixon Jr. and the Birth of Modern America*, ed. Michelle K. Gillespie and Randal L. Hall (Baton Rouge: Louisiana State University Press, 2006), 136–137. See also Walter Benn Michaels, *Our America: Nativism, Modernism, and Pluralism* (Durham, NC: Duke University Press, 1995), 17–23.

79. W. E .B. Du Bois, "The Problem of Tillman, Vardaman, and Thomas Dixon, Jr." (1905), quoted in W. Fitzhugh Brundage, "American Proteus," in Gillespie and Hall, *Thomas Dixon Jr. and the Birth of Modern America*, 41.

80. See John David Smith, "'My Books Are Hard Reading for a Negro': Tom Dixon and His African American Critics, 1905–1939," in Gillespie and Hall, *Thomas Dixon Jr. and the Birth of Modern America*, 46–79.

81. "Mr. Dixon's 'The Leopard's Spots,'" *New York Times*, April 5, 1902, BR10. The *Times* also affirmed Dixon's representation of Reconstruction, commenting, "The author does not overstate the evils resulting to both races from the bestowal of the ballot upon the negro, nor the carnival of insolent misrule attending negro domination." The review reflects the extent to which the North came to accept black disfranchisement and loss of rights.

82. Thomas Dixon, Jr., "An Author's Answer to His Critics," *New York Times Saturday Review of Books and Art*, August 9, 1902, BR10.

83. "Amusements," *The Times-Picayune*, September 23, 1905.

84. "Protest," *Morning Herald* (Lexington, KY), October 25, 1901.

85. Twelfth Census of the United States—1900, Census Reports Volume I—Population Report Volume I, 540.

86. "Protest," *Morning Herald* (Lexington, KY), October 25, 1901.

87. Gregory A. Waller, *Main Street Amusements: Movies and Commercial Entertainment in a Southern City, 1896–1930* (Washington, DC: Smithsonian Institution Press, 1995), 44.

88. While "the standard Opera House policy consigned African Americans to the gallery, the cheapest and least visible section of the theater," "for *Uncle Tom's Cabin*, all of the fifty-cent balcony seats were also 'reserved for colored people.'" Ibid., 33.

89. "Protest against 'Uncle Tom' Shows," *Morning Herald* (Lexington, KY), January 11, 1902.

90. A typical broadside, for a production at New York's Provincetown Playhouse, assured audiences that *Uncle Tom's Cabin* "is not simply an amusement, it is a drama of our country, and the only one that is a part of our Nation's history. Take the children and give them an ideal and lasting lesson in American history." In like manner, an 1880 Jarrett & Palmer production billed itself as a "new dramatic arrangement of Mrs. Harriet Beecher Stowe's ante-bellum picture of Southern Life and Plantation Customs," while an 1897 broadside for Stetson's Big Double Spectacular Uncle Tom's Cabin Co. called it "This Grand Old Historical Play." "Uncle Tom's Cabin," Provincetown Playhouse, New York, November 8 [n.d.], New-York Historical Society Print Collection; *Uncle Tom's Cabin* playbill, Jarrett & Palmer's European Combination, Booth's Theatre, New York, December 28, 1880, Harvard Theatre Collection, Harvard University; *Uncle Tom's Cabin* broadside, Stetson's Big Double Spectacular Uncle Tom's Cabin Co., February 22, 1897, New-York Historical Society Print Collection.

91. Barbara Hochman describes such an effect in the use of *Uncle Tom's Cabin* in "a self-congratulatory narrative of moral and social progress in U.S. culture" during the 1890s. See Barbara Hochman, "*Uncle Tom's Cabin* at the World's Columbian Exposition," *Libraries and Culture* 41.1 (2006): 82–108.

92. "Protest against 'Uncle Tom' Shows," *Morning Herald* (Lexington, KY), January 11, 1902.

93. Ibid.

94. "Uncle Tom's Cabin," *Columbus Enquirer-Sun*, January 12, 1902.

95. "Uncle Tom's Cabin Wins," *Fort Worth Morning Register*, February 11, 1902; "Uncle Tom's Cabin Is Denounced as Partisan History," *Lexington Herald*, November 5, 1905.

96. *The Freeman* (Detroit), March 1, 1902.

97. "Barring Uncle Tom," *Macon Telegraph*, January 3, 1904.

98. "Uncle Tom's Cabin," *Duluth News-Tribune*, July 11, 1903.

99. "'Uncle Tom' Excluded from a Maryland Town," *Charlotte Daily Observer*, July 18, 1903.

100. Ibid.

101. Gregory A. Waller prints the text of the Uncle Tom's Cabin Law in the appendix of *Main Street Amusements*. This law became a selectively deployed tool for whites to censor anything that challenged the racial hierarchy. For example, Lexington's mayor cited the law in banning the showing of a film of the famous boxing match between Jack Johnson and Jim Jeffries, in which the black pugilist defeated the "Great White Hope." Meanwhile, black efforts to use the law to ban the 1915 showing of *Birth of a Nation* were unsuccessful: in this case, city commissioners argued that the Uncle Tom's Cabin Law was inapplicable to film, a medium "in a nebulous and undeveloped state when these laws were enacted." Anne E. Marshall, *Creating a Confederate Kentucky: The Lost Cause and Civil War Memory in a Border State* (Chapel Hill: University of North Carolina Press, 2010), 165–171.

102. "Kentucky Law May Be Copied in South," *Lexington Herald*, April 16, 1906, 8.

103. *Cleveland Gazette*, July 18, 1903.

104. "Baltimore, April 21, 1906," *The Afro-American* (Baltimore), April 21, 1906, 4. With the bill's passage, the paper saluted Kentucky for "shut[ting] out Tom Dixon and his Clansman. Poor 'Uncle Tom's Cabin' went along with it, but we can do without 'Old Uncle Tom' if we thereby get rid of that noxious weeds of prejudice now being reared by that notorious slanderer of Negro womanhood, Tom Dixon."

105. "Position and Place Where Colored Actors Actually Figure," *The Freeman* (Indianapolis), February 29, 1908.

106. "Ashamed of Their Record," *The Freeman* (Detroit), January 18, 1902.

107. Ibid., 4.

Chapter 4: Writing the Old Negro

1. "'Uncle Tom's Cabin to Show Next Week but under New Name," *Atlanta Constitution*, February 19, 1915, 5.

2. Ibid.

3. The black newspaper Topeka *Plaindealer*, for example, pointed out the unfairness of the NAACP having to struggle to convince the National Board of Censorship to reconsider its approval of *Birth of a Nation*, while protesters in Atlanta had easily forced *Uncle Tom's Cabin* to be renamed and ridden of "all disagreeable scenes," including the whipping post. "Clansman [illegible] Moving Picture," *The Plaindealer* (Topeka), March 19, 1915, 6.

4. James Weldon Johnson, "Uncle Tom and the Clansman," *New York Age*, March 4, 1915, in *The Selected Writings of James Weldon Johnson*, ed. Sondra Kathryn Wilson (New York: Oxford University Press, 1995), 1:12.

5. James Weldon Johnson, "Sam Lucas," *New York Age*, January 20, 1916, in ibid., 126.

6. In Aristotelian tragedy, the protagonist or hero should be well-born and basically

good, but with a tragic flaw—the "tragic hero" type. Unlike the later romantic form of the bildungsroman, in which the formation of the character *is* the story, in Aristotelian tragedy characters derive their effectiveness by effacing individuality in the service of a tragic plot. For more on character, see Stanley Bates, "Character," in *The Oxford Handbook of Philosophy and Literature* (New York: Oxford University Press, 2009), 393–419.

7. In my interpretation of Chesnutt's literary aesthetics, his fiction draws on both romantic and realist techniques. Moreover, despite Howells' praise of Chesnutt as a realist writer, his recurrent interest in representing a variety of "types" signals a realist aesthetic more in line with the continental realism of Balzac than the American version promoted by Howells.

8. See Mary Church Terrell, *A Colored Woman in a White World*. (1940; New York: Arno Press, 1980).

9. See Elizabeth McHenry, "Toward a History of Access: The Case of Mary Church Terrell," *American Literary History* (2007), 381–401.

10. Terrell, *Colored Woman in a White World*, 279.

11. Terrell was the most prominent representative of a group of African American women who viewed Stowe's novel as a political and literary triumph both for the race and for women. Celebrating the efficacy and literary genius of what Jane Tompkins (1986) has called the "sentimental power" of *Uncle Tom's Cabin*, these women understood feminine love and sympathy as the engine of the novel's remarkable influence. Among these women, Henrietta Vinton Davis, whom *The Freeman* called "the race's premier elocutionist," planned to stage a production of *Uncle Tom's Cabin* as "a fitting adjunct" to the birthday celebration: she would play Eliza and would call upon the veteran Sam Lucas to see if he would play his old role of Uncle Tom, "a part in which he has achieved enviable fame over the country." "At the Chicago Theaters," *The Freeman*, September 17, 1910.

12. Mary Church Terrell, *Harriet Beecher Stowe: An Appreciation* (Washington, DC: Murray Bros. Press, 1911), 22.

13. Ibid., 13.

14. Ibid., 18.

15. Ibid., 12.

16. Ibid., 13.

17. "The Saturday Review," *Chicago Defender*, February 7, 1920.

18. Terrell, *Colored Woman in a White World*, 233.

19. W. E. B. Du Bois, "The Negro in Literature and Art," *Annals of the American Academy of Political and Social Science* 49 (September 1913): 237.

20. Ibid.

21. Quoted in Williams L. Andrews, *The Literary Career of Charles W. Chesnutt* (Baton Rouge: Louisiana State University Press, 1980), 126.

22. The publisher's additions to the text of Tourgée's novel included excerpts of several reviews pronouncing it "The New 'Uncle Tom'" for both its literary excellence—its "vivid scene-painting, subtle intuitions of character, and colloquial raciness and humor" (*New York Tribune*)—and its documentary function, "enlightening the North about the startling events of the reconstruction period" just as Stowe's novel "illustrat[ed] the phases of an earlier epoch" (*Christian Union*). See [Albion W. Tourgée], *A Fool's Errand* (New York: Fords, Howard, and Hulbert, 1879), 2–3.

23. Chesnutt was hardly alone in regarding *Uncle Tom's Cabin* as a praiseworthy literary model. In 1900, Chesnutt wrote to his friend John P. Green thanking him for

comparing his novel *The House behind the Cedars* to *Uncle Tom's Cabin*, writing, "[I]f I could write a book that would stir the waters in any appreciable degree like that famous book, I would feel that I had vindicated my right to live & the right of a whole race." And he was so flattered by a note from T. Thomas Fortune calling *Marrow* "the strongest work of fiction since *Uncle Tom's Cabin*, which it equals in dramatic power and excels in plot and literary finish," that he excerpted Fortune's praise in a 1901 letter to Booker T. Washington. Charles W. Chesnutt, Joseph R. McElrath, and Robert C. Leitz, *To Be an Author: Letters of Charles W. Chesnutt, 1889–1905* (Princeton, NJ: Princeton University Press, 1997), 156, 169.

24. Albon Lewis Holsey, "Young Writer Reviews Book by Former Teacher," *The Afro-American* (Baltimore), December 16, 1911.

25. A decade later, a subscription book publisher gave the reprint of *Darkwater*, Du Bois' autobiographical work, the subtitle "The Twentieth Century Completion of 'Uncle Tom's Cabin.'" See advertisements in the March 1921, August 1921, and July 1923 issues of *The Crisis*. (The first printing by Harcourt, Brace earlier that year used the standard subtitle, "Voices from within the Veil.")

26. Stowe's novel was a featured text in the 1928 Negro History Week reading recommendations of Roscoe Conkling Simmons, who instructed his readers not to overlook works by white authors: "[B]ooks by white men and women will help you when studying up your past," he wrote. "Whatever you do, read 'Uncle Tom's Cabin.' There you drink from a spiritual well. While on that book, look up a picture of Mrs. Stowe, frame it and hang it on the wall." Roscoe Simmons, "The Week," *The Afro-American* (Baltimore), March 3, 1928.

27. Felix J. Koch, "Where Eliza Crossed the Ice," *The Crisis* (January 1920).

28. Charles Chesnutt, "The Writing of a Novel" (undated speech written after 1899), in *Charles W. Chesnutt: Essays and Speeches*, ed. Joseph R. McElrath, Jr., Robert C. Leitz III, and Jesse S. Crisler (Stanford, CA: Stanford University Press, 1999), 550.

29. Ibid., 551.

30. Joseph R. McElrath, Jr., suggests that Howells saw Chesnutt as a realist despite the latter's clear romanticism because his characters hewed to his preconceptions about black Americans. McElrath, "Why Charles W. Chesnutt Is Not a Realist," *American Literary Realism* 32.2 (2000): 94.

31. Peter Demetz, "Balzac and the Zoologists: A Concept of the Type," in *The Disciplines of Criticism: Essays in Literary Theory, Interpretation, and History*, ed. Peter Demetz, Thomas Greene, and Lowry Nelson, Jr. (New Haven, CT: Yale University Press, 1968), 408.

32. Charles Chesnutt, "The Negro in Books," in *The New Negro: Readings on Race, Representation, and African American Culture, 1892–1938*, ed. Henry Louis Gates, Jr., and Gene Jarrett (Princeton, NJ: Princeton University Press, 2007), 179.

33. Charles W. Chesnutt, "The Negro in Books" (December 5, 1916), in McElrath, Leitz, and Crisler, *Charles W. Chesnutt: Essays and Speeches*, 430.

34. Honoré de Balzac, *Honoré de Balzac in Twenty-Five Volumes*, vol. 1 (New York: Peter Fenelon Collier and Son, 1900), 22.

35. Charles Chesnutt, "Remarks of Charles Waddell Chesnutt, of Cleveland, in Accepting the Spingarn Medal at Los Angeles," July 3, 1928, in McElrath, Leitz, and Crisler, *Charles W. Chesnutt: Essays and Speeches*, 513.

36. Chesnutt, "The Negro in Books," 434. Eric J. Sundquist has shown how the conjure tales cannily manipulate the "Old Negro" type through the character of Uncle

Julius, the genial former slave who tells all but one of the tales. See Sundquist, *To Wake the Nations: Race in the Making of American Literature* (Cambridge, MA: Harvard University Press, 1993), 271–454.

37. Charles Chesnutt, "The Negro in Present Day Fiction" (speech delivered at Oberlin, ca. 1929), in McElrath, Leitz, and Crisler, *Charles W. Chesnutt: Essays and Speeches*, 521.

38. Ibid., 520.

39. Ibid.

40. Sterling Brown, *Negro Poetry and Drama and the Negro in American Fiction* (New York: Atheneum, 1969), 49.

41. Ibid., 52.

42. Ibid., 84.

43. Gary Gallagher delineates four postbellum narratives of the Civil War: the Lost Cause, the Union Cause, the Emancipation Cause, and the Reconciliation Cause, which involved Northern assent to the Lost Cause tradition. See Gary Gallagher, *Causes Won, Lost, and Forgotten: How Hollywood and Popular Art Shape What We Know about the Civil War* (Chapel Hill: University of North Carolina Press, 2008).

44. Nina Silber, *The Romance of Reunion: Northerners and the South, 1865–1900* (Chapel Hill: University of North Carolina Press, 1993), 108.

45. "Abraham Lincoln: An Appreciation," speech to the Bethel Literary and Historical Association, Washington, DC, October 7, 1913, in McElrath, Leitz, and Crisler, *Charles W. Chesnutt: Essays and Speeches*, 350.

46. Silber, *The Romance of Reunion*, 141.

47. William L. Van Deburg, *Slavery and Race in American Popular Culture* (Madison: University of Wisconsin Press, 1984), 67–68.

48. Ibid., 84.

49. See Stephen Budiansky, *The Bloody Shirt: Terror after the Civil War* (New York: Penguin, 2008).

50. Benjamin Brawley, *A Social History of the American Negro, Being a History of the Negro Problem* (New York: Macmillan, 1921), 232.

51. "'Uncle Tom's Cabin' Blacklisted," *Charlotte Daily Observer*, April 25, 1903.

52. Joel Chandler Harris, *The Complete Tales of Uncle Remus*, comp. Richard Chase (Boston: Houghton Mifflin, 1983), xxi.

53. Francis A. Shoup, "Uncle Tom's Cabin Forty Years After," *Sewanee Review* 2, no. 1 (November 1893): 92. In 1898, another Southern writer, pointing out an example of what he called "the irony of genius," similarly argued that despite the anti-slavery agenda of *Uncle Tom's Cabin*, the novel's best and most noble parts were the products of Southern slavery. Uncle Tom, in particular, "intelligent, refined, loyal and imbued with a tenderness most touching," was evidence of how even an anti-slavery novel could not help but show the good effects of slavery. "The Irony of Genius," *Atlanta Constitution*, November 25, 1898.

54. Anna Julia Cooper, *A View from the South* (Xenia, OH: Aldine Printing House, 1892), 180 (via UNC's *Documenting the American South*, http://docsouth.unc.edu/church/cooper/cooper.html).

55. Ibid., 157.

56. Brawley, *The Negro in Literature and Art*, 149.

57. Dickson D. Bruce, *Black American Writing from the Nadir: The Evolution of a Literary Tradition 1877–1915* (Baton Rouge: Louisiana State University Press, 1989), 11.

58. James Weldon Johnson, *The Autobiography of an Ex–Colored Man* (1912; repr.,

New York: Penguin, 1990), 29. For a more extensive account of Johnson's *Autobiography*, see Spingarn, "Writing the Old Negro in a New Century," *American Literature* 89.1 (March 2017).

59. See Spingarn, "Writing the Old Negro in a New Century." As far as I can tell, I am the first scholar to discuss Johnson's planned operatic cantata of *Uncle Tom's Cabin*, a detailed nine-page synopsis of which is located in the James Weldon Johnson papers at Beinecke Library, Yale University. My dating of this undated typescript to 1917 is based on a letter from the American critic H. L. Mencken to Johnson, who apparently wanted to keep his *Uncle Tom's Cabin* adaptation a secret. Mencken wrote to Johnson, "I am sorry I spilled the 'Uncle Tom's Cabin' beans. Why not announce the work, and so protect your priority? What an opera it would make. I have a prejudice against cantatas, largely, I suppose, because they are often given in Methodist churches." H. L. Mencken to James Weldon Johnson, November 27, 1917, James Weldon Johnson Papers, Beinecke Rare Book and Manuscript Library, Yale University.

60. James Weldon Johnson, *Along This Way* (New York: Viking, 1933), 317.

61. Ibid.

62. Ibid., 318.

63. Jacqueline Goldsby suggests this in her introduction to the 2015 Norton edition of *The Autobiography of an Ex–Colored Man*.

64. In this tradition, "the threat or occurrence of a lynching, past or present, has major impact on the dramatic action." See Kathy A. Perkins and Judith L. Stephens, eds. *Strange Fruit: Plays on Lynching by American Women* (Bloomington: Indiana University Press, 1998), 3.

65. Koritha Mitchell suggests that lynching dramas highlighted "the lasting damage that mob violence did to households, not just bodies, and to communities, not just individuals." See Mitchell, *Living with Lynching: African American Lynching Plays, Performance, and Citizenship, 1890–1930* (Urbana: University of Illinois Press, 2011), 9.

66. James Weldon Johnson, "The Dilemma of the Negro Author," *American Mercury* (December 1928): 479.

67. Ibid., 478.

Chapter 5: Uncle Toms and New Negroes

1. "People and Things," *Inter Ocean* (Chicago), February 10, 1877.

2. "Another 'Original' Uncle Tom," *Washington Bee*, August 1, 1903.

3. In May 1877, for example, Stowe released a statement that the character of Uncle Tom was informed by the autobiography of Josiah Henson but that no one man formed the basis for the character.

4. After the success of Stowe's novel, Josiah Henson's newly titled *Truth Is Stranger Than Fiction* was advertised as the work of "The Real Uncle Tom." See *Sandusky Register*, June 26, 1858. Indeed, in advertisements for Henson's tours and books, Uncle Tom's name got more prominent billing than his own. See, for example, *Boston Daily Journal*, March 24, 1875, 3.

5. "Multum in Parvo," *Santa Fe Daily New Mexican*, July 29, 1889.

6. "The Federal Election Law," *New York Times*, June 27, 1890.

7. "Victories of the Pen," *Daily Picayune*, October 10, 1886.

8. As Henry Louis Gates, Jr., has shown, the "New Negro" was a recurrent rhetorical strategy that would over time develop many different meanings, from the politically radical to the aesthetically anti-political. See Henry Louis Gates, Jr., "The Trope of

a New Negro and the Reconstruction of the Image of the Black," *Representations* 24 (1988): 129–155.

9. Martha Jane Nadell (2004) suggests that the Old Negro was "not quite invented but rather culled from a wide variety of nineteenth-century literary and visual images of African Americans" (10–11). See also Marlon B. Ross, *Manning the Race: Reforming Black Men in the Jim Crow Era* (New York: New York University Press, 2004).

10. See Gail Bederman, *Manliness and Civilization: A Cultural History of Gender and Race in the United States, 1880–1917* (Chicago: University of Chicago Press, 1995).

11. See, for example, Booker T. Washington, "The Negro and the Signs of Civilization," *Tuskegee Student*, November 9, 1901, in *African American Political Thought 1890–1930*, ed. Cary D. Wintz (Armonk, NY: M. E. Sharpe, 1996), 41–42.

12. Crummell's inaugural address before the American Negro Academy in 1897 was titled "Civilization: The Primal Need of the Race."

13. David W. Blight, *Beyond the Battlefield: Race, Memory, and the American Civil War* (Amherst: University of Massachusetts Press, 2002), 311.

14. Fannie Barrier Williams, "The Intellectual Progress of the Colored Women of the United States since the Emancipation Proclamation," in *The World's Congress of Representative Women*, ed. May Wright Sewall (Chicago: Rand, McNally, 1894), 697.

15. Ibid., 698.

16. "Self-Made Men: An Address Delivered in Carlisle, Pennsylvania, in March 1893," in *The Frederick Douglass Papers: Series One, Speeches, Debates, and Interviews*, vol. 5, ed. John W. Blassingame and John R. McKivigan (New Haven, CT: Yale University Press, 1992), 561.

17. Rev. W. E. C. Wright, "The New Negro" (1894), in *The New Negro: Readings on Race, Representation, and African American Culture, 1892–1938*, ed. Henry Louis Gates, Jr., and Gene Andrew Jarrett (Princeton, NJ: Princeton University Press, 2007), 24.

18. Ibid., 25.

19. The theologian and former slave J. W. E. Bowen offered a similar account of the race's ignorant origins and its strong efforts toward civilization at the 1895 exposition, where Booker T. Washington gave his famous Atlanta Compromise address. Bowen's narrative of the race's progress began with "the virus of degrading sin" that plagued the race during slavery, and which it was now "making a heroic effort to expel from its system." In what was an essentially conservative program of slow and steady progress toward civilization, he saw education and training as the keys to the race's progress; the new Negro, he asserted, "when educated in all of the disciplines of civilization and thoroughly trained in the arts of civil and moral life, cannot fail to be an invaluable help to our American life." J. W. E. Bowen, "An Appeal to the King" (1895), in Gates and Jarrett, *The New Negro: Readings*, 26–32.

20. Williams, "The Intellectual Progress of the Colored Women," 705.

21. John Henry Adams, Jr., "Rough Sketches: The New Negro Man" (1904), in Gates and Jarrett, *The New Negro: Readings*, 67.

22. Albery A. Whitman, *The Rape of Florida* (St. Louis: Nixon-Jones, 1884), 3–4.

23. Founded in 1881 and active until at least 1915, the Bethel Literary invited speakers (including prominent race leaders such as Frederick Douglass, Booker T. Washington, and W. E. B. Du Bois) to give formal public presentations on the major intraracial issues of the day, always followed by discussion among the audience. A major topic of the group's meetings was Negro education, and particularly the relative merits of industrial and higher education. See Elizabeth McHenry, *Forgotten Readers: Recovering*

the Lost History of African American Literary Societies (Durham, NC: Duke University Press, 2002), 141–186.

24. Walter G. Christopher, "The Educational Problem," *The Globe* (New York), March 31, 1883, 1.

25. Ibid.

26. For Christopher, Uncle Tom was neither a role model nor a race traitor. We can see the boundaries of Christopher's conception of the Uncle Tom model in an angry critique of "the arch traitor Frederick Douglass," published just two months later. He castigated Douglass as "the pliant and humble tool of the dominant [Republican] party," standing "ready at all times to betray and sacrifice the race"—but he made no mention of Uncle Tom, who was not yet a figure for a race traitor. *New Haven Evening Register*, May 3, 1883.

27. See Darrel E. Bigham, "The Black Press in Indiana, 1879–1985," in *The Black Press in the Middle West, 1865–1985*, ed. Henry Lewis Suggs (Westport, CT: Greenwood Press, 1996), 51–69.

28. "Humble Niggers in Politics," *The Freeman* (Indianapolis), November 11, 1893, 4.

29. "Announcement," *The Freeman* (Indianapolis), November 18, 1883.

30. "'Uncle Tom' Says, Say He," *The Freeman* (Indianapolis), November 18, 1893, 1.

31. "Uncle Tom Puts His Knife in the Fetid Carcass of a Terrible Moral Evil," *The Freeman* (Indianapolis), December 2, 1883, 3.

32. "Uncle Tom Mad, Very Mad!" *The Freeman* (Indianapolis), December 9, 1893, 7.

33. "Stained with Negro Blood," *The Freeman* (Indianapolis), September 14, 1895.

34. John D. Howard, "The Beginning of the Dawn," *The Freeman* (Indianapolis), October 24, 1903.

35. See Rayford Logan, *The Negro in American Life and Thought: The Nadir, 1877–1901* (New York: Dial Press, 1954).

36. See W. E. B. Du Bois, *Black Reconstruction in America* (1935; repr., New York: Simon and Schuster, 1992); Eric Foner, *Reconstruction: America's Unfinished Revolution 1863–1877* (New York: Harper and Row, 1988); James McPherson, *Ordeal by Fire: The Civil War and Reconstruction* (1982; repr., Boston: McGraw-Hill, 2001); August Meier, *Negro Thought in America 1880–1915: Racial Ideologies in the Age of Booker T. Washington* (1966; repr., Ann Arbor, MI: Ann Arbor Paperbacks, 1988); Kenneth M. Stampp, *The Era of Reconstruction, 1865–1877* (New York: Knopf, 1966).

37. This "crisis of masculinity," a shift from the nineteenth-century masculine ideal of hard work and self-sacrifice to one of aggression and acquisitiveness, developed out of market and social changes in the United States around the turn of the century. See E. Anthony Rotundo, *American Manhood: Transformations in Masculinity from the Revolution to the Modern Era* (New York: Basic Books, 1993); Bederman, *Manliness and Civilization*; Mark C. Canes and Clyde Griffen, eds., *Meanings for Manhood: Constructions of Masculinity in Victorian America* (Chicago: University of Chicago Press, 1990).

38. See Clifford Putney, *Muscular Christianity: Manhood and Sports in Protestant America, 1880–1920* (Cambridge, MA: Harvard University Press, 2001); Donald E. Hall, ed., *Muscular Christianity: Embodying the Victorian Age* (Cambridge: Cambridge University Press, 1994).

39. Bret E. Carroll, *American Masculinities: A Historical Encyclopedia* (Thousand Oaks, CA: Sage, 2003), 247–248. See also Bruce Barton, *The Man Nobody Knows* (Indianapolis: Bobbs-Merrill, 1925), which contradicted feminized notions of Christ by

portraying him as an energetic businessman and outdoorsman in line with twentieth-century masculine values.

40. According to Blassingame, the lecture changed little over the course of the thirty-five years Douglass delivered it, though he continually updated it with current challenges facing blacks.

41. Speaking at the dedication of the Robert Gould Shaw Monument in Boston in 1897, for example, Washington said that the progress of the race would come "through the effort of the Negro himself, in his effort to withstand temptation, to economize, to exercise thrift, to disregard the superficial for the real—the shadow for the substance, to be great and yet small, in his effort to be patient in the laying of a firm foundation, to so grow in skills and knowledge that he shall place his services in demand by reason of his intrinsic and superior worth." "A Speech at the Unveiling of the Robert Gould Shaw Monument," accessed May 6, 2012, http://teachingamericanhistory.org/library/index.asp?document=934.

42. Booker T. Washington, "Atlanta Exposition Address" (September 18, 1885), in Wintz, *African American Political Thought*, 24.

43. Ibid., 35.

44. Booker T. Washington to Timothy Thomas Fortune, April 4, 1899, in *The Booker T. Washington Papers*, vol. 5, ed. Louis D. Harlan (Urbana: University of Illinois Press, 1975), 70.

45. W. E. B. Du Bois, *The Souls of Black Folk* (1903; repr., New York: Norton, 1999), 41.

46. Ibid., 36.

47. Ibid., 43.

48. Ibid.

49. William H. Ferris to Booker T. Washington, January 1902, in *Booker T. Washington Papers*, vol. 6, ed. Louis R. Harlan (Urbana: University of Illinois Press, 1977), 384–386.

50. William H. Ferris, *The African Abroad* (New Haven, CT: Tuttle, Morehouse, and Taylor Press, 1913), 90–91.

51. Cited in "No Pride in Oppression and Servility," *Broad Ax* (Chicago), July 15, 1905. Here *The Advance* alluded to Lord Brougham's 1830 speech on Negro slavery to the House of Commons, in which he passionately argued that there could be no valid law allowing man to own man. A higher law of liberty for all men, "unchangeable and eternal," had been "written by the finger of God upon the heart of man," and it required British landowners to "reject with indignation the wild and guilty phantasy that man can hold property in man."

52. *The Plaindealer* (Topeka), May 25, 1906, 2.

53. "The World Needs Men," *The Freeman* (Indianapolis), August 28, 1909, 2.

54. "Afro-American Cullings," *Cleveland Gazette*, November 27, 1915.

55. "The Negro in the Tenth Place," *Chicago Defender*, July 2, 1910.

56. James R. Grossman, *Land of Hope: Chicago, Black Southerners, and the Great Migration* (Chicago: University of Chicago Press, 1989); Allan H. Spear, *Black Chicago: The Making of a Negro Ghetto 1890–1920* (Chicago: University of Chicago Press, 1967). On "respectability politics," see Evelyn Brooks Higginbotham, *Righteous Discontent: The Women's Movement in the Black Baptist Church, 1880–1920* (Cambridge, MA: Harvard University Press, 1994).

57. "Jim Crow School in Chicago," *Chicago Defender*, November 12, 1910.

58. John R. Winston, "In the Railroad Center," *Chicago Defender*, February 4, 1911.

59. "Sparks from the Rail," *Chicago Defender*, June 22, 1912.

60. "Railroad Rumblings," *Chicago Defender*, November 18, 1916, 11.

61. "No Separate Headquarters," *Chicago Defender*, October 28, 1916, 10.

62. X. Y. Z., "Resorting to Petty Tactics," *Cleveland Gazette*, October 21, 1922.

63. "Capt. R.P. Roots' Letter to Lindley M. Garrison, Secretary of War," *Chicago Defender*, December 18, 1915.

64. Mark Ellis, "'Closing Ranks' and 'Seeking Honors': W. E. B. Du Bois in World War I," *Journal of American History* 79, no. 1 (June 1992): 96–124.

65. C. Vann Woodward, *The Strange Career of Jim Crow* (1955; repr., Oxford: Oxford University Press, 2002), 115.

66. Robert T. Kerlin, ed., *The Voice of the Negro 1919* (New York: E. P. Dutton, 1920), 72.

67. Hubert H. Harrison, "The New Politics" (1920), in Gates and Jarrett, *The New Negro: Readings*, 101.

68. Ibid., 104.

69. "Former Alderman Oscar De Priest," *Broad Ax* (Chicago), January 19, 1918.

70. "Colored Traitors," *Washington Bee*, October 18, 1919, in Kerlin, *The Voice of the Negro*, 28. This article was a response to a rumor that two black men from Georgia had gone to Washington to oppose an anti–Jim Crow bill.

71. "Special Expert," *The Appeal*, October 1, 1921; reprinted from *The Chicago Whip*.

72. In Chicago, Bishop C. D. Smith told a meeting of the Bishop's Council of the A.M.E. church that "the men of the church have got to look the problems of the race in the face and fight them with the courage to do and die.... He made it clear that the A.M.E. church wants no more 'Uncle Tom' preachers." "Exit Uncle Tom," *The Appeal*, July 9, 1921.

73. X. Y. Z., "Resorting to Petty Tactics," *Cleveland Gazette*, October 21, 1922.

74. Reprinted in "Symposium of President's Southern Speeches," *The Appeal*, November 12, 1921.

75. Richard Slotkin, *Lost Battalions: The Great War and the Crisis of American Nationality* (New York: Henry Holt, 2005), 439.

76. Kerlin, *The Voice of the Negro*, 77.

77. Carita Owens Collins, "Be a Man!" (1919), in ibid., 185.

78. Kerlin, *The Voice of the Negro*, 25.

79. From the New York *World*, August 7, 1920, in *"Uncle Tom's Cabin" and American Culture*, ed. Stephen Railton, accessed July 25, 2010, http://utc.iath.virginia.edu.

80. A. Philip Randolph, "Dialogue of the Old and New," *The Messenger* 9.3 (1927): 94.

81. The Uncle Tom Porter's language here is very similar to Ralph Ellison's *Invisible Man* (1952), in which the narrator's grandfather confesses that he has been "a traitor all my born days" and urges his descendants to "overcome 'em with yeses, undermine 'em with grins, agree 'em to death and destruction, let 'em swoller you till they vomit or bust wide open." Ralph Ellison, *Invisible Man* (1952; repr., New York: Vintage, 1995), 16.

Chapter 6: Writing Off Uncle Tom

1. "Mr. Garvey's Speech," *Negro World*, September 17, 1921, in *"Uncle Tom's Cabin" and American Culture*, ed. Stephen Railton, accessed July 25, 2010, http://utc.iath.virginia.edu.

2. Judith Stein, *The World of Marcus Garvey: Race and Class in Modern Society* (Baton Rouge: Louisiana State University Press, 1991), 166–169.

3. Advertisement, *Washington Post*, December 20, 1925. The same language appeared in full-page advertisements published in the *Worker's Herald* (March 27, 1926, at 5) and the *Gold Coast Leader* (March 27, 1926, at 3). Robert A. Hill, ed., *The Marcus Garvey and Universal Negro Improvement Association Papers* (Berkeley: University of California Press, 2006), 10: 368.

4. Brawley, *The Negro in Literature and Art in the United States* (New York: Duffield, 1918), 157; originally printed as "The Negro in American Fiction," *The Dial*, May 11, 1916, 445–450.

5. Alain Locke, "The New Negro," in *The New Negro: Voices of the Harlem Renaissance* (New York: Touchstone, 1997), 3.

6. Deborah E. McDowell, "Telling Slavery in 'Freedom's' Time: Post-Reconstruction and the Harlem Renaissance," in *The Cambridge Companion to the African American Slave Narrative*, ed. Audrey Fisch (Cambridge: Cambridge University Press, 2007), 163.

7. Locke, "The New Negro," 3.

8. Ibid., 4.

9. In a 1929 speech to Oberlin students, Charles Chesnutt observed that the contemporary category of "Negro literature" included "books by colored writers and books about the Negro." Chesnutt, "The Negro in Present Day Fiction," in *Charles W. Chesnutt: Essays and Speeches*, ed. Joseph R. McElrath, Jr., Robert C. Leitz III, and Jesse S. Crisler (Stanford, CA: Stanford University Press, 1999), 518.

10. William Stanley Braithwaite, "The Negro in American Literature," in Locke, *The New Negro*, 29. On the relationship between realism and American racial politics, see Kenneth W. Warren, *Black and White Strangers: Race and American Literary Realism* (Chicago: University of Chicago Press, 1993).

11. Alain Locke, "American Literary Tradition and the Negro," in *Interracialism: Black-White Intermarriage in American History, Literature, and Law*, ed. Werner Sollors (New York: Oxford University Press, 2000), 272. Sollors identifies a 1916 *Modern Quarterly* as the essay's source, but this appears to be a typo; in fact, *Modern Quarterly* did not begin publication until 1923, and the essay appeared in 1926.

12. Alain Locke, "Negro Youth Speaks," in *The New Negro*, 52.

13. Alain Locke, "The Saving Grace of Realism: Retrospective Review of the Negro Literature of 1933," *Opportunity* 13 (January 1934); Sterling Brown, *Negro Poetry and Drama and the Negro in American Fiction* (New York: Atheneum, 1969), 4, 82. Characteristic of Brown's faith in realism are the discussion questions he attached to his account; one asks, "Why would realism improve poetry about Negro life?" (102).

14. Henry Louis Mencken, *A Book of Prefaces* (New York: Knopf, 1917), 214. Along with Dickens' *David Copperfield* and Alexandre Dumas' *La dame aux camélias*, H. L. Mencken placed *Uncle Tom's Cabin*, which he dismissed as a "crude politico-puritan tract," in a group of three texts that exemplified mid-nineteenth-century sentimental romanticism. Lea Jacobs, *The Decline of Sentiment: American Film in the 1920s* (Berkeley: University of California Press, 2008), 16. On the challenges *Uncle Tom's Cabin* posed to literary realists, see Warren, *Black and White Strangers*, 72–108.

15. William Stanley Braithwaite, "The Negro in American Literature," in Locke, *The New Negro*, 30.

16. Ibid., 30–31.

17. Locke, "American Literary Tradition," 272.

18. Ibid.

19. Ibid.

20. Ibid.

21. Wallace Thurman, "Negro Artists and the Negro," *New Republic*, August 31, 1927, 198.

22. See Wallace Thurman, "Cordelia the Crude," *Fire!!* 1.1 (November 1926), 5–6.

23. Wallace Thurman, "Fire Burns: A Department of Comment," *Fire!!* 1.1 (November 1926), 47, 48. Note: in the original essay, Octavus is misspelled as "Octavius."

24. Thurman, "Negro Artists and the Negro," 199.

25. Ibid.

26. Ibid.

27. Gustavus Adolphus Stewart, "The New Negro Hokum," *Social Forces* 6.3 (March 1928): 439.

28. Of the nine *Uncle Tom's Cabin* film adaptations produced between 1903 and 1927, five have been lost. See Stephen Railton, "Readapting *Uncle Tom's Cabin*," in *Nineteenth-Century American Fiction on Screen*, ed. R. Barton Palmer (Cambridge: Cambridge University Press, 2007).

29. Janet Staiger, *Interpreting Films: Studies in the Historical Reception of American Cinema* (Princeton, NJ: Princeton University Press, 1992), 105–118.

30. "'Uncle Tom' in Natural Colors," *Variety*, October 14, 1925, 31; "'Uncle Tom' for U with Colored Actor," *Variety*, March 3, 1926, 26.

31. Thomas Cripps, *Slow Fade to Black: The Negro in American Film, 1900–1942* (New York: Oxford University Press, 1977), 118; Floyd C. Covington, "The Negro Invades Hollywood" (*Opportunity*, 1929), in *Black Films and Filmmakers: A Comprehensive Anthology from Stereotype to Superhero*, ed. Lindsay Patterson (New York: Dodd, Mead, 1975), 122.

32. During the silent film era, the black press approached black achievement in film with an "ebullient, optimistic, and ultimately naïve" attitude. Anna Everett, *Returning the Gaze: A Genealogy of Black Film Criticism, 1909–1949* (Durham, NC: Duke University Press, 2000), 8.

33. "Gilpin Out of Role in *Uncle Tom's Cabin*," *The Afro-American* (Baltimore), September 18, 1926. Initially the studio cast Charles Gilpin as Uncle Tom, but he left the production under mysterious circumstances.

34. "An Uncrowned Champion," *Pittsburgh Courier*, February 5, 1927, A4.

35. Pollard looked for what he called "perfect types" of each character as portrayed in Stowe's novel. While Mona Ray, the actress who played Topsy, was reportedly white, her blackface is so convincingly rendered and her appearance in her one other film credit so visually obscured that, as Michele Wallace points out, her racial identity is unclear. "Complete Cast of 'Uncle Tom's Cabin' Is Announced," *Los Angeles Times*, June 5, 1927, 18; Michele Wallace, "*Uncle Tom's Cabin*: Before and after the Jim Crow Era," *TDR: The Drama Review* 44.1 (2000): 140.

36. "Bathing Beauty Gets Parts in *Uncle Tom's Cabin* at Universal," *The Plaindealer* (Topeka), December 31, 1926.

37. See Cripps, *Slow Fade to Black*, 100–110.

38. Rodney Ayers, "Lowe Completes Role of Uncle Tom Movie," *The Afro-American* (Baltimore), June 18, 1927.

39. Railton, "Readapting *Uncle Tom's Cabin*," 67.

40. "'Uncle Tom' Must Be 'Cut' in Natchez," *The Afro-American* (Baltimore), January 16, 1926, 4.

41. "Protest 'Uncle Tom's Cabin' Film Being Made," *New Journal and Guide*, November 13, 1926, 1.

42. Grace Kingsley, "Eddie Cantor on His Way West," *Los Angeles Times*, November 18, 1926, A10. Jacobsen specified that "the School Commissioners refused to permit the children to work for us; the War Department representative refused to permit us to paint 'Kate Adams' out and substitute 'La Belle Rivere' as the name of the boat."

43. David Pierce, "'Carl Laemmle's Outstanding Achievement': Harry Pollard and the Struggle to Film 'Uncle Tom's Cabin,'" *Film History* 10.4 (1998): 465.

44. "White South Won't Allow Filming of 'Uncle Tom's Cabin,'" *Pittsburgh Courier*, January 16, 1926. Similarly, when Pollard's team moved on to Atlanta, residents did not formally oppose production but instead called for the film to incorporate a Lost Cause narrative of the Civil War and its aftermath. Insistent that the film could not "fairly tell the story" by following Stowe's novel, Atlantans suggested that Pollard's script needed to show the South's suffering from the "ruthlessness" of Sherman's March and the city set on fire, and then "the south rebuilt, pulsating, progressive." If *Uncle Tom's Cabin* was a verdict on the South, then Atlantans wanted it to be a forward-looking one. "Peachtree Creek Battle Site to Be Scene of Movie," *Atlanta Constitution*, October 17, 1926, 13.

45. Thomas R. Cripps calls this "the myth of the Southern box office." See Cripps, "The Myth of the Southern Box Office: A Factor in Racial Stereotyping in American Movies, 1920–1940," in *The Black Experience: Selected Essays*, ed. James C. Curtis and Lewis L. Gould (Austin: University of Texas Press, 1970), 116–144.

46. Matthew Bernstein, "The 'Professional Southerner' in the Hollywood Studio System: Lamar Trotti at Work, 1934–1952," in *American Cinema and the Southern Imaginary*, ed. Deborah Barker and Kathryn B. McKee (Athens: University of Georgia Press, 2011), 123–124.

47. Ruth Vasey, "Beyond Sex and Violence: 'Industry Policy' and the Regulation of Hollywood Movies, 1922–1939," in *Controlling Hollywood: Censorship and Regulation in the Studio Era*, ed. Matthew Bernstein (New Brunswick, NJ: Rutgers University Press, 1999).

48. "As Four Women Hear It!," *Atlanta Constitution*, November 21, 1926, E7.

49. See Bernstein, "The 'Professional Southerner.'"

50. Stephen Railton notes that these scenes are still described in the film's souvenir program, suggesting that the edits were made at the last minute, after the souvenir program was printed. Railton, "Readapting *Uncle Tom's Cabin*," 69–70; Pierce, "'Carl Laemmle's Outstanding Achievement,'" 464.

51. *Uncle Tom's Cabin*, dir. Harry Pollard, Universal, 1927.

52. For an analysis of Universal's *Uncle Tom's Cabin* as a response to *Birth of a Nation*, see Linda Williams, *Playing the Race Card: Melodramas of Black and White from Uncle Tom to O. J. Simpson* (Princeton, NJ: Princeton University Press, 2001), 96–135.

53. Reflecting the continuing presence of *Birth of a Nation* in American culture, responses to the 1927 Universal adaptation, like those of the 1910s, suggested that *Uncle Tom's Cabin* was an offset to *Birth of a Nation*. See, for example, "The Week," *Chicago Defender*, November 17, 1928.

54. Underhill described the film as "one of the most thrilling and satisfying melodramas we have seen in a long time" but confessed that she was unable to watch the scene in which "Legree tells Uncle Tom he is going to kill him and then does it. He strings him up to the rafters and whips him to death." The scene made her realize the cruelty of slavery in a way she "never" had before. Harriette Underhill, "On the Screen," *New York Herald-Tribune*, November 5, 1927, 11.

55. March Church Terrell, "Up to Date," *Chicago Defender*, February 23, 1929, A2.

56. Eugene D. Genovese, *Roll, Jordan Role: The World the Slaves Made* (New York: Vintage, 1976), 159–284.

57. Floyd J. Calvin, "'Uncle Tom's Cabin' Reviewed by Calvin," *Pittsburgh Courier*, December 3, 1927, 15.

58. Given that the actors who played Eliza and George were white and wore no darkening makeup, Calvin suggested that "[i]It must be quite humiliating to some whites to see their own color treated as the blackest slave, as many mixed bloods actually were during the slavery." Calvin, "'Uncle Tom's Cabin' Reviewed."

59. Deborah McDowell notes the "striking . . . frequency with which shame appears in writings of the period, even in the manifestoes of the new." McDowell, "Telling Slavery in 'Freedom's' Time," 165.

60. William Pickens, "Apologies to 'Uncle Tom,'" *New York Amsterdam News*, November 18, 1925, 9. Pickens' essay quotes and responds to an essay published in the first black newsmagazine, the short-lived *Heebie Jeebies* by the Chicago newspaperman Percival L. Prattis. In this essay, according to Pickens, Prattis argues that the term "Uncle Tom Negro" should be shelved. Noting the gap between the "hero of 'Uncle Tom's Cabin,'" "one of the noblest characters in all literature," and the "Uncle Tom Negro," Prattis suggests that "[c]owards and sycophants ought to be classified by a less worthy prototype."

61. Ibid.

62. "The Week," *Chicago Defender*, September 3, 1927, A1.

63. Ibid.

64. Calvin, "'Uncle Tom's Cabin' Reviewed."

65. Emmet V. Mittlebeeler, "Forget 'Uncle Tom's Cabin,'" *Chicago Tribune*, April 18, 1929, 14.

66. In the view of James Wingate, director of the New York Board of Censors, "the scenes portraying cruel and inhuman treatment were so overdone and prolonged" that the film "offended the audience's idea of good taste." Pierce, "'Carl Laemmle's Outstanding Achievement,'" 469.

67. "Review of Universal Pictures' *Uncle Tom's Cabin*," *Billboard*, November 12, 1927; cited in Railton, "Readapting *Uncle Tom's Cabin*," 71.

68. Pierce, "'Carl Laemmle's Outstanding Achievement,'" 469.

69. Ibid.

70. Ibid.

71. "'Uncle Tom' Cut," *Variety*, November 23, 1927, 12.

72. "'Uncle Tom' in Fla.," *Variety*, April 25, 1928, 23; reprinted in the Baltimore *Afro-American*, May 5, 1928, 9; "Pictures: Small Town Tests on 'Uncle Tom' Pleasing to U," *Variety*, May 9, 1928, 14.

73. Nelson B. Bell, "Two Complaints, a Slight Conflict and a New Book," *Washington Post*, December 9, 1928; Sam W. Small, "Looking and Listening: The Serpent of Sectionalism and the Hope That Its Head Is Bruised," *Atlanta Constitution*, December 9, 1928, 2F.

74. "Atlanta Bars 'Uncle Tom' after Uproar," *Variety*, August 15, 1928, 2.

75. Ibid.; see also "'Uncle Tom's Cabin' Barred in Atlanta," *Atlanta Constitution*, August 16, 1928, 8.

76. "Atlanta Bars a Picture," *Pittsburgh Courier*, August 25, 1928, A8.

77. Ibid.

78. Ibid.; "Birmingham Prohibits 'Uncle Tom's Cabin," *The Afro-American* (Baltimore), December 29, 1928.

79. "What Is Good for the Goose Is Sauce for the Gander," *Chicago Defender*, September 8, 1928.

80. "No Bloodhounds," *Boston Daily Globe*, August 17, 1928, 14.

81. "Revise Uncle Tom's Cabin for Texas; Legree a Yankee," *New York Times*, August 23, 1928, 26; "'Uncle Tom's Cabin' Film Revamped in Texas," *Chicago Defender*, August 25, 1928.

82. *Montgomery Advertiser*, April 21, 1929; *Nashville Banner*, April 21, 1929. Cited in Edward D. C. Campbell, *The Celluloid South: Hollywood and the Southern Myth* (Knoxville: University of Tennessee Press, 1981), 69–70.

83. William N. Jones, "Day by Day," *The Afro-American* (Baltimore), September 8, 1928, 6.

84. "U.D.C. Chapter Meetings Interest Readers of Official Page," *Atlanta Constitution*, November 4, 1928, 8M.

85. In Tampa, Florida, a local theater manager gave a preview of the film for the local United Daughters of the Confederacy in January, specifying that he would not present the film if the women objected. They did, strongly: the group's president declared that the story was "enough to cause a race riot" and other members concurred, asserting that the film was "an insult to southern women; brutal beyond words; worse than the original book" and therefore "should be banned everywhere." "Uncle Tom's Cabin in Motion Pictures Taboo in Tampa," *Atlanta Constitution*, January 22, 1929, 8. Women's Confederate groups in Georgia also successfully prevented presentation of the film. In a letter to the *Atlanta Constitution*, the head of the Georgia division of the UDC urged members to follow the examples of Atlanta and Augusta in stopping any showings of the film, asking, "Why stir up strife by showing the children pictures that misrepresented our fathers and the south?" In Valdosta, a scheduled midnight premiere provoked such "vigorous opposition" from local groups including the Better Films Committee of the Wimodausis Club, the Valdosta chapter of the UDC, and the Valdosta Ministerial Association, that the police suppressed the film. "Mrs. Bankston Issues Letter to Georgia Daughters," *Atlanta Constitution*, February 10, 1929, F6; "'Uncle Tom's Cabin,' Film, Gets Police Ban in Valdosta," *Atlanta Constitution*, April 23, 1929, 30.

86. William N. Jones, "Day by Day," *The Afro-American* (Baltimore), September 8, 1928, 6.

87. J. Ernest Webb, "Naptown Doings," *Chicago Defender*, December 1, 1928.

88. Thomas Cauldwell, "Atlanta Is Right," *Chicago Defender*, September 29, 1928.

89. O'Dell Hatchett, "Atlanta Is Wrong," *Chicago Defender*, October 13, 1928.

90. James Weldon Johnson, "The Dilemma of the Negro Author," *American Mercury* 15 (December 1928).

91. Emco's production was staged in various locations under the auspices of churches including the St. James A.M.E. Church, Carron Baptist Church, and Ebenezer Baptist Church. "Principals in Drama," *Pittsburgh Courier*, April 20, 1929, A6; "Additional Society," *Pittsburgh Courier*, May 25, 1929, A8; "Clubs," *Pittsburgh Courier*, June 8, 1929. According to *The Courier*, a number of churches, clubs, and lodges requested that the Emco Players stage *Uncle Tom's Cabin* for their groups. "'Uncle Tom's Cabin' Was Big Success," *Pittsburgh Courier*, May 11, 1929, 9. The same year, students at Dunbar High School in Norfolk, Virginia, staged the play, and in 1936, a black civic group in Kentucky staged an *Uncle Tom's Cabin* drama at the local school auditorium, giving all proceeds to the local

Christian church. "Clubs," *Pittsburgh Courier*, June 8, 1929; "Elizabeth City," *New Journal and Guide*, March 30, 1929, 11.

92. "Race Movie Fans Object to 'Uncle Tom's Cabin,'" *The Afro-American* (Baltimore), July 6, 1929, 8.

93. "'Uncle Tom's Cabin Hits a Snag in Gary, Indiana," *Chicago Defender*, July 26, 1929.

94. An American bishop claimed that the drama's presentation would provoke racial strife and bitterness. See "Ban Uncle Tom's Cabin in Philippine College," *Chicago Defender*, February 23, 1929, 1.

95. Geraldyn Dismond, "The Negro Actor and the American Movies," in *Black Films and Filmmakers: A Comprehensive Anthology from Stereotype to Superhero*, 119; originally published in 1929 in *Close-Up* magazine.

96. Cripps, *Making Movies Black*, 11.

97. Quoted in Alice Maurice, "'Cinema at Its Source': Synchronizing Race and Sound in the Early Talkies," *Camera Obscura* 17.1 (2002): 44.

98. Donald Bogle is critical of these films, writing that black actors presented "for mass consumption black life as seen through the eyes of white artists." Bogle, *Toms, Coons, Mulattoes, Mammies, and Bucks: An Interpretive History of Blacks in American Films* (New York: Continuum, 2002), 27.

99. Quoted in Maurice, "'Cinema at Its Source,'" 32.

100. Cedric J. Robinson, *Forgeries of Memory and Meaning: Blacks and the Regimes of Race in American Theater and Film before World War II* (Chapel Hill: University of North Carolina Press, 2007), 272.

101. According to Karen L. Cox, films set in the South usually depicted an Old South of "plantations, southern belles, and loyal slaves." Cox, *Dreaming of Dixie: How the South Was Created in American Popular Culture* (Chapel Hill: University of North Carolina Press, 2011), 83.

102. Guerrero, *Framing Blackness: The African American Image in Film* (Philadelphia: Temple University Press, 1993), 21, 19.

103. Campbell, *The Celluloid South*, 80, 75.

104. On racial representation in sound films, see Barbara Tepa Lupack, *Literary Adaptations in Black American Cinema* (Rochester, NY: University of Rochester Press, 2010), 183–241.

105. Cripps, *Slow Fade to Black*, 266.

106. The black press frequently celebrated the achievements of individual actors "as though reflecting a general rise in African American fortunes." Cripps, *Making Movies Black*, 20.

107. Dismond, "The Negro Actor," 121.

108. Cripps, *Slow Fade to Black*, 236.

109. Ellen Scott suggests that during this time activists preferred to focus on "legitimate theater" and that, in the few black protests of film from 1930 to 1935, "activists did not explicitly address epithets as a civil rights issue, discussing it instead in terms of 'insult' and 'offense.'" Ellen Scott, *Cinema Civil Rights* (New Brunswick, NJ: Rutgers University Press, 2015), 149.

110. For example, the Chicago social worker Jane Addams devoted a chapter of *The Spirit of Youth and City Streets* (1909) to moving pictures' pernicious potential. See Garth S. Jowett, *Children and the Movies: Media Influence and the Payne Fund Controversy* (Cambridge: Cambridge University Press, 1996), 25–26.

111. Quoted in ibid., 21.

112. The process of stereotyping, according to the *Oxford English Dictionary*, involved the following: "a solid plate of type-metal, cast from a papier-mâché or plaster mould taken from the surface of a forme of type, is used for printing from instead of the forme itself." *Oxford English Dictionary*, June 2017, s.v. "stereotype, n. and adj.," OED Online, accessed November 28, 2017, http://www.oed.com.stanford.idm.oclc.org/view/Entry/189956?rskey=rkPE7C&result=1&isAdvanced=false.

113. Ruth Amossy's work on the history of stereotype and its relationship to adjacent terms such as type and cliché is crucial to my analysis of the conceptual shifts enabled by Lippmann's book. According to Amossy, through Lippmann "the stereotype becomes a concept through which the relation of man to his environment can be re-evaluated." Ruth Amossy, "Commonplace Knowledge and Innovation," *SubStance* 19.2–3 (1990): 149.

114. Walter Lippmann, *Public Opinion* (New York: Harcourt, Brace, 1922), 89.

115. Amossy, "Commonplace Knowledge and Innovation," 145.

116. See John P. Jackson, Jr., *Social Scientists for Social Justice: Making the Case against Segregation* (New York: New York University Press, 2001), 18.

117. Quoted in Jackson, *Social Scientists for Social Justice*, 27.

118. See Amossy, "Commonplace Knowledge and Innovation." Amossy points out the irony that social scientific research on stereotype ended up codifying or creating stereotypes by asking subjects to identify terms that they associated with various groups.

119. See Bruno Lasker, *Race Attitudes in Children* (New York: Henry Holt, 1929). Edgar Dale describes a number of studies on the influence of motion pictures on children's racial attitudes in "The Movies and Race Relations," *The Crisis* 44 (October 1937): 294–296.

120. Loren Miller, "Uncle Tom in Hollywood," *The Crisis* (November 1934): 329.

121. Ibid.

122. Ibid.

123. Ibid.

124. John Tidwell, "Wants Colored Movies," *The Afro-American* (Baltimore), February 15, 1936.

125. Lillian Johnson, "There Were Ups and Downs, but 1937 Was Good to Those Who Trod the Boards," *The Afro-American* (Baltimore), January 1, 1938.

126. Ralph Matthews, "Dixie Prejudice Still Dominates the Movies but Not the Stage," *The Afro-American* (Baltimore), February 8, 1936.

127. Ibid.; Rienzi B. Lemus, "Uncle Tom Roles for Stars on Screen Beat a Blank, Points Out Lemus," *The Afro-American* (Baltimore), February 22, 1936.

128. Ralph Matthews, "Looking at the Stars," *The Afro-American* (Baltimore), February 13, 1932; Ralph Matthews, "All-White Cast Present Play 81 Years Old," *The Afro-American* (Baltimore), June 3, 1933, 10.

129. Helena Wilson, "Open Letter to Mr. Lawes," *Chicago Defender*, September 29, 1934, 14.

130. Ibid.

131. For example, according to Ellen Scott the only action taken against *Imitation of Life* was an open letter written by Shirley Graham to the manager of the Apollo Theater, urging him not to show *Imitation* because it portrayed black women assenting to unequal treatment. Scott, *Cinema Civil Rights*, 151.

132. For example, in 1938 a conglomerate of exhibitors in several Southern states

announced their intention to ban "Negroes in scenes with white people on a social equality basis." In response, thousands of black students in Greensboro conducted a boycott of the exhibitors. Ibid., 157.

133. In both its title and subject matter, Hughes' "Colonel Tom's Cabin" referenced two Shirley Temple pictures: *The Little Colonel* (1935), set in the postbellum South, and *Dimples* (1936), in which Temple plays a nineteenth-century street urchin who takes a turn on the stage as Little Eva.

134. Joseph McLaren, *Langston Hughes: Folk Dramatist in the Protest Tradition, 1921–1943* (Westport, CT: Greenwood Press, 1997), 130.

135. Langston Hughes, "Colonel Tom's Cabin," in *The Collected Works of Langston Hughes*, vol. 5, ed. Arnold Rampersad (Columbia: University of Missouri Press, 2001), 575–577.

136. Langston Hughes, "Introduction to *Uncle Tom's Cabin*" (1952), in *Critical Essays on Harriet Beecher Stowe*, ed. Elizabeth Ammons (Boston: G. K. Hall, 1980), 104. Hughes' familiarity with the *Uncle Tom's Cabin* stage tradition went back to his childhood in Kansas, when his mother took him to see "all the plays that came to Topeka, like *Buster Brown*, *Under Two Flags*, and *Uncle Tom's Cabin*." His positive experience of the play is reflected in his glowing 1946 review of Maxine Wood's *On Whitman Avenue*, a play about a black family's attempt to move into a white neighborhood. Hughes commented that the play "ranks high in the social drama of our day, and it takes its place in a long line of fine plays—'Uncle Tom's Cabin,' 'In Abraham's Bosom,' 'Stevedore,' 'Big White Fog,' 'Deep Are The Roots'—that our theatre has given as its contribution towards a solution of our ever dramatic race problem." Hughes also praised the Gilpin Players in 1943 for being one of the few black theater groups that didn't almost exclusively stage white-authored plays about whites (for example, Oscar Wilde's *Lady Windemere's Fan*) instead of Negro dramas. As he approvingly informed his readers, the group staged "everything from 'Uncle Tom's Cabin' to 'Stevedore,' from 'Mulatto' to their own cooperatively written comedy, 'One Hundred In the Shade.' When they temporarily exhaust the supply of good plays by Negro writers, they put on plays about Negroes by white writers. But they consistently try to interpret Negro life through the drama." Langston Hughes, *The Big Sea* (1940; New York: Hill and Wang, 1993), 15; Langston Hughes, "Here to Yonder," *Chicago Defender*, June 22, 1946; Langston Hughes, "Here to Yonder: Plays for a Negro Theater," *Chicago Defender*, May 8, 1943.

137. Kennard Williams, "Growth of American Slave Spirituals Is Marvelous," *The Afro-American* (Baltimore), February 14, 1925; Lucius C. Harper, "Dustin' Off the News," *Chicago Defender*, May 6, 1939. Criticism of spirituals went hand in hand with criticism of folklore. Both, according to *The Defender*'s editor Robert S. Abbott, in an October 27, 1924, article, "seek but to glorify the plantation and the log cabin."

138. Langston Hughes was initially involved in conceiving this program and wrote a few songs and sketches but left before it was complete, resigning from the Hollywood Theatre Alliance. Ellington then took the helm, ultimately keeping just one of Hughes' sketches in the program. See Michael Denning, *The Cultural Front: The Laboring of American Culture in the Twentieth Century* (London: Verso, 1998), 312.

139. Lawrence F. LaMar, "Swing Fans Ready for Duke's 'Jump for Joy': 'I'm Ready,'" *Chicago Defender*, June 28, 1941.

140. Quoted in Denning, *The Cultural Front*, 312.

141. Quoted in Krin Gabbard, *Jammin' at the Margins: Jazz and the American Cinema* (Chicago: University of Chicago Press, 1996), 177–178.

142. "Epitaph [2]," in *The Collected Poems of Langston Hughes*, ed. Arnold Rampersad (New York: Knopf, 1994); originally published in *Amsterdam News*, October 8, 1941, 8.

143. Langston Hughes, "Uncle Tom [1]," in ibid., 302. See also "Uncle Tom [2]," in ibid., 467.

144. Denning, *The Cultural Front*, 314.

145. Interestingly, a nightclub alternately called "Uncle Tom's Cabin" and "Uncle Tom's Plantation," in which the local black community held events including weddings, cabarets, and dances, operated on Eight Mile Road in Detroit during the late 1930s and early 1940s.

146. "Editorials: 'Gone with the Wind,'" *The Crisis*, January 1940. See also Cripps, *Making Movies Black*, 16–21. Cripps further argues that both the black and the liberal press "were seduced by the quality of *Gone With the Wind* and took little notice of its confused ideological view . . . conservative and somewhat *avant garde* at the same time." Cripps, *Slow Fade to Black*, 363.

147. "Editorials: 'Gone with the Wind,'" *The Crisis*, January 1940.

148. "'Gone with the Wind," *Chicago Defender*, January 13, 1940.

149. Scott, *Cinema Civil Rights*, 147.

150. A. B. Johnson, "Hit the Nail on the Head," *Chicago Defender*, June 16, 1934.

151. Clarence Muse, "What's Going On in Hollywood," *Chicago Defender*, December 23, 1939. My citation has standardized the format of Muse's article, which is PRINTED with every FEW words CAPITALIZED.

152. "Show Power of Radio to Promote Race Amnesty," *Chicago Defender*, May 13, 1944.

153. W. F. Davis, "'Uncle Tom' Actors Make Bad Name for the Race," *Chicago Defender*, December 9, 1944.

154. John S. Brown, Jr., "What Afro Readers Say," *The Afro-American* (Baltimore), September 16, 1944; Harry Levette, "Canada Lee has 'Uncle Tom' Phrases Cut from Script in Fox's 'Lifeboat,'" *The Afro-American* (Baltimore), September 11, 1943.

155. Harry Levette, "Say! Bill Is No 'Thomas,'" *Chicago Defender*, March 13, 1943.

156. Ralph Matthews, "The Truth about Hollywood and the Race Issue from the Actors' Viewpoint," *The Afro-American* (Baltimore), January 9, 1943.

157. Mrs. B. H. W., "What Afro Readers Write," *The Afro-American* (Baltimore), February 17, 1945.

158. Langston Hughes, "Here to Yonder: Jews, Negroes, and Hollywood," *Chicago Defender*, April 17, 1943.

159. See "One Reason Why They Segregate Our Gold Star Mothers," *Chicago Defender*, April 5, 1930, 14; "Watson an 'Uncle Tom' Says N.A.A.C.P. Head," *Chicago Defender*, March 11, 1939, 5; "Expose Plans to Bar Race Beauty School Operators," *Chicago Defender*, November 24, 1934, A1.

160. "Hollywood News," *New York Herald Tribune*, January 28, 1944, 11.

161. Within a week of the announcement, Robeson announced that he "could not and would not possibly accept" the role if it was offered to him. Horne soon followed suit, explaining that the production "would hardly meet the approval of members of her race." E. B. Rea, "Robeson Won't Play Role of Uncle Tom," *The Afro-American* (Baltimore), February 5, 1944; Leon H. Hardwick, "Lena Horne Turns Down Lead in Filming of 'Uncle Tom's Cabin,'" *Atlanta Daily World*, February 15, 1944, 2.

162. Hardwick told Hornblow that "we Negroes would prefer to forget the slave background as American history." Leon H. Hardwick, "'Uncle Tom's Cabin' to Be Made with Lena Horne in Main Role," *Chicago Defender*, February 12, 1944, 8.

163. Ibid.

164. E. B. Rea, "The 'March of Slaves' Will Be Propaganda as Inflaming for Us as the 'March of Death' against Japan," *The Afro-American* (Baltimore), February 12, 1944.

165. "No Uncle Tom Revival," *The Afro-American* (Baltimore), March 18, 1944, 4; see also "Public Views in re: 'Uncle Tom's Cabin,'" *The Afro-American* (Baltimore), February 26, 1944.

166. Quoted in Scott, *Cinema Civil Rights*, 173.

167. "Protests Force MGM to Shelve Uncle Tom Film," *Chicago Defender*, February 19, 1944, 1.

168. The *Chicago Sun* is quoted in Lucius C. Harper, "Dustin' Off the News: It Seems after All, That Old 'Uncle Tom' Is Dead," *Chicago Defender*, October 27, 1945.

169. Ibid., 1.

170. W. E. B. Du Bois, "The Winds of Time," *Chicago Defender*, October 27, 1945, 13.

171. Wallace Lee, "Is 'Uncle Tom's Cabin' Anti-Negro?," *Negro Digest*, January 1946, 68.

Conclusion: Twentieth-Century Uncle Toms

1. Deborah E. McDowell, "Telling Slavery in 'Freedom's' Time: Post-Reconstruction and the Harlem Renaissance," in *The Cambridge Companion to the African American Slave Narrative*, ed. Audrey Fisch (Cambridge: Cambridge University Press, 2007), 163.

2. Richard Wright, "Blueprint for Negro Writing," in *Within the Circle: An Anthology of African American Literary Criticism from the Harlem Renaissance to the Present*, ed. Angelyn Mitchell (Durham, NC: Duke University Press), 100.

3. Richard Wright, "How 'Bigger' Was Born," in *Native Son* (1940; repr., New York: Harper Perennial, 1993), 517.

4. Wright, "Blueprint for Negro Writing," 105.

5. Tess Chakkalakal, "'Uncle Tom' and the Making of a Modern African American Literature," *Review of Black Political Economy* 33.2 (2005): 80.

6. The epigraph is not attributed in the text, but Chakkalakal (2005) has traced it to Edward Strong, executive secretary of the Southern Negro Youth Congress, whom Wright interviewed for the *Daily Worker* in 1937.

7. Richard Wright, *Uncle Tom's Children* (New York: Harper and Row, 1965), 69.

8. Joel Dinerstein reads the Uncle Tom invoked in Wright's collection as well as several other works of that era as "the *lived embodiment of deference* marked by the mask in the public sphere." Dinerstein, "'Uncle Tom Is Dead!': Wright, Himes, and Ellison Lay a Mask to Rest," *African American Review* 43.1 (2009): 83.

9. Wright, *Uncle Tom's Children*, 4.

10. Ibid., 8.

11. Wright, "How 'Bigger' Was Born," 531.

12. Ibid.

13. Ibid., 523.

14. Ibid., 521.

15. See Harold Bloom, *The Anxiety of Influence: A Theory of Poetry* (New York: Oxford University Press, 1997).

16. James Baldwin, "Everybody's Protest Novel" (1949), in *Critical Essays on Harriet Beecher Stowe*, ed. Elizabeth Ammons (Boston: G. K. Hall, 1980), 92.

17. Ibid., 97.

18. Ibid., 96.

19. Ibid., 97.

20. "Everybody's Protest Novel" has had a tremendous influence over American perceptions of *Uncle Tom's Cabin*. Henry Louis Gates, Jr., in his introduction to *The Annotated "Uncle Tom's Cabin"* (2007), spends as many pages discussing Baldwin's essay as he does Stowe's novel.

21. Daryl Lorenzo Wellington, "Uncle Tom's Shadow," *The Nation*, December 7, 2006.

22. James Baldwin, "The Devil Finds Work," in *The Price of the Ticket: Collected Nonfiction, 1948–1985* (New York: St. Martin's Press, 1985), 562, 565, 561.

23. Ibid., 565.

24. Ibid., 563.

25. Ralph Ellison, *Invisible Man* (1952; repr., New York: Vintage, 1995), xvi.

26. Farrah Jasmine Griffin, *"Who Set You Flowin'?": The African-American Migration Narrative* (New York: Oxford University Press, 1995), 130.

27. Ellison, *Invisible Man*, 16.

28. Ibid., 33.

29. Ibid., 315.

30. Ibid., 354.

31. See Ashraf Rushdy, *Neo-Slave Narratives: Studies in the Social Logic of a Literary Form* (New York: Oxford University Press, 1999).

32. Louis Lomax, "Louis Lomax Interviews Malcolm X," in *When the Word Is Given: A Report on Elijah Muhammad, Malcolm X, and the Black Muslim World* (Cleveland: World Publishing, 1963), 198.

33. Ibid., 203.

34. See Malcolm X, "The Race Problem," African Students Association and NAACP Campus Chapter, Michigan State University, East Lansing, January 23, 1963, accessed May 17, 2017, http://ccnmtl.columbia.edu/projects/mmt/mxp/speeches/mxt17.html.

35. New York Radical Women, *Notes from the First Year* (New York: New York Radical Women, 1968), 28.

36. "I Hate Women: A Diatribe by an Unreconstructed Feminist," *The Ladder*, February 1, 1965, 7.

37. Eddie Huang, *Fresh off the Boat: A Memoir* (New York: Spiegel and Grau, 2013), 157.

INDEX